"This timely and well-researched book takes stock of how far Caribbean women have come in their struggle for equality and social justice. While acknowledging the gains made through the campaigns of named activists, this book draws on statistical data and testimonies/narratives to reveal the serious gaps in addressing violence against women and girls and ensuring that all women can access their legal and constitutional rights as citizens, especially in a global context where patriarchy and homophobia are being reasserted."

Patricia Daley, *University of Oxford, UK*

"Gender Justice! Women's rights as human rights! The dominant themes of this impressive scholarly work are firmly grounded in research and rigorous analysis. Its contribution to the literature on public policy issues related to gender equity is significant. It will also serve as an invaluable resource for facilitating the necessary attitudinal, policy and cultural shifts the authors identify as crucial for dismantling barriers to gender justice."

Maxine Henry-Wilson, *Former Minister of Education, Jamaica*

"This is a fairly large volume of well-researched and insightful chapters, written by Campbell and Johnson-Myers, on gender inequalities and the effort to achieve greater gender justice in the Anglo-Caribbean. The more expansive and deeper the body of knowledge, the more that is required of new work in terms of rigour of method and reasoning, as well as its yield in terms of new insights into the phenomenon of gender inequality. This book meets the above stated requirements. It is a well-planned and well-executed (if I may borrow from the vocabulary of athletics) account of the state of gender inequalities in the region. It is rich in insights."

Anthony Harriott, *University of the West Indies, Jamaica*

"This book offers a deep and contextual examination of gender in the Anglo-Caribbean. The authors marshal a range of evidence to demonstrate and explain the persistence of gender-based inequalities in the region. Spanning the fields of politics, healthcare, human rights and domestic violence, this book makes a meaningful contribution to the discourse on women's equality in the Caribbean."

Se-shauna Wheatle, *Associate Professor, Durham University, UK*

Gender Inequality and Women's Citizenship

Gender Inequality and Women's Citizenship combines cases across Barbados, Guyana, Jamaica and Trinidad and Tobago to highlight the range of systemic inequalities that impact women in the Anglo-Caribbean.

Using empirical and secondary data and drawing on feminist theoretical insights, Yonique Campbell and Tracy-Ann Johnson-Myers examine a range of pertinent and intersecting social, political and economic challenges facing women in the Anglo-Caribbean. The issues explored include gender-based violence, barriers to women in politics, the effects of COVID-19 on women and debates around the illegality of abortion rights and failure to protect the health of women by allowing them to exercise autonomy over their bodies. They raise questions about systemic inequalities resulting from patriarchal gender relations, heteronormativity, women's social and economic status and state inaction.

This book is unique in its interdisciplinary analysis of gender inequality in the Anglo-Caribbean, mapping the intersection of women's multiple identities and positionalities to determine the obstacles they encounter. It will be of interest to scholars and researchers of International Relations, Caribbean Studies, Gender and Sexuality Studies, Development Studies, Sociology and Anthropology.

Yonique Campbell is a senior lecturer in the Department of Government at the University of the West Indies, Mona. She is the author of *Citizenship on the Margins: State Power, Security and Precariousness in 21st-Century Jamaica* (2020) and co-editor (with Professor John Connell) of *COVID in the Islands: A Comparative Perspective on the Caribbean and the Pacific* (2021). Her work has also appeared in *Commonwealth and Comparative Politics* and books published by Oxford University Press, Cambridge University Press and Routledge.

Tracy-Ann Johnson-Myers is a researcher and a former lecturer in the Department of Government at the University of the West Indies, Mona. She is the author of *The Mixed Member Proportional System, Providing Greater Representation for Women? A Case Study of the New Zealand Experience* (2017). She has researched and published on gender and identity politics in the Anglo-Caribbean and Canada. She adopts an intersectional approach to research to gain a more nuanced understanding of how different social categories, such as race, gender, sexuality, class, and ability, interact and shape people's experiences of oppression or privilege.

Routledge Advances in International Relations and Global Politics

Positive Security
Collective Life in an Uncertain World
Gunhild Hoogensen Gjørv and Ali Bilgic

Globalization, Multipolarity and Great Power Competition
Hanna Samir Kassab

Asymmetric Neighbours and International Relations
Living in the Shadow of Elephants
Edited by Ian Roberge, Nara Park and Thomas R. Klassen

Non-Western Nations and the Liberal International Order
Responding to the Backlash in the West
Edited by Hiroki Kusano and Hiro Katsumata

Power Vacuums and Global Politics
Areas of State and Non-state Competition in Multipolarity
Hanna Samir Kassab

Evolution of the United Nations System
An East Asian Perspective
Edited by The Japan Association for United Nations Studies (JAUNS)

Australia's Pursuit of an Independent Foreign Policy under the Whitlam Labor Government
The Achievements and Limitations of a Middle Power
Changwei Chen

Gender Inequality and Women's Citizenship
Evidence from the Caribbean
Yonique Campbell and Tracy-Ann Johnson-Myers

For information about the series: https://www.routledge.com/Routledge-Advances-in-International-Relations-and-Global-Politics/book-series/IRGP

Gender Inequality and Women's Citizenship
Evidence from the Caribbean

Yonique Campbell and
Tracy-Ann Johnson-Myers

NEW YORK AND LONDON

First published 2024
by Routledge
605 Third Avenue, New York, NY 10158

and by Routledge
4 Park Square, Milton Park, Abingdon, Oxon OX14 4RN

Routledge is an imprint of the Taylor & Francis Group, an informa business

© 2024 Yonique Campbell and Tracy-Ann Johnson-Myers

The right of Yonique Campbell and Tracy-Ann Johnson-Myers to be identified as authors of this work has been asserted in accordance with sections 77 and 78 of the Copyright, Designs and Patents Act 1988.

All rights reserved. No part of this book may be reprinted or reproduced or utilised in any form or by any electronic, mechanical, or other means, now known or hereafter invented, including photocopying and recording, or in any information storage or retrieval system, without permission in writing from the publishers.

Trademark notice: Product or corporate names may be trademarks or registered trademarks, and are used only for identification and explanation without intent to infringe.

British Library Cataloguing-in-Publication Data
A catalogue record for this book is available from the British Library

Library of Congress Cataloging-in-Publication Data
Names: Campbell, Yonique, 1983- author. | Johnson-Myers, Tracy-Ann, author.
Title: Gender inequality and women's citizenship : evidence from the Caribbean / Yonique Campbell and Tracy-Ann Johnson-Myers.
Description: Abingdon, Oxon ; New York, NY : Routledge, 2024. | Series: Routledge advances in international relations and global politics | Includes bibliographical references and index.
Identifiers: LCCN 2023023102 (print) | LCCN 2023023103 (ebook) | ISBN 9780367650858 (hardback) | ISBN 9780367673574 (paperback) | ISBN 9781003130987 (ebook)
Subjects: LCSH: Women's rights. | Equality.
Classification: LCC HQ1236 .C345 2024 (print) | LCC HQ1236 (ebook) | DDC 305.42--dc23/eng/20230712
LC record available at https://lccn.loc.gov/2023023102
LC ebook record available at https://lccn.loc.gov/2023023103

ISBN: 978-0-367-65085-8 (hbk)
ISBN: 978-0-367-67357-4 (pbk)
ISBN: 978-1-003-13098-7 (ebk)

DOI: 10.4324/9781003130987

Typeset in Times New Roman
by Taylor & Francis Books

Contents

List of Tables	viii
Acknowledgements	xi

1 Introduction: Gender Challenges in the Caribbean   1

Introduction 1
    Intersectionality 4
    Women's Citizenship 8
    Women's Agency 11
Chapter Overviews 13

2 Barriers, Biases, Boys' Club: A Qualitative Study of the Underrepresentation of Female Politicians in Barbados, Jamaica and Trinidad and Tobago   21

Introduction 21
Barriers to Women in Politics Globally 23
    Supply-Side Barriers to Women's Political
      Representation 24
    Demand-Side Barriers 27
Barriers to Women in Politics: Caribbean Perspectives 29
*Women in Politics in the Anglo-Caribbean: A Historical
    Overview 31*
*Results/Findings: Challenges and Deterrents for Female
    Politicians in the Caribbean 36*
    Double Bind: Domestic Roles/Responsibilities 36
    Lack of Networks and Support 41
    Political Financing/Funding 44
    Role Congruency and Gender Stereotypes 46
    Violence against Female Politicians in the
      Anglo-Caribbean 48

viii   *Contents*

*Solutions to Increasing Women's Political Participation in the
Anglo-Caribbean 51*
    Assets: The Recipe to Survive Politics as a Woman 55
Conclusion 59
Notes 60

3   Debating the Illegality of Abortion Rights in Jamaica:
Challenges for Gender Equality and Collaborative
Governance Approaches   67

Introduction 67
*The Illegality of Abortion in Jamaica and Its
  Consequences 70*
Collaborative Governance 73
Abortion and Collaborative Governance 74
*Failure of Collaborative Governance? Power, the Christian
  Lobby and the Election Cycle 76*
    State Power 77
    Public Opinion 79
    The Christian Lobby 80
    The Political Cycle 84
Conclusion 84

4   The Invisibility of LGBTQ Women in Violence against
Women Legislation in the Anglo-Caribbean: An Intersectional
Analysis   90

Introduction 90
Gender-Based Violence 92
Violence against Women in the Caribbean 94
Violence against LGBTQ Women Globally 96
Violence against LGBTQ People in the Anglo-Caribbean 98
Gender-Based Violence Laws in the Anglo-Caribbean 102
Domestic Violence Legislation in the Caribbean 103
Sexual Offences Legislation in the Anglo-Caribbean 105
*The Invisibility of LGBTQ Women in Domestic Violence
  Laws in the Anglo-Caribbean 107*
*The Invisibility of LGBTQ Women in Sexual Offences
  Legislation in the Anglo-Caribbean 111*
    Definition of Rape in the Anglo-Caribbean 112
    Gross Indecency 114

Contents ix

Conclusion 116
Note 117

5   Health Inequalities and the Gendered Impact of COVID-19
    on Women   125

   Introduction 125
   Health Inequalities and Social Determinants of Health 127
   Health Inequalities in the Caribbean 127
   The Gendered Impact of COVID-19 129
       Social and Economic Impacts 131
       Gender-Based Violence 132
   Research Findings: Impact of COVID-19 on Women 134
       Childcare Responsibilities/Unpaid Employment 134
       Economic Impacts on Caribbean Women 136
       Mental and Physical Health 141
   Conclusion 144

6   Conclusion   150

   Index   153

Tables

2.1	Women's Entry to Formal Political Participation (Anglo-Caribbean)	32
2.2.	Caribbean Countries with Females in Political Positions of Power	34
2.3	Women in National Parliaments in the Anglo-Caribbean	35
4.1	Homophobic Laws in the Anglo Caribbean	99
4.2	Legislation Governing Gender-Based Violence in the Anglo-Caribbean	104

Acknowledgements

This book is a testament to the contributions and support of many individuals. Without their dedication, insights, and encouragement, this endeavour would not have been possible.

We extend our heartfelt gratitude to those who generously devoted their time, shared their expertise, and engaged us in profound intellectual discussions during the development of the initial manuscript. The invaluable insights provided by these individuals have undeniably shaped the direction of this body of work and our research. Special appreciation goes to the women across the Caribbean who shared, through surveys and interviews, their political and lived gender experiences with us.

We are deeply grateful to Natalja Mortensen and the team at Routledge for their dedication, expertise and commitment to bringing this book to fruition.

We also want to acknowledge the invaluable contributions of Patricia Daley, Se-shauna Wheatle, Maxine Henry-Wilson, John Connell, and Anthony Harriott, who read, constructively critiqued or endorsed the book.

Our respective families have been unwavering pillars of support, inspiring us to persevere in our scholarly pursuits, guiding our thinking on gender issues and supporting our efforts to continue to study and understand Caribbean societies. They include Kathleen Campbell, Icelyn Fearon, Kristian Campbell, Veronica Caine and Calvin Campbell.

Dalton Myers, Alia Myers, Jaheem Myers, Marjorie Hines and Doreen Morris, your support and encouragement throughout the writing process have been invaluable.

To our friends and colleagues, too numerous to name individually, we appreciate your unwavering love, patience, and understanding throughout this journey.

Finally, we dedicate this book to the resilient and indomitable women across the Caribbean who tirelessly champion gender equality and social justice. Their courage and determination serve as a beacon of inspiration, reminding us of the importance of our collective efforts in shaping a more just and equitable society.

1 Introduction
Gender Challenges in the Caribbean

Introduction

Gender equality is a fundamental human right, achieved when women can live with dignity and freedom from want, fear and violence. Women's rights are protected under almost every human rights treaty, including the Universal Declaration of Human Rights, which stipulates that "all human beings are born free and equal in dignity and rights" (1948, art. 1) and "everyone is entitled to all the rights and freedoms—without distinction of any kind, such as race, colour, sex, language, religion, political or other opinion, national or social origin, property, birth or other status" (1948, art. 2). Still, many women who live in the Caribbean and the global South have yet to achieve this. Although this book is about a set of intersectional challenges confronting a broader group of Caribbean women, it is shaped by our understanding and interpretation of the world. As black Caribbean women, who have worked in different places and spaces, we have seen how gender intervenes in women's socioeconomic and professional experiences. We are also women who have studied abroad in the UK and Canada, predominantly white countries. Moreover, as single and married women with and without children, patriarchy has affected us in similar and disparate ways. We are aware, too, that, as women with PhDs and academic jobs, alongside whatever disadvantages we face that are related to our gender and intersectional challenges, we have certain privileges and perhaps enjoy greater degrees of gender rights that are by no means universally guaranteed.

We focus primarily on Barbados, Guyana, Jamaica and Trinidad and Tobago, but the gender challenges identified are reflective of inequalities that exist elsewhere in the Anglo-Caribbean. We are using the Anglo-Caribbean to refer to the independent English-speaking countries in the Americas that are members of the Caribbean Community (CARICOM). They include Antigua and Barbuda, Barbados, the Bahamas, Belize, Dominica, Grenada, Guyana, Jamaica, St Kitts and Nevis, St Lucia, St Vincent and the Grenadines, Trinidad and Tobago. These countries are generally characterised by small size, lack of economic diversification and coastal geographies (Alonso, Cortez & Klasen, 2014; OECD, 2015;Briguglio, 2018). They also have a

DOI: 10.4324/9781003130987-1

2 Introduction

shared experience of slavery and colonialism and only gained their independence from Britain in the 1960s. There are also overseas territories in the Caribbean which include Anguilla, the British Virgin Islands, the Cayman Islands, Montserrat, Puerto Rico, the Turks and Caicos Islands and the US Virgin Islands.

While the Anglo-Caribbean countries that we focus on share a similar Westminster/Whitehall political system, there are variations in terms of socioeconomic progress and stability. Barbados, for example, has traditionally maintained a more robust economy and greater social cohesion. There are also ethnic, religious and cultural differences between these countries. Guyana and Trinidad and Tobago are divided along ethnic and religious lines. This divide is also reflected in the politics of the countries. The gender challenges these countries face are influenced by their socioeconomic, historical and political characteristics. In 2019, UNICEF ranked Latin America and the Caribbean as the region with the most global inequality, discrimination and violence, all of which affect women's citizenship and gender equality.

The Fourth World Conference on Women in 1995 marked a significant turning point in the commitment of the international community to achieve gender equality and eliminate all forms of discrimination against women and girls. Embedded in the Beijing Platform for Action (1995) is the conviction that "women's rights are human rights." Also included is the commitment to "take all necessary measures to eliminate all forms of discrimination against women and the girl child and remove all obstacles to gender equality and the advancement and empowerment of women" (United Nations, 1995). Countries in the Anglo-Caribbean have made strides towards achieving these commitments, particularly in education and the labour force (World Bank, 2018). Much of this progress can be attributed to the efforts of Caribbean women's movements and organisations and the work of feminists and women's rights activists, such as Lucille Mathurin Mair, Amy Bailey, Amy Garvey, Maxine Henry-Wilson and Gema Ramkeesoon, who have worked, in various capacities, to increase the voice and visibility of women in the region and achieve full gender equality in law and practice (Antrobus, 2004). Feminist scholars and activists, such as Eudine Barriteau, Rhoda Reddock, Verene Shepherd, Patricia Mohammed, Linette Vassell and Tracy Robinson, have contributed to the discourse on gender justice, racial equality and discrimination in the Anglo-Caribbean. These women are among those who have made critical contributions to the gender project, allowing us to study and understand the role of women in the Caribbean.

By tracing the roots of fractured gender and power relations in the region, Shepherd has highlighted the history of women in the Caribbean from slavery to independence and the struggle by women to survive in a patriarchal society. Eudine Barriteau, in her contribution to the growing body of feminist scholarships, also draws attention to "the constantly mutating social relations of gender and its effect on women in the

Commonwealth Caribbean" (2001, p. 6). By addressing gender justice and inequality issues in the Anglo-Caribbean, these women have exposed obstacles to gender equality in the region.

State action in advancing gender equality has been insufficient. States' commitment to gender equality in the Anglo-Caribbean has resulted in efforts to eradicate violence against women and eliminate patriarchal practices and societal norms that limit women's autonomy and the full exercise of their rights. Countries have ratified international and regional conventions such as the 1993 Declaration on the Elimination of All Forms of Discrimination Against Women and the Inter-American Convention on the Prevention, Punishment, and Eradication of Violence against Women. They have also implemented regional state legislation, such as the Domestic Violence Act and the Sexual Violence Act, to address gender equality in the region. In conjunction with international conventions and state legislation, some countries have developed plans or policies that include equal opportunities for women and some have government ministries or cabinet positions dedicated, in part, to gender. For example, Jamaica has a Ministry of Culture, Gender, Entertainment and Sport, a Bureau of Gender Affairs, and a Gender Advisory Committee. In Guyana, there is a National Gender and Social Inclusion Policy and a Strategic Plan for Women's and Gender Development.

Despite these efforts, there remains a gap between ratification and implementation, with women mostly enjoying *de jure* equality at the expense of *de facto* equality. The result is that women continue to face multiple and intersecting challenges based on gender, sexual orientation and gender identity. These challenges include unpaid care work, lower pay, poverty and unemployment and gender-based discrimination (Budlender & Iyahen, 2019; ECLAC, 2019; FAO, 2017; World Bank, 2022). Women suffer disproportionately from gender-based violence and have been affected by patriarchal tendencies, discriminatory laws and gender norms across various institutions. Women are also underrepresented at all levels of political leadership and decision-making in the region, despite the emergence of prominent female Prime Ministers, such as Eugenia Charles, Portia Simpson-Miller, Kamla Persad-Bissessar, and Mia Mottley.

Twenty-seven years after the Fourth World Conference on Women, there have been some advances in the status of women and girls, but the progress has been marginal, slow and uneven at best. Inequalities between women and men persist: women are subjected to violence, abuse and unequal treatment at home, work and in their communities and are denied opportunities to learn, earn and lead. They are also underrepresented in leadership and decision-making positions. This situation has been exacerbated by the COVID-19 pandemic, which has affected the lives of most of the world's people, particularly women and children. A 2020 study by the United Nations has shown that "across every sphere, from health to the economy, security to social protection, the impacts of COVID-19 are exacerbated for women and girls

4 *Introduction*

simply by virtue of their sex" (United Nations, 2020). It has threatened gains made in addressing domestic and intimate partner violence, led to a loss of employment for women—especially those in insecure, informal and lower-paying jobs—and increased health risks to women who predominantly occupy healthcare jobs and fulfil caregiving roles. The pandemic also increased the unpaid care work that women and girls mainly provide.

Using empirical and secondary data and drawing on feminist theoretical insights, we examine in this book a range of pertinent and intersecting social, political and economic challenges to women in the Anglo-Caribbean. In particular, we raise questions about systemic inequalities resulting from patriarchal gender relations, heteronormativity, the social and economic status of women and state inaction. The book is divided into four chapters, each focusing on one of four challenges to gender equality in the region—gender-based violence, barriers to women in politics, the effects of COVID-19 on women, and debates around the illegality of abortion rights and the failure to protect the health of women by allowing them to exercise autonomy over their bodies. Underlying each chapter is the recognition that gender inequality remains a persistent threat to the fundamental human rights of Anglo-Caribbean women. The uniqueness of this book lies in its multifaceted approach to understanding gender challenges in the Anglo-Caribbean. Along with mapping the intersection of women's multiple identities and positionalities to determine the challenges they face, this book also has the advantage of being inter-disciplinary in its analysis of gender inequality in the Caribbean. The chapters are organised around three central themes: intersectionality, women's citizenship and power relations and challenges for women in their quest to exercise agency.

Intersectionality

Intersectionality is a theme that runs throughout the chapters of this book. There is no question that the gender challenges we describe—whether related to abortion rights, political representation, sexuality or violence against LGBTQ women—are compounded by intersectional challenges. Feminists and critical race theorists use the concept of intersectionality to explain how the current social order perpetuates discrimination and how certain groups within society face multiple forms of discrimination. Research has shown, for example, that women with disabilities are likely to experience physical, sexual and emotional violence at a significantly higher rate than women without disabilities (Morris, 2022; Koistinen et al., 2019; Cotter & Savage, 2019; Cotter, 2018; Jones et al., 2012). They are also "up to 10 times more likely to experience sexual violence" (UNFPA & Management Sciences for Health, 2016).

Suppose women with disabilities fall into other vulnerable groups, such as the elderly, indigenous peoples, migrants and other minorities. In that

Introduction 5

case, they may face additional risks of abuse and violence due to intersecting forms of discrimination (Garcia Ozemela et al., 2019). They also experience forms of violence that women without disabilities do not. Poor women are also more likely to suffer from the effects of restrictive abortion rights in the Caribbean and elsewhere. They are less likely to have insurance, to run for political office and are usually not included in policy-making processes that seek to tackle the very inequalities they are confronted with. While it was designed primarily to assess, address and explain the lives of black women, intersectionality is a useful conceptual tool for considering the experiences of minority groups in the Anglo-Caribbean who face discrimination and multiple forms of oppression.

Throughout our discussion in each chapter, we have demonstrated that gender inequalities in the Anglo-Caribbean intersect with class, race, gender identity, geography and health status, worsening vulnerabilities and creating multiple forms of oppression. Moreover, as we have shown in Chapter 3, LGBTQ women in the Anglo-Caribbean experience multiple forms of discrimination, placing them at increased risk of violence.

Rooted in Black Feminism and Critical Race Theory, the term "intersectionality" gained notoriety from Kimberlé Crenshaw (1989; 1991), who used it to denote "the various ways race and gender interact to shape the multiple dimensions of black women's employment experiences" in the United States of America (Crenshaw, 1991, p. 1244). Before Crenshaw's use of the term, black feminists, activists and minority scholars in the United States of America used it to examine the complex and intertwining factors and processes that shape human lives (hooks, 2014 [1984]; Collins, 1986). In her landmark essay, Demarginalising the Intersection of Race and Sex: A Black Feminist Critique of Antidiscrimination Doctrine, Feminist Theory, and Antiracist Politics, Crenshaw detailed how African American women were subjected to sex and racial discrimination:

> Many of the experiences Black women face are not subsumed within the traditional boundaries of race or gender discrimination as these boundaries are currently understood, and the intersection of racism and sexism factors into Black women's lives in ways that cannot be captured wholly by looking at the race or gender dimensions of those experiences separately.
>
> (Crenshaw, 1991, p. 1244)

In short, these women were not discriminated against because they were women or black. They were discriminated against because they were black women. Using an analysis of three discrimination suits brought against white corporate employees by black women, she further illustrated how the US judicial system's refusal "to acknowledge that black women encounter combined race and sex discrimination implies that the boundaries of sex and race discrimination doctrine are defined respectively by

6 Introduction

white women's and black men's experiences" (Crenshaw, 1989, p. 143). Black women are, therefore, protected only to the extent that their experiences of discrimination "coincide" with those of black men or white women (Crenshaw, 1989). Crenshaw also noted in her analysis that by treating race and gender as mutually exclusive categories of experience and analysis, traditional feminist ideas and antiracist policies excluded black women by failing to acknowledge the overlapping identities, discrimination and oppression unique to them.

For Collins, intersectionality is "the critical insight that race, class, gender, sexuality, ethnicity, nation, ability, and age operate not as unitary, mutually exclusive entities, but as reciprocally constructing phenomena that in turn shape complex social inequalities" (Collins, 2015, p. 2). She further explains that "intersectional paradigms remind us that oppression cannot be reduced to one fundamental type and that oppressions work together in producing injustice" (Collins, 2000, p. 18). Hankivsky also offered a working definition of intersectionality, explaining that it:

> promotes an understanding of human beings as shaped by the interaction of different social locations, e.g., race, ethnicity, indigeneity, gender, class, sexuality, geography, age, disability/ability, migration status, and religion. These interactions occur within a context of connected system[s] and structures of power, e.g., law, policies, state governments, religious institutions, [and] media. Through such processes, interdependent forms of privilege and oppression shaped by colonialism, imperialism, racism, homophobia, ableism, and patriarchy are created.
>
> (Hankivsky, 2014, p. 2)

According to these definitions, intersectionality is built on the following key tenets:

a   there are multiple and complex intersecting identities (race, gender, age, sex, sexual orientation, religion, etc.) which cannot be understood in isolation
b   the focal point of analysis is historically marginalised and oppressed people (women, blacks, indigenous, gays, lesbians)
c   forces of oppression and inequality intersect in complex and compounding ways
d   people can experience privilege and oppression simultaneously: they can also experience multiple oppressions

Today, the term "intersectionality" is used in a multiplicity of disciplines and different ways—as a theoretical framework, approach, lens and tool to explain how various aspects of people's social identity converge to produce different experiences of marginalisation and discrimination (Collins & Bilge, 2016; Mik-Meyer, 2015; Kelan, 2014; Atewologun & Sealy, 2014; Cho,

Introduction   7

Crenshaw & McCall, 2013; Holvino, 2010; Davis, 2008). Central to intersectionality is the fact that that inequity and oppression are the outcomes of "different social locations, power relations, and experiences" (Hankivsky, 2014). Everyone has unique experiences of discrimination and oppression, defined by gender, race, sexual orientation, nationality, disability and age, among other things. It also explains how systems of oppression overlap to create distinct experiences for people with multiple identities. When used as a tool of analysis in Feminist or Gender Studies, it addresses how "racism, patriarchy, class oppression and other systems of discrimination create inequalities that structure the relative positions of women" (Women's Rights and Economic Change, 2004, p. 2).

In this book, intersectionality is understood as the intersecting of identities and power structures, like traffic in an intersection, to create different experiences of gender inequality for women in the Anglo-Caribbean. We borrow from Crenshaw's traffic metaphor which explains that "race, gender, class and other forms of discrimination or subordination are the roads that structure the social and economic or political terrain" (United Nations, 2001). These avenues often overlap to create complex intersections and crossroads at which marginalised women are located because of their multiple intersecting identities. Intersectional injuries occur when multiple disadvantages or collisions interact to create a distinct and compound dimension of disempowerment (UNDAW, OHCHR & UNIFEM, 2000). Women must, therefore, "negotiate the traffic that flows through these intersections to avoid injury and to obtain resources for the normal activities of life" (UNDAW, OHCHR & UNIFEM, 2000). This, however, can be dangerous when the traffic flows simultaneously from many directions. Injuries are sometimes caused when the impact from one direction throws victims into the path of oncoming traffic, while on other occasions, injuries occur from simultaneous collisions (UNDAW, OHCHR & UNIFEM, 2000).

Intersectionality, as a theoretical framework and analytical tool, is especially useful in assessing violence against women in the Anglo-Caribbean as it challenges the notion that women form a homogenous group. It helps us understand how women's multiple or complex identities converge to create different struggles, discrimination and oppression. It acknowledges that as a "pluralistic" group, the lives of women in the region vary. Other factors relating to women's social identities, such as race, age, religion, ethnicity, class, national origin, disability and sexuality, can also intersect with and, therefore, compound gender discrimination (Patel, 2001). These multiple identities of Anglo-Caribbean women—race, marital status, disability, age, religion and sexual orientation—also influence the forms and nature of the violence they experience (UN Women, 2012).

Women are also more at risk of experiencing violence because of various forms of oppression, such as racism, colonialism, sexism, homophobia, transphobia and ableism. Intersectionality also challenges the tendency of gender-based violence (GBV) policies/measures to define violence towards

8   *Introduction*

people from the LGBTQ community as a problem of gendered violence or homophobic violence. Through an interrogation of Domestic Violence and Sexual Violence Acts in select Anglo-Caribbean countries, we reveal in this chapter the inequalities and discrimination inherent in state legislation, ultimately demonstrating how these laws create burdens that flow along intersecting axes, creating discrimination for LGBTQ women. We also explain how the complexity of different identity categories and their intersections create varying experiences of violence for LGBTQ women in Anglo-Caribbean countries.

Abortion rights also create discrimination against all women. However, poor lower-class women are mainly affected because of their inability to afford safe medical care, which women in the middle or upper strata have access to. The stigma associated with abortion is also more prevalent among poorer and younger women, who are often discriminated against because of their socioeconomic status. Marginalised women are also more likely to be impacted by inequalities in health, as demonstrated by women's experiences with the COVID-19 pandemic (CARE International & UN Women, 2020; PAHO, 2022).

Women's Citizenship

Citizenship is important for achieving gender justice, improving democracy and challenging exclusionary power systems. It has provided an important lens for Caribbean feminists to consider legal and non-legal mechanisms through which women are excluded from full equality. It has also provided a tool for examining how women's legal and social status in the Anglo-Caribbean has been (re-)configured through various political and economic struggles and claims-making. Traditionally, citizenship is understood as a set of political, civil and social rights (Marshall, 1950). Here we are using citizenship to "encapsulate the relationship between the individual, state and society" (Yuval-Davis, 1997, p. 4) and as both a socio-legal status and a practice. As a status, it captures the legal context as well as the social norms and expectations that govern membership and belonging in a society. As a practice, it "addresses the deeper constitutive struggles over embodied freedom and embodied constraints within unequal interpersonal and international relations" (Sheller, 2012, p. 23).

In this way, the concepts of transnational and cosmopolitan citizenship also have relevance in the Anglo-Caribbean. Both cosmopolitan and transnational citizenship reject the monopolisation of political subjectivity by the nation-state and frame citizenship in a global context. The cosmopolitan citizen is "someone who is empowered and has the capacity to participate in a global democratic system and demand cosmopolitan justice" (Tan, 2017). Intergovernmental organisations such as UN Women and the WHO enable women to work across borders and engage with each other on women's

Introduction 9

citizenship issues such as GBV, health inequalities, abortion rights, women's underrepresentation in the political arena and the pay gap. One challenge is that Western epistemologies and liberal notions of citizenship tend to dominate notions of what it means to be a global citizen.

Another challenge is the tension between state actors, who frame citizenship in relation to the nation state and "national culture," and citizens, who frame citizenship beyond the nation-state. After all, "the bodily politics of freedom extend both below and beyond the nation state" (Sheller, 2012, p. 23). Caribbean states regard this framing of citizenship as a threat to national identity and have pushed back at transnational theorisations of citizenship, arguing that national identity supersedes "foreign" ways of being and belonging. It is not uncommon, therefore, for states in the Caribbean to label new claims for citizenship and bodily autonomy as being outside a Christian national identity (Perkins, 2011; Lazarus, 2020). These claims threaten gendered power relations and the cultural and religious norms that inscribe them. This denial of equal citizenship is not new.

Traditionally, women in the Caribbean have been excluded from full citizenship (Alexander, 1994; Beckles 1998; 2003), both *de jure* and *de facto*. According to Tracy Robinson, who has dealt with the question of state laws and the problem of women's citizenship:

> The early independence constitutions in the Caribbean explicitly created classes of citizenship for men and women. Men were given rights—not afforded to women—to pass on citizenship to their foreign spouses and children born outside the jurisdiction. Only unwed mothers of children born outside the jurisdiction automatically passed on citizenship to those children. Here citizenship passing through the maternal line was entirely by default because, under the common law, that child was filius nullius, belonging to no one. The patriarchal family, therefore, was the constitutional foundation, and the male head of household was the paradigm of a citizen.
>
> (Robinson, 2003, p. 235)

She believes that the focus on social and economic issues, a pragmatic response to inequality, has overshadowed a more challenging question of how Caribbean feminists can challenge constructions of citizenship. This problem underpins the gender *problématique*. While contesting the law offers one way out of this dilemma, and Robinson has shown how it can be utilised in the interest of the "gender equality project," the law in several Caribbean countries is yet to answer Robinson's call for equal citizenship. As Biholar has shown:

> by retaining limited definitions and conceptualisations of rape, accompanied by the offences of grievous/sexual assault, serious

10 *Introduction*

indecency or unlawful sexual connection, and the restrictive criminalisation of marital rape, some Caribbean sexual violence laws reinforce gender stereotyping that reflect fixed codes of femininity and masculinity.

(Biholar, 2022, p. 50)

Even though a set of fundamental rights and freedoms are now enshrined in the constitutions of countries in the Anglophone Caribbean, and although women in the Caribbean have won important rights such as the right to vote and run for office, they are still denied important rights over their bodies. These rights, which include LGBTQ and abortion rights, were established in the 1900s in many Western countries. Even so, certain rights, such as abortion rights, that were thought to be decidedly settled are now being contested or are in danger even in the West. In several Caribbean countries, owing to savings clauses in Caribbean constitutions which preserve discriminatory laws and state inaction in the face of opposition from powerful groups, these laws remain unchanged. Citizenship, however, is not static; women have claimed new rights and challenged states to move away from fixed notions of gender identity. This can be seen in increasingly more fluid ways of defining gender beyond the male–female binary to include demands that the state affords rights to LGBTQ people and provide citizenship rights for groups that do not fit into a binary, heteronormative framework. Non-binary, trans- and LGBTQ people disrupt the assumptions of discrete male/female categories that underpin the institutions of heterosexuality and homosexuality (Butler, 1990). In the Caribbean, this disruption and demands that the state recognise and grant new rights to women have not gone unchallenged by religious and secular groups. Many religious groups and Christian denominations, especially the Evangelical Churches in the Caribbean space, have been firmly against LGBTQ groups claiming citizenship rights. They are also firmly against abortion rights. Setting the tone for the Catholic Church in 2019, the Vatican issued a guidance document entitled *Male and Female He Created Them*, establishing that there should be no deviation from and recognition of identities beyond cisgender as this posed dangers to society and the family and could "annihilate the concept of nature" (Congregation for Catholic Education, 2019). Failure to protect women's rights and recognise gender diversity has affected women's citizenship claims.

Power continues to affect women's citizenship in the Anglo-Caribbean and is a central theme throughout the chapters in this book. Power manifests in various dimensions and across the social, economic and political spheres. It is evident and operates in and through public and private institutions and across formal and informal norms and practices. Feminists have conceptualised power in different ways: capacity to act (Arendt, 1958), a resource which can be redistributed (Young, 1990), something to be possessed and exercised and power as subordination and domination. Power-over is the

Introduction 11

most common conception of power, where one actor can exercise power over another (Dahl, 1957; Foucault, 1983; Lukes, 1974). By regulating women's conduct, whether in explicit or in insidious ways, gender operates through a "regulatory power that not only acts upon a pre-existing subject but also shapes and forms that subject" (Butler, 2014, p. 141). And in this way, gendered power relations position women and men differently, both structurally and strategically (Beckwith, 2015 p. 132).

From domestic and gender-based violence to sexual harassment, gender stereotypes and gender norms that place expectations and burdens on women, there are many ways in which power is evident in women's social experiences in the Anglophone Caribbean. Economically, there is still the glass ceiling that women have to contend with in the workplace, and women are still underrepresented in decision-making roles, despite workplace equality laws. Women globally earn less than men. Although the power dynamic between men and women in the Caribbean has not been static, women still operate within gendered paradigms of power that are overdetermined by men. Caribbean states have not done enough to change this. Recognising the centrality of the state in the distribution of rights and the enjoyment of citizenship, we place our gaze on the "masculinist" state but also look beyond it.

Caribbean feminist Barriteau (2001) has problematised the flawed nature of the state paradigm. For Barriteau, the problem lies with the state and its institutions which create mechanisms and policies to have women's interests serve the goals of the states. Similar to Barriteau, we are suggesting that failure to connect women's adverse conditions to unequal power relations between women and men in society and between women and the state points to an important fault line in gender policies. We contend that there is also a failure that arises from power relations among a broader coalition of actors, including the Christian lobby, which has been involved in debates about gender rights in relation to women's sexuality and abortion rights through the state and outside of it.

Women's Agency

Agency is another theme that has relevance in this book. Not only are we concerned with how the exercise and institutionalisation of gender power affect women, but we are also interested in how agency has been, and can be, enabled. In each chapter, however modestly, we have tried to show how women have attempted to resist, subvert and emancipate themselves from multiple gender challenges across different domains, with various challenges. Despite some of the challenges we have pointed to in this book, women have also been able to create meaningful identities, whether within or against the dominant cultural norms. No country in the Anglophone Caribbean, and indeed globally, has been able to challenge patriarchy without the struggles of women's movements. Although agency, "both individual

12 *Introduction*

and collective, is at the heart of the feminist, and indeed, all radical political projects" (Clegg, 2006, pp. 309–310), there have been many controversies surrounding how agency should be understood, especially from a non-Western liberal approach, and how it has been used in the work of post-structuralist theorists. Agency has been troubled by problems related to the silence–voice binary and how it has been theorised by post-structuralism.

Mahmood (2005), working through a decolonial and global South framework, has critiqued the Western neoliberal epistemology for framing women's agency in relation to the power of men and through Western epistemologies and for how it locates the political and moral autonomy of the subject in the face of power. She has also critiqued its logic of subversion and resignification of hegemonic norms. Instead of treating agency as analogous to resistance in the face of domination, she defines it as "a capacity for action that specific relations of subordination create and enable" (Mahmood, 2005, p. 45). There are numerous examples of how feminists challenge agency as resistance against patriarchy and look through other intersectional lenses, such as racism and imperialism, which also inscribe privileges (Hudson, 2009). They also point to the deployment of strategic silence as a "negotiated survival strategy" in a highly patriarchal context (Glenn, 2004).

Caribbean feminists have tackled the question of agency in various ways, showing how female autonomy, capacity for action, embodied citizenship and gender performativity can take many forms. Judith Butler makes a distinction between performativity that takes linguistic and bodily form, arguing that although they overlap, they are not identical. Consequently, speech, silence, movement and immobility are all political enactments. (Butler, 2015, p. 172). In the Caribbean both dancehall and carnival have been sites where women challenge oppressive power structures, the moral order and gender norms through bodily performances (Cooper, 2004; Hope, 2006; Perkins, 2011). In the Jamaican context, Cooper argues that "in dancehall, the affirmation of the pleasures of the body, which is often misunderstood as a devaluation of female sexuality, also can be theorized as an act of self-conscious female assertion of control over the representation of her person" (2004, pp. 125–126). In confrontation with security forces, inner-city women have also used bodily exposures to directly challenge state power, making the naked body a site of protest. Members of the LGBTQ community have also challenged heteronormativity by disrupting gender norms, challenging the status quo and demanding "erotic agency." Agency has also been exercised in subtler forms in the Caribbean. Some women use silence as a way of negotiating and challenging power. Subtler forms of resistance can be hard to locate for an outsider, especially when they take a discursive and symbolic form.

Collective resistance to dealing with women's issues has also been evident in the Anglophone Caribbean. Women's Empowerment for Change (WE-Change), a community-based association, is one such organisation

Introduction   13

that is "committed to increasing the participation of lesbians, bisexuals and transgender women in social justice advocacy in Jamaica and the Caribbean" (Equality Fund, 2022). In 2016, Stella Gibson, founder of WE-Change, and member of the Tambourine Army (Jamaica), was involved in an incident where, during a protest by survivors of sexual abuse at the Nazareth Moravian Church, she hit Dr Paul Gardner, the Jamaican Moravian Church leader, on the head with a tambourine. She alleged that Gardner abused her partner as a child (Lewis, 2017). The protests followed a widely publicised sexual assault case against a female minor by Rupert Clarke, a 64-year-old pastor at the Nazareth Moravian Church. Women have also acted collectively to improve their lives. Sistren Theatre Collective was established in Jamaica in 1977 to confront gender issues, including the oppression of women, and incite social change for both genders in some of Jamaica's most vulnerable communities. While the women involved in and affected by this initiative have not confronted power in the ways we have come to expect, their work has been meaningful and has produced changes in the lives of both the "sistrens" who founded and benefited from the movement. In Guyana, the Red Thread plays a similar role in empowering women at the grassroots level who experience exploitation owing to unequal power relations. Caribbean women's struggle for equality has been most successful in labour force participation, education (UN Women, 2019; ILO, 2018) and in sports. Women have also made strides to increase political representation and participation. This is evident in the number of female heads of state in the Anglo-Caribbean, relative to other regions.

Chapter Overviews

In Chapter 2, we conduct an exploratory analysis of barriers to women's political participation in three Anglo-Caribbean countries. We do so through elite interviews with female politicians in Barbados, Jamaica and Trinidad and Tobago. Drawing on supply- and demand-side market-frame theory to account for why women were systematically excluded from political office, we try to determine what might account for the underrepresentation of women in politics in the Anglo-Caribbean. Despite the proven political leadership of female politicians, there still exist visible and invisible obstacles to women's political participation in the Anglo-Caribbean. Politics remains a highly patriarchal space in all aspects of Caribbean life. Except for Guyana and Trinidad and Tobago, women in the region generally do not hold more than 30 per cent of elected political positions, and only 22 per cent of ministerial portfolios/cabinet positions in the Anglophone Caribbean are held by women (UN Women, 2018). An interesting finding from this study is that the underrepresentation of women in politics in the region can be attributed mainly to the supply of female political aspirants or the qualifications of women as a group to run for political office (supply-side barriers). This

14 *Introduction*

undersupply is rooted in larger intersecting and deep-rooted factors—patriarchal norms and traditions, gender discrimination and oppressive structural systems—that affect women's political entry and retention. The women interviewed for the study identified increased political funding/financing and stronger support or network systems as potential solutions for overcoming the barriers women face in politics in the Anglo-Caribbean. They also stated that women entering politics must equip themselves with the critical attributes and leadership skills needed to survive. Ultimately, the impetus for change must also come from women themselves. The chapter concludes with recommended solutions to removing barriers to women's political representation in the Anglophone Caribbean.

In Chapter 3, we focus on abortion rights, using the public policy concept of collaborative governance to interrogate how the Jamaican government has approached demands from different groups to either change or retain current policies and laws. For many years, abortion legislation and women's reproductive rights have been contentious issues in Jamaica. Abortion is illegal in Jamaica under the 1864 Offences of the Person's Act. The Act stipulates that anyone guilty of having or facilitating an abortion could be sentenced to life in prison. Abortion laws in Jamaica and other Anglo-Caribbean countries are vestiges of a colonial past. Though these laws are rarely enforced, having them on the statute book instils fear in pregnant women, leads to significant delay in care-seeking and forces women into unsafe abortion practices, which can lead to death and injuries. Restrictive abortion laws also prevent doctors from performing primary care.

We use these reproductive rights and abortion debates to highlight the contested nature of gender policies and the female body as a site of moral, religious and political conflict. We suggest that the main approach of the state is policy inaction. The chapter begins with an overview of abortion rights in Jamaica, followed by an exploration of collaborative governance as a public policy tool for solving "wicked" public policy problems. We round off the chapter with a critical analysis of the use of collaborative governance to examine abortion laws and policies in Jamaica by exploring the use of policy advisory bodies, Joint Select and Special Select Committees of Parliament. We consider several shortcomings in using a collaborative, multi-sector governance approach and question why it has failed to achieve policy and legislative shifts related to abortion in Jamaica. Finally, we point to state power, the influence and power of "the Church" or the Christian lobby (institutional), sharp ideological differences and the political cycle.

Using an intersectional approach to analysing violence against women, in Chapter 4 we highlight multiple inequalities in policies on violence against women in the Anglo-Caribbean, focusing on women in the LGBTQ community. Gender-based violence remains a challenge for women in the Anglo-Caribbean. Historically women and girls are the victims of severe forms of violence and tragic encounters (UN Women, 2022; WHO, 2021a;

2021b; UNODC, 2018; Fleming et. al., 2015; Hester, 2013; Kimmel, 2002; Lacey, Jeremiah & West, 2021). In some Caribbean countries, sociopolitical conditions result in violence against women becoming a way of life within their societies (Hayes & Franklin, 2017). While gender-based violence affects everyone, those who exist at the intersection of multiple identities are at a higher risk of experiencing all forms of violence due to various forms of oppression, such as sexism, racism, colonialism, homophobia, transphobia, ageism and ableism. Among the most disadvantaged minority groups in Anglo-Caribbean countries are LGBTQ women. They face unique challenges and disproportionately higher levels of discrimination and violence but receive the least attention.

Through an interrogation of Domestic Violence and Sexual Violence Acts in selected Anglo-Caribbean countries, we reveal in this chapter the inequalities and discrimination inherent in state legislation, ultimately demonstrating how these laws create burdens that flow along intersecting axes, creating discrimination for LGBTQ women. We also explain how the complexity of different identity categories and their intersections create varying experiences of violence for LGBTQ women in Anglo-Caribbean countries.

Using qualitative data-collection methods, we further examine our arguments about challenges to gender equality and women's citizenship in the Anglo-Caribbean in Chapter 5. We examine health and gender inequalities through the lens of the COVID-19 pandemic, using both secondary and primary data to critically explore the health inequalities and the impact of COVID on the social, economic and mental of women in the Caribbean. Evidence was drawn from interviews conducted across four Caribbean countries (Barbados, Guyana, Jamaica and Trinidad and Tobago). The findings of our research support general arguments in the literature on the impact of the COVID-19 pandemic on gender equality. COVID-19 has revealed the vulnerability of women in crisis moments and the lack of gender-based policies to cushion the socioeconomic shocks and impacts that women experience (World Bank, 2021). It has also exacerbated gender inequality in the region, shifting the power dynamic in favour of men and creating hardship for many women (UN Women, 2021).

References

Alexander, M. J. (1994). Not just (any) body can be a citizen: The politics of law, sexuality and post coloniality in Trinidad and Tobago and the Bahamas. *Feminist Review* 48(1), 5–23.

Alonso, J. A., Cortez, A. L., & Klasen, S. (2014). *LDC and Other Country Groupings: How Useful are Current Approaches to Classify Countries in a More Heterogeneous Developing World?* Department of Economic & Social Affairs. CDP Background Paper No. 21 ST/ESA/2014/CDP/21. Retrieved on November

16 Introduction

22, 2022, from https://www.un.org/development/desa/dpad/wp-content/uploads/sites/45/publication/bp2014_21.pdf.

Antrobus, P. (2004). Feminist activism: The CARICOM experience. *In* B. Bailey and E. Leo-Rhiney (Eds.), *Gender in the 21st Century: Caribbean Perspectives, Visions and Possibilities* (pp. 35–58). Kingston, Jamaica: Ian Randle Publishers.

Arendt, H. (1958). *The Human Condition.* Chicago: University of Chicago Press.

Atewologun, D., & Sealy, R. (2014). Experiencing privilege at ethnic, gender and senior intersections. *Journal of Managerial Psychology* 29(4), 423–439.

Barriteau, E. (2001). *The Political Economy of Gender in the Twentieth Century Caribbean.* New York: Palgrave.

Beckles, H. (1998). Centering woman: The political economy of gender in West African and Caribbean slavery. In *Caribbean Portraits: Essays on Gender Ideologies and Identities* (pp. 93–114). Kingston, Jamaica: Ian Randle Publishers.

Beckles, H. (2003). Perfect property: Enslaved black women in the Caribbean. In *Confronting Power, Theorizing Gender: Interdisciplinary Perspectives in the Caribbean* (pp. 3–24). Kingston, Jamaica: University of the West Indies Press.

Beckwith, K. (2015). Before prime minister: Margaret Thatcher, Angela Merkel, and gendered party leadership contests. *Politics & Gender* 11(4), 718–745.

Biholar, R. (2022). Discriminatory laws: The normalization of sexual violence in Anglophone Caribbean sexual violence laws. In R. Biholar and D. Leslie (Eds.), *Critical Caribbean Perspectives on Preventing Gender-Based Violence* (pp. 44–64). London and New York: Routledge.

Briguglio, L. (Ed.) (2018). *Handbook of Small States: Economic, Social and Environmental Issues.* New York: Routledge.

Budlender, D., & Iyahen, I. (2019). *Status of Women and Men Report: Productive Employment and Decent Work for All.* Barbados: UN Women. Retrieved on November 22, 2022, from https://caribbean.unwomen.org/sites/default/files/Field%20Office%20Caribbean/Attachments/Publications/2019/Status%20of%20Women%20and%20Men-WEB.pdf.

Butler, J. (1990). *Gender Trouble: Feminism and the Subversion of Identity.* Abingdon: Routledge.

Butler, J. (2014). *Undoing Gender.* New York and London: Routledge.

Butler, J. (2015). *Notes Toward a Performative Theory of Assembly.* Cambridge, MA: Harvard University Press.

CARE International & UN Women (2020). *Latin America and the Caribbean Rapid Gender Analysis for COVID-19.* Retrieved on November 22, 2022, from https://www.care-international.org/news/care-international-and-un-women-advocate-rapid-gender-analysis-crisis-response-reduce.

Cho, S., Crenshaw, K. W., & McCall, L. (2013). Toward a field of intersectionality studies: Theory, applications, and praxis. *Signs* 38(4), 785–810.

Clegg, S. (2006). The problem of agency in feminism: A critical realist approach. *Gender and Education* 18(3), 309–324. doi:10.1080/09540250600667892.

Collins, P. H. (1986). Learning from the outsider within: The sociological significance of Black feminist thought. *Sociological Problems* 33(6),14–32.

Collins, P. H. (2000). *Black Feminist Thought: Knowledge, Consciousness, and the Politics of Empowerment.* New York: Routledge.

Collins, P. H. (2015). Intersectionality's definitional dilemmas. *Annual Review of Sociology,* 41(1), 1–20.

Collins, P. H., & Bilge, S. (2016). *Intersectionality.* Cambridge: Polity Press.

Introduction 17

Congregation for Catholic Education (2019). *Male and Female He Created Them: Towards a Path of Dialogue on the Question of Gender Theory in Education.* Retrieved on June 16, 2023, from https://www.vatican.va/roman_curia/congregations/cca theduc/documents/rc_con_ccatheduc_doc_20190202_maschio-e-femmina_en.pdf.

Cooper, C. (2004). *Sound Clash: Jamaican Dancehall Culture at Large.* New York: Palgrave MacMillan.

Cotter, A. (2018). Violent victimization of women with disabilities. *Juristat.* Statistics Canada Catalogue no. 85–002-X.

Cotter, A., & Savage, L. (2019). Gender-based violence and inappropriate sexual behaviour in Canada, 2018: Initial findings from the Survey of Safety in Public and Private Spaces. *Juristat.* Statistics Canada Catalogue no. 85–002-X.

Crenshaw, K. (1989). Demarginalizing the intersection of race and sex: A black feminist critique of antidiscrimination doctrine, feminist theory and antiracist politics. *University of Chicago Legal Forum* 1, art. 8. Retrieved on June 16, 2023, from https://chicagounbound.uchicago.edu/cgi/viewcontent.cgi?article= 1052&context=uclf.

Crenshaw, K. (1991). Mapping the margins: Intersectionality, identity politics, and violence against women of color. *Stanford Law Review* 43(6), 1241–1299.

Dahl, R. (1957). The concept of power. *Behavioral Science* 2, 201–215.

Davis, K. (2008). Intersectionality as buzzword: A sociology of science perspective on what makes a feminist theory successful. *Feminist Theory* 9(1),67–85. Retrieved on June 16, 2023, from https://doi.org/10.1177/1464700108086364.

ECLAC (2019). *Femininity Index of Poor Households.* Retrieved on September 8, 2022, from https://oig.cepal.org/en/indicators/feminity-index-poor-households.

Equality Fund (2022). *Women's Voice and Leadership-Caribbean.* Retrieved on June 9, 2023, from https://equalityfund.ca/wvl-caribbean/womens-voice-and-lea dership-caribbean-july-update.

FAO (2017). *Women in Latin America and the Caribbean Face Greater Poverty and Obesity than Men.* Retrieved on September 8, 2022, from https://www.fao. org/americas/noticias/ver/en/c/473028/.

Fleming, P. J., Gruskin, S., Rojo, F., & Dworkin, S. L. (2015). Men's violence against women and men are inter-related: Recommendations for simultaneous intervention. *Social Science & Medicine* 146: 249–256. Retrieved on November 22, 2022, from https://doi.org/10.1016/j.socscimed.2015.10.021.

Foucault, M. (1983). The subject and power. In H. Dreyfus, & P. Rabinow (Eds.), *Michel Foucault: Beyond Structuralism and Hermeneutics*, 2nd edn (pp. 208–226). Chicago: University of Chicago Press.

Garcia Ozemela, L. M., Ortiz, D. and Urban, A. (2019). *Violence against Women and Girls with Disabilities: Latin America and the Caribbean.* Retrieved on June 20, 2022, from https://publications.iadb.org/en/violence-against-women-and-girls-disa bilities-latin-america-and-caribbean.

Glenn, C. (2004). *Unspoken: A Rhetoric of Silence.* Carbondale, IL: Southern Illinois Press.

Hankivsky, O. (2014). *Intersectionality* 101. Vancouver, BC: Institute for Intersectionality Research & Policy, SFU.

Hayes, B. E., & Franklin, C. A. (2017). Community effects on women's help-seeking behaviour for intimate partner violence in India: Gender disparity, feminist theory, and empowerment. *International Journal of Comparative and Applied Criminal Justice* 41(1–2), 79–94.

18   *Introduction*

Hester, M. (2013). Who does what to whom? Gender and domestic violence perpetrators in English police records. *European Journal of Criminology* 10(5), 623–637.

Holvino, E. (2010). Intersections: The simultaneity of race, gender and class in organization studies. *Gender Work and Organization* 17(3), 248–277.

hooks, b. (2014) [1984]. *Feminist Theory: From Margin to Center* (3rd edn). New York: Routledge.

Hope, D. P. (2006). *Inna di dancehall: Popular Culture and the Politics of Identity in Jamaica.* Kingston, Jamaica: University of the West Indies Press.

Hudson, H. (2009). Peacebuilding through a gender lens and the challenges of implementation in Rwanda and Côte d'Ivoire. *Security Studies* 18(2), 287–318. doi:10.1080/09636410902899982.

ILO (2018). *Women in Business and Management: Gaining Momentum in the Caribbean.* Retrieved on November 22, 2022, from https://www.ilo.org/wcmsp5/group s/public/—ed_dialogue/—act_emp/documents/publication/wcms_645810.pdf.

Jones, L., Bellis, M. A., Wood, S., Hughes, K., McCoy, E., Eckley, L., Bates, G., Mikton, C., Shakespeare, T., & Officer, A. (2012). Prevalence and risk of violence against children with disabilities: A systematic review and meta-analysis of observational studies. *The Lancet* 380(9845), 899–907.

Kelan, E. K. (2014). From biological clocks to unspeakable inequalities: The intersectional positioning of young professionals. *British Journal of Management* 25(4), 790–804.

Kimmel, M. S. (2002). Gender symmetry in domestic violence: A substantive and methodological research review. *Violence against Women* 8(11), 1332–1363.

Koistinen, M., McClaon-Nhlapo. C., Arango, D., & Gandini, C. (2019). *Five Facts to Know about Violence against Women and Girls with Disabilities.* Retrieved on November 22, 2022, from https://blogs.worldbank.org/sustainablecities/five-fa cts-know-about-violence-against-women-and-girls-disabilities.

Lacey, K. K., Jeremiah, R., & West, C. (2021). Domestic violence through a Caribbean lens: Historical context, theories, risks and consequences. *Journal of Aggression, Maltreatment & Trauma* 30(6), 761–780. doi:10.1080/10926771.2019.1660442.

Lazarus, L. (2020). Enacting citizenship, debating sex and sexuality: Conservative Christians' participation in legal processes in Jamaica and Belize. *Commonwealth & Comparative Politics* 58(3), 366–386.

Lewis, E. (2017). "Tambourine Army" gathers recruits as Jamaicans anger over child sexual abuse grows. Retrieved on November 222, 2022, from https://globalvoices.org/ 2017/02/07/tambourine-army-gathers-recruits-as-jamaicans-anger-over-child-sexual-abuse-grows/.

Lukes, S. (1974). *Power: A Radical View,* London: Macmillan.

Mahmood, S. (2005). Feminist theory, agency and the liberatory subject. In F. Nouraie-Simone (Ed.), *On Shifting Ground: Muslim Women in the Global Era* (pp. 111–152). New York: The Feminist Press.

Marshall, T. H. (1950). *Citizenship and Social Class and Other Essays.* Cambridge: Cambridge University Press.

Mik-Meyer, N. (2015). Gender and disability: Feminizing male employees with visible impairments in Danish work organizations. *Gender, Work and Organization,* 22(6), 579–595.

Morris, F. (2022). Violence against persons with disabilities and the responsiveness of the justice system in Jamaica. In R. Biholar and D. Leslie (Eds.), *Critical*

Caribbean Perspectives on Preventing Gender-Based Violence (pp. 10–26). London and New York: Routledge.

OECD (2015). *Small Island Developing States (SIDS) and the Post-2015 Development Finance Agenda*. Retrieved on November 22, 2022, from https://www.oecd.org/dac/financing-sustainable-development/Addis%20Flyer%20SIDS%20FINAL.pdf.

PAHO (2022). *COVID-19 Pandemic Disproportionately Affected Women in the Americas*. Retrieved on November 22, 2022, from https://www.paho.org/en/news/8-3-2022-covid-19-pandemic-disproportionately-affected-women-americas.

Patel, P. (2001). *Notes on Gender and Racial Discrimination: An Urgent Need to Integrate an Intersectional Perspective to the Examination and Development of Policies, Strategies and Remedies for Gender and Racial Equality*. United Nations Commission on the Status of Women, Forty-Fifth Session, 6–16 March. Retrieved on June 2, 2023, from https://www.un.org/womenwatch/daw/csw/Patel45.htm.

Perkins, A. K. (2011). Carne vale (goodbye to flesh?): Caribbean carnival, notions of the flesh and Christian ambivalence about the body. *Sexuality & Culture* 15 (4), 361–374.

Ray, T. (2022). *Caribbean Women Fight through the Challenge of COVID-19*. Retrieved on November 22, 2022, from https://www.ifc.org/wps/wcm/connect/news_ext_content/ifc_external_corporate_site/news+and+events/news/caribbean-women-fight-through-covid-19.

Robinson, T. (2003). Beyond the Bill of Rights. In E. Barriteau (Ed.), *Confronting Power, Theorizing Gender: Interdisciplinary Perspectives in the Caribbean* (pp. 231–261). Kingston, Jamaica: University of the West Indies Press.

Sheller, M. (2012). *Citizenship from Below: Erotic Agency and Caribbean Freedom*. Durham, NC: Duke University Press.

Tan, K.-C. (2017). Cosmopolitan citizenship. In A. Shachar, R. Bauböck, I. Bloemraad and M. Vink (Eds.), *The Oxford Handbook of Citizenship* (pp. 694–714). Oxford: Oxford University Press.

UN Women (2012). *Handbook for National Action Plans on Violence Against Women*. New York: UN Women.

UN Women (2018). *Women in Political Leadership in the Caribbean*. Retrieved on June 30, 2023 from https://parlamericas.org/uploads/documents/WomensPoliticalLeadershipUNWomen.pdf.

UN Women (2019). *Status of Women and Men Report: Productive Employment and Decent Work for All: A Gender Analysis of Labour Force Data and Policy Frameworks in Six CARICOM Member States*. Retrieved on June 21, 2022, from https://caribbean.unwomen.org/sites/default/files/Field%20Office%20Caribbean/Attachments/Publications/2019/Status%20of%20Women%20and%20Men-WEB.pdf.

UN Women (2021). *Measuring the Shadow Pandemic: Violence against Women during COVID-19*. Retrieved on June 21, 2022, from https://data.unwomen.org/sites/default/files/documents/Publications/Measuring-shadow-pandemic.pdf.

UN Women (2022). *Facts and Figures: Ending Violence against Women*. Retrieved on June 12, 2022, from https://www.unwomen.org/en/what-we-do/ending-violence-against-women/facts-and-figures#notes.

UNDAW, OHCHR & UNIFEM (2000). *Gender and Racial Discrimination*. Report of the Expert Group Meeting 21–24 November 2000, Zagreb, Croatia. Retrieved on June 21, 2022, from https://www.un.org/womenwatch/daw/csw/genrac/report.htm.

20 *Introduction*

UNFPA & Management Sciences for Health (2016). *We Decide: Young Persons with Disabilities Call for Equal Rights and a Life Free of Violence.* Retrieved on June 21, 2022, from https://www.msh.org/blog/2016/08/12/we-decide-young-persons-with-disabilities-call-for-equal-rights-and-alife-free-of.

UNICEF (2019). *Gender Equality.* Retrieved on November 23, 2022, from https://www.unicef.org/lac/en/gender-equality.

United Nations (1995). *Beijing Declaration and Platform for Action.* Retrieved on June 21, 2022, from https://www.un.org/womenwatch/daw/beijing/pdf/BDPfA%20E.pdf.

United Nations (2001). *Gender and Racial Discrimination, Report of the Expert Group Meeting in Zagreb, 21–24 November 2000.* Retrieved on June 6, 2023, from https://www.un.org/womenwatch/daw/csw/genrac/report.htm.

United Nations (2020). *Policy Brief: The Impact of COVID-19 on Women.* Retrieved on June 21, 2022, from https://www.un.org/sites/un2.un.org/files/policy_brief_on_covid_impact_on_women_9_apr_2020_updated.pdf.

Universal Declaration of Human Rights (1948). Retrieved on June 21, 2022, from https://www.un.org/sites/un2.un.org/files/2021/03/udhr.pdf.

UNODC (2018). *Global Study on Homicide: Gender-Related Killing of Women and Girls.* Vienna: UNODC.

WHO (2021a). *Devastatingly Pervasive: 1 in 3 Women Globally Experience Violence.* Retrieved on June 12, 2022, from https://www.who.int/news/item/09-03-2021-devastatingly-pervasive-1-in-3-women-globally-experience-violence.

WHO (2021b). *Violence against Women Prevalence Estimates, 2018.* Retrieved on June 15, 2022, from https://apps.who.int/iris/bitstream/handle/10665/341338/9789240026681-eng.pdf.

Women's Rights and Economic Change (2004). *Intersectionality: A Tool for Gender and Economic Justice,* 9. Retrieved on November 22, 2022, from https://www.awid.org/sites/default/files/atoms/files/intersectionality_a_tool_for_gender_and_economic_justice.pdf.

World Bank (2018). *The Time is Now for Gender Equality in the Caribbean.* Retrieved on November 7, 2022, from https://www.worldbank.org/en/news/feature/2018/03/07/the-time-is-now-for-gender-equality-in-the-caribbean.

World Bank (2021). *The Gendered Impacts of COVID-19 on Labor Markets in Latin America and the Caribbean.* Retrieved on November 8, 2022, from https://www.worldbank.org/en/results/2021/05/05/the-gendered-impacts-of-covid-19-on-labor-markets-in-latin-america-and-the-caribbean.

World Bank (2022). *Women, Business and the Law.* Washington DC: World Bank.

Young, I. M. (1990). *Justice and the Politics of Difference,* Princeton, NJ: Princeton University Press.

Yuval-Davis, N. (1997). Women, citizenship and difference. *Feminist Review,* 57(1), 4–27. https://doi.org/10.1080/014177897339632.

2 Barriers, Biases, Boys' Club
A Qualitative Study of the Underrepresentation of Female Politicians in Barbados, Jamaica and Trinidad and Tobago

Introduction

Women comprise at least 50 per cent of the world's population (World Bank, 2020). Despite this, they remain underrepresented as candidates for public and political offices. Since the Fourth World Conference on Women in Beijing in 1995, the number of women in national parliaments has doubled, but they still comprise only 25 per cent of members of national parliaments (Inter-Parliamentary Union, 2020). In 1995, the Beijing Platform for Action (BPA) called for 30 per cent of national legislative seats to be held by women, asserting that "without the active participation of women and the incorporation of women's perspective at all levels of decision-making, the goals of equality, development and peace cannot be achieved." In short, unless women form a critical mass (at least 30 per cent) in a legislative body, they are but "token" participants. The Convention on the Elimination of Discrimination against Women (CEDAW) also proposed 30 to 35 per cent as the critical mass of women required to affect decision-making. According to CEDAW's General Recommendation No. 23, "if women's participation reaches 30 to 35 per cent (generally termed a 'critical mass'), there is a real impact on political style and the content of decisions, and political life is revitalized" (CEDAW, 1997). This approach, often referred to as "critical mass theory," suggests that to have any substantial effect on legislative outcomes, women need to move from mere tokens in the legislative assembly to a considerable minority of all legislators (Dahlerup, 1988; Kanter, 1977; Mansbridge, 2005). Today, only 61 countries have reached this critical mass. Only five countries worldwide now have gender parity or a more significant share of women in parliament—Rwanda, Cuba, Nicaragua, Mexico and the United Arab Emirates (Inter-Parliamentary Union, 2022).

In the Anglo-Caribbean, women gained the right to vote and stand for elections over 75 years ago. They also possess *de jure* equality. The region also boasts prominent female leaders. Despite this, the Anglo-Caribbean lacks a critical mass of women in the legislative branches of nearly every country in the region. According to the United Nations, on average,

DOI: 10.4324/9781003130987-2

22 Barriers, Biases, Boys' Club

22 per cent of ministerial portfolios/cabinet positions in the Anglophone Caribbean are held by women. Across the region, women generally do not hold more than 30 per cent of elected positions, with the exception of Guyana (which has a legislated quota of one-third of the number of political nominees must be women) (UN Women, 2018, p. 5).

In countries like Antigua and Barbuda, St Lucia, Belize, the Bahamas and St Vincent and the Grenadines, women comprise less than 20 per cent of the lower house. Several factors contribute to this underrepresentation of women in politics in the Anglo-Caribbean. One factor is cultural attitudes towards women's societal roles, which may discourage women from seeking political office. Additionally, there may be structural barriers, such as the need for more access to education and training opportunities for women and limited financial resources and networks to support their political campaigns.

Using Norris and Lovenduski's (1995) supply-and-demand model to account for why women were systematically excluded from political office, we will attempt to explain in this chapter what might account for the underrepresentation of women in politics in the Anglo-Caribbean. This is amid the growing demand for gender equality in the region. It offers a critical analysis of the challenges faced by female politicians and political aspirants through the voice of the women themselves. Interviews were conducted with female politicians from Jamaica, Barbados and Trinidad and Tobago.[1] Overall, 13 interviews were conducted: Barbados (6), Jamaica (5) and Trinidad and Tobago (2). Of the 13 interviewees, eight currently serve in parliament, while the remaining five are former politicians or women who ran in an election but did not win a seat. Respondents were asked to (i) explain whether they perceived women to be underrepresented in politics in their respective countries, (ii) identify the barriers to women's political representation, (iii) recount their experiences (or those of other female politicians) in political office or while seeking to enter politics, (iv) make recommendations on what they believe needs to be done to increase the number of women in politics in the Anglo-Caribbean. These elite interviews provided insight into the barriers and gender-related constraints to women's political participation and representation in the Anglo-Caribbean.

Thematic analysis was employed to analyse the interview data. First, transcripts were read through twice, and initial notes were taken. Next, initial codes were developed manually using NVivo (a programme for qualitative and mixed-methods research) and descriptive coding at the first level. One hundred and twelve codes emerged, were revised, and condensed to 15 categories. These categories were reviewed to ensure that the data formed a coherent pattern, and a thematic map was developed to establish relationships among the categories. Two major themes emerged. The first theme is: "Challenges and Deterrents for Female Politicians in the Caribbean." The second is "Assets: The Recipe to Survive Politics as a

Woman." Subsequently, categories were refined and collapsed into four sub-themes for the identified challenges and assets/recommendations. The supporting sub-themes are (1) perceived female roles/domestic roles, (2) lack of funding, (3) lack of network and support and (4) violent politics. Findings are reported from an emic perspective using direct quotes from the respondents.

The chapter is organised into several broad sections. First, an overview of the barriers to women in politics literature is provided. This is followed by a historical overview of the entry of women into elected political offices in the Anglo-Caribbean and the struggles they endured in doing so. Next, it explores the challenges and solutions to the marginalisation of women in national parliaments in the Anglo-Caribbean, highlighting the views of female politicians.

Barriers to Women in Politics Globally

According to Norris and Lovenduski, there is an intersection between the demand and supply of female candidates: "the political system sets the general context, the recruitment process sets the steps from aspiration to nomination, while selectors demand and candidate supply determine the outcome" (1995, p. 4). The supply-side analysis emphasises factors that affect women's interest in pursuing political offices, such as lack of confidence, resource constraints (money, time, political experience), motivation, career choices or lack of support networks. In short, women's decision to run for political office or not will be based on factors such as personal considerations about family and career, perception of politics, and motivation. Demand-side factors reflect the active selection, recruitment and nomination of candidates by political parties, whether they are run in winnable or lost-cause ridings, and the public's willingness to vote. Political parties looking for the best candidate presenting the least electoral risk will "choose candidates depending upon their perceptions of the applicant's abilities, qualifications and experience" (Norris & Lovenduski, 1995, p. 14). Political parties and elites act as gatekeepers to politics, determining through the nomination and selection of candidates the composition of the government, the opposition, and the legislature, as well as the choices before voters (Ashe, 2020). In short, demand-side factors are those factors of the political system that limit women's political participation. Separately or combined, both supply and demand factors can affect women's political representation; a decision in one process can affect a decision in the other. If, for example, fewer women than men put themselves up as potential candidates, political parties will only have a pool of men from whom to choose. Likewise, if women perceive that they will not be selected or nominated by political parties, they will be less likely to put themselves forward as potential candidates.

Supply-Side Barriers to Women's Political Representation

Education, the number of women in the labour force, occupational segregation and the socioeconomic status of women are some of the factors that influence women's participation in politics (Krook, 2004; Reynolds, 1999; Matland, 1998). Other factors include levels of education and the dual burden of domestic tasks and professional obligations (Shvedova, 2005). Gender scholars also point out that gender norms and stereotypes tend to put women seeking to enter politics in a double bind (Dittmar, 2015; Jamieson, 1995). Women are traditionally socialised to carry a disproportionate portion of household labour (Bianchi et al., 2012; Iversen & Rosenbluth, 2006). Moreover, women with full-time jobs and a family face an even greater battle. Entering politics becomes a choice between public or private life. They must work twice as hard as their male counterparts to be successful in their careers and prove their worth. Not only is a woman's political activity negatively correlated to marriage and raising a family (Crowder-Meyer, 2018), her political involvement and interests tend to be at their lowest during child-bearing years. Some women, after giving birth, might lose interest in politics, or may struggle to balance the demands of motherhood with the demands of political life. This can be especially challenging in contexts where there is limited support for working parents, such as affordable childcare options and parental leave policies.

Political involvement requires time, effort, and commitment that many women, especially those with families, may be unwilling or unable to give. For Kalla and Rosenbluth, the double bind in politics "emerges because female candidates without families—who could better afford the time to invest in political careers— may face greater degrees of voter disapproval, while women in more demanding family roles have less time for political work" (2018, p. 526). The intersection of voter preferences for families with traditional family structures, a woman's family roles and the demand of a political office contributes to women's underrepresentation in politics in many societies, not excluding the Anglo-Caribbean.

Society's views about cultural norms, attitudes, values and perceptions of gender roles also present significant challenges to women's representation (Darcy, Welch & Clark, 1994). Most children are socialised to believe that women should be passive, domesticated and demure, while boys should be assertive and aggressive. According to Matland, "men, across virtually all cultures, are socialized to see politics as a legitimate sphere for them to act in. This leads to men having a greater knowledge of and interest in politics, and greater political ambition" (2005, p. 94). Women tend to view politics as a dirty game played only by men. This perception, unfortunately, reflects the reality in most countries worldwide. Shvedova explains that this perception "has jarred [women's] confidence in their ability to participate in the political process" (2005, p. 45).

The incongruence between leadership roles and commonly held gender stereotypes further creates a double bind for female politicians. Not only are girls and boys socialised to view positions of power differently, but women are commonly ascribed communal traits (sensitivity, kindness, compassion), while men are ascribed agentic traits such as confidence, assertiveness, charisma and authority (Burns & Kattelman, 2017; Abele, 2003; Fiske & Stevens, 1993). Female politicians' roles as political leaders require them to be agentic, but stereotypical gender roles prescribed to women expect them to be communal. When women display agentic characteristics, they are perceived as less cooperative because they violate gender role expectations (Eagly & Karau, 2002). Female politicians are, therefore, faced with the double bind of creating the perfect balance between the agentic traits assigned to the prototypical leaders and the communal characteristics attributed to women. This complex expectation of women is summed up by Jamieson, who claimed that:

> women are penalized both for deviating from the masculine norm and appearing masculine. When women try to establish their competence, they are scrutinized for evidence that they lack masculine (instrumental) characteristics and for signs that they no longer possess female (expressive) ones. They are taken to fail, in other words, both as a male and as a female.
>
> (Jamieson, 1995, p. 125)

This double bind can make it difficult for women to navigate the complex and often hostile terrain of politics and can discourage them from running for office or speaking out on issues they care about. It can also make it challenging for women in politics to be taken seriously and to be effective in their roles, particularly if they are subject to gender-based discrimination and harassment.

Many women simply lack the confidence to run for public office. Women who are accomplished with comparable education, skills and experience to men tend to perceive themselves as less qualified for elected office. Although men and women use similar evaluative criteria in their decision-making process to run for office, women are more likely to feel that they fail to meet these criteria. Moreover, these women also feel they do not have the traits for crude politics. All these barriers affect women's sense of self-efficacy (Fox & Lawless, 2011). However, it is not enough to get women to run for political office, because more women who run for public office tend to lose elections compared to men. Whenever and wherever they perceive gender barriers to their political participation, women tend to become very cynical and apathetic towards politics and avoid it. This sceptical outlook is reflected in their low levels of political efficacy and political ambition. Therefore, women's concerns tend to be neglected in the design and implementation of public policies. This presents a barrier to the supply of women in politics.

26 *Barriers, Biases, Boys' Club*

Lack of money and support also act as deterrents for female politicians, who, without finances, cannot contest electoral campaigns or conduct political duties once elected to office (Lawless & Fox, 2005; 2008). Women's difficulties in funding election campaigns or raising funds needed to win party nominations are due to multiple factors, including "the lack of access to moneyed networks and credit, and political clientelism" (Ballington & Kahane, 2014, p. 307). In a 2008 survey of 300 MPs, the Inter-Parliamentary Union (IPU) found that campaign finance was one of the biggest obstacles for women entering politics (Inter-Parliamentary Union, 2008). A 2013 survey by UN Women reported similar findings wherein over 80 per cent of respondents identified the lack of access to funding as one of the biggest challenges to women's entry into politics (iKnowPolitics, 2015). One possible explanation is that women generally have fewer resources than men.

There is evidence to suggest that wealthy men dominate politics, particularly in countries with privately funded political systems (Ballington & Khane, 2014; Cigane & Ohman, 2014). The concentration of funding among a small group of wealthy individuals can create a significant barrier to entry for candidates who lack the financial resources or access to networks of wealthy donors. Political parties are also less likely to fund female politicians, in part because of perceptions that women are less likely to win elections. This can create a self-fulfilling prophecy, as the lack of funding and support can make it more difficult for women to mount successful campaigns and win elections.

Male politicians also have access to influential networks that women are excluded from. This gives them greater access both to wealthy donors and to well-needed resources. This points to another political barrier for women: a lack of access to influential networks and support. Men are more likely than women to donate or contribute large sums to party campaigns (Barber, Canes-Wrone & Thrower, 2017; Swers & Thomson, 2020). Swers and Thomson also pointed to a homosocial dimension to fundraising, in which men obtain a significant proportion of campaign donations from men and women from other women. If more men donate more money to political campaigns, women face a more significant challenge in raising funds for their campaigns. In the United States, for example, it was found that "more men than women donated to general election candidates for state legislative office in the 2020 election. The total amount contributed by men also exceeded the total amount contributed by women" (Gothreau & Sanbonmatsu, 2020, p. 1). This helps to explain why men are over-represented in parliaments worldwide. In Canada, Ouellet, Shiab, and Gilchrist (2021) found that in the 2015 and 2019 general elections, white men received 10 per cent ($68,001) more funding from their parties than did other candidates ($61,724).

Another supply-side barrier that affects the number of women willing to put themselves up for public and political office is violence against women in politics (VAWIP). Violence against women in politics is acknowledged globally as a human rights violation and a barrier to women's political representation. It "cuts across all political sectors and targets women in-person and online regardless of their political role, age, background or station in life" (National Democratic Institute, 2017). UN Women and UNDP define VAWIP, including in and beyond elections, as:

> Any act of, or threat of, gender-based violence resulting in physical, sexual, psychological harm or suffering to women that prevents them from exercising and realizing their political rights, whether in public or private spaces, including the right to vote and hold public office, to vote in secret and to freely campaign, to associate and assemble, and to enjoy freedom of opinion and expression. Such violence can be perpetrated by a family member, community member and/or by the State.
>
> (UN Women & UNDP, 2017, p. 20)

It is pervasive and seriously violates women's enjoyment of their human rights. Not to be confused with political violence (PV), VAWIP is a subset of violence against women in the political sphere and specifically targets women. It differs slightly from violence against women in elections, which primarily takes place during a period of election. Violence against women in politics occurs during elections and after women have assumed their positions as politicians (Krook & Restrepo Sanín, 2016; Johnson-Myers, 2019). Unlike political violence, VAWIP seeks to violate, repress, deter and control women's political rights based on gender identity. It is "behaviours that specifically target women to leave politics by pressuring them to step down as candidates or resign from a particular political office" (Krook & Restrepo Sanín, 2016, p. 128).

Acts of violence against women in politics can take several forms, including physical, psychological, economic and sexual violence. (Krook, 2020; Krook & Restrepo Sanín, 2020; UN Women, 2018). These acts of violence are usually done to enforce patriarchal control of democratic institutions (Bardall, 2011) and prevent women from exercising their political rights. Violence against women in politics also manifests in the unequal distribution of power between men and women, in both the private and public spheres. It embodies "a form of backlash to women's greater inclusion in the political sphere, resisting the gains made possible by gender quotas and other mechanisms to empower women in decision-making" (Krook & Restrepo Sanín, 2016, p. 137).

Demand-Side Barriers

Matland (2005) identifies three crucial barriers women must overcome to enter national parliaments. They need to nominate themselves or express an interest in running for office, be selected as candidates by their

28   Barriers, Biases, Boys' Club

respective political parties, and be elected by the voters. Earlier research on women's political participation highlighted overt discrimination against women by voters and political parties as barriers to female candidates (Githens & Prestage, 1977; Rule, 1981; Darcy, Welch & Clark, 1994). A key deterrent to women's political representation on the demand side is the ability of political parties to recruit, nominate and select female candidates. Political parties, as the gatekeepers to political life, are often responsible for recruiting legislative candidates (Cross, 2006; Ashe, 2020). They and the political elites "control the recruitment and selection of candidates, determine the rules, the procedures, and often the criteria according to which candidates will be recruited" (Pitre, 2003, p. 103). Many political parties, however, do not provide financial or mentorship support for female candidates. The selection and nomination processes are sometimes biased against women, using "male characteristics" to determine their suitability (Shvedova, 2005). Also, women are often not placed in winnable positions on party lists, thus minimising their chances of being elected. Party support is, therefore, essential for the removal of partisan exclusion and for improving the electoral success of the women who run for public office (Bucchianeri, 2018).

Other structural and institutional factors explaining women's underrepresentation are the political system and the process by which candidates are recruited for political office (Norris, 1997). A related issue is that some electoral systems' structures are barriers to women's political participation. According to Norris, "electoral systems represent, perhaps, the most powerful instrument available for institutional engineering, with far-reaching consequences for party systems, the composition of legislatures, and the durability of democratic arrangements" (2004, p. 209). Studies have shown that proportional-representation systems such as parallel and mixed-member proportional (MMP) systems provide the best political opportunities for women to get elected to parliament (Matland, 2005; Reynolds, Reilly & Ellis, 2005; Norris & Lovenduski, 1995; Bakopanos, 2004; Ogai, 2001; Kenworthy & Malami, 1999; Paxton, 1997; Darcy, Welch & Clark, 1994). Electoral systems that rely on single-member districts (such as the first-past-the-post or the alternative vote systems) often fail to guarantee proportional representation or a minimum percentage of seats for women (unless there are special provisions in place or additional seats are elected by party lists) (Lijphart, 1994; Shugart, 1994; Rule, 1994).

There is also a media-related barrier to women's political representation. Female politicians are less likely to receive newspaper and TV news coverage compared with male politicians (Gilmartin, 2001; Kahn 1992; 1994; 1996; Norris, 1997; O'Neill & Savigny, 2014; Sampert & Trimble, 2003). They also receive more "horse-race" coverage than their male counterparts. This type of coverage "emphasizes which candidates are ahead and behind and the strategies and tactics of campaigning necessary to position a candidate to get

Barriers, Biases, Boys' Club 29

ahead or to stay ahead" (Cappella & Jamieson, 1997, p. 74). How women are represented or portrayed in the media is also a barrier to getting elected or achieving parity with men (Johnson-Myers, 2021; Braden, 1996; Bystrom et al., 2001 Dolan, 2004; Kahn, 1996; Norris, 1997; Ross, 2002).

The frame through which the media portray female politicians has helped to perpetuate certain negative stereotypes and biases, especially as they relate to the roles of men and women. Gender bias in the media results in the underrepresentation of women in politics, and the portrayal of women perpetuates negative stereotypes. It is not uncommon for the media to objectify women by focusing on their physical appearance, character traits, family and sexual orientation rather than on issues or policies (Aday & Devitt, 2001; Conroy et al., 2015; Devitt, 1999; Garcia-Blanco & Wahl-Jorgensen, 2011; Haraldsson & Wängnerud, 2019; Heron, 2008; Johnson-Myers, 2021; Jamieson, 1995; Kahn, 1992; 1996; Robinson & Saint-Jean, 1991; Ross & Comrie, 2012). Using gender frames to cover female politicians, the media trivialises their position and importance in the political sphere, diminishing them to their gender. Media coverage of women candidates and politicians is disproportionately negative, and justified expectations of media hostility are likely to discourage women from standing for election. Media sexism also affects the number of women willing to put themselves up for elections. Haraldsson and Wängnerud's study on the relationship between media and sexism in politics found, for example, that "the higher the level of media sexism, the lower the share of women candidates." They hypothesised that "sexist portrayals of women in the media stifle ambition among women who, in a less sexist media environment, would be willing to stand as political candidates" (2019, p. 524).

Barriers to Women in Politics: Caribbean Perspectives

There is a paucity of information on women in politics in the Anglo-Caribbean, despite attempts by women's rights activists and feminist scholars such as Linette Vassell, Eudine Barriteau, Patricia Mohammed, Verene Shepherd, Maxine Henry-Wilson and Rhoda Reddock to understand and interpret the challenges women face in politics and at the decision-making table. With so few women in parliament, what are some of the factors preventing women from entering or remaining in politics? Before the granting of universal suffrage, starting in 1944 in Jamaica, restrictions in the electoral system presented systemic discrimination to women in the Caribbean, making them ineligible to vote or run for public office. Those voting barriers have since been removed, but not much has changed for women, especially those running for political office. In addition to institutional barriers, "women in commonwealth Caribbean countries continue to experience a combination of sub-systemic material and ideological barriers that thwart their full participation in the practices of governance nationally and at the community level" (Barriteau, 1998, p. 203).

30 Barriers, Biases, Boys' Club

Writing in 1987, former female Member of Parliament in Jamaica, Maxine Henry-Wilson (1987), found several cultural and historical challenges facing female political aspirants and politicians. Many of these barriers remain today. These include lack of confidence among women to act as political representatives; women's activities in the home, which leave very little time for public life and office; lack of funding for campaigns and constituency activities; women uniting to exclude other women from politics; the perception that politics is a "dirty game"—and one in which women will not be able to cope; and finally, the portrayal of politics as a male-dominated area and one that worked to exclude women.

Vassell (2003; 2013) also identified similar factors impeding women's political participation and advancement in the region. Among these are discriminatory cultural and social attitudes and negative stereotypes about and against women and the negative political culture of violence and partisan politics that exists in the country. A 2015 study by the Caribbean Institute for Women in Leadership (CIWiL) and UN Women also found that women were not inclined to participate in representational politics due to similar reasons found by Henry-Wilson (1987) and Vassell (2003; 2013). These include verbal abuse; how women are portrayed in the media; condescension and discrimination by male colleagues; lack of support from both male and female colleagues; lack of intra-party democracy and the persistence of the exclusionary male network. The Commonwealth Parliamentary Association also reported that women in Commonwealth parliaments, including the Caribbean, "are awarded a disproportionate number of seats, have little influence on party policy and little leverage to push nominees for electoral office. They still largely make the tea and not the policy" (cited in Barriteau, 1998, p. 23).

Political violence is another barrier to women's entrance and durability in politics in the Anglo-Caribbean (Johnson-Myers, 2021). Political violence, especially in Jamaica, can be attributed to the violent nature of the country and its history of electoral violence. The violence ranges from character assassination and verbal abuse to being shot. These acts of violence ordinarily peaked during the election campaigns, especially in communities with a history of violence. Violent politics, patronage and aggressive partisanship in Jamaica can be attributed to the intense rivalry between the two major political parties (the People's National Party (PNP) and the Jamaica Labour Party (JLP)) in their quest for votes (Gray, 2004; Sives, 2003; Campbell, 2020). By the 1960s, and especially the 1980s, violence had become institutionalised in modern Jamaican politics. Between 1980 and the present, political violence has become less of a feature of the general elections, but violence itself has become a feature of daily everyday life. Female politicians must compete with their male counterparts in this treacherous and often intimidating political environment. It is understandable, therefore, why many of them leave politics prematurely or do not enter at all.

Women in Politics in the Anglo-Caribbean: A Historical Overview

Caribbean women's political activity dates to the period of enslavement, where they were active agents in the resistance movement and the fight for freedom and independence (Bush, 1990; Mair, Beckles & Shepherd, 2006; Mathurin-Mair, 2006; Shepherd, 2011; Wilmot, 2011). Politics during the colonial era in the Anglo-Caribbean was monopolised by white men who excluded women, blacks and Jews from the political space. By 1886, the right to vote was extended to "wealthy" non-white males, but women continued to be excluded. In Guyana, for example, "1891 electoral reforms ... lowered property and income qualifications and diversified the 'racio-ethnic' composition of the still limited electorate, but women were still excluded until well into the 1920s" (Reddock, 2011, p. 5). During the post-slavery era, women's role and participation in politics would see them running for political office, participating actively in trade unions, and forming women's groups. Women's involvement in politics also took the forms of letter-writing, campaigns, petitions to colonial governors and protest marches (Reddock, 1994; 2004; Bissessar, 2014).

In Jamaica, the franchise was extended in 1919 to women over 25 with an earned income of £50 or who paid taxes of over £2 per year (Reddock, 2011, p. 5). Women were still excluded from running in an election or holding public office. With the right to vote so inextricably linked to income and property ownership, it is no surprise that women were excluded from voting or running for public office. As depicted in Table 2.1, it was not until after the granting of universal adult suffrage, during the period 1944 to 1962, that women of all classes and colours gained the right to vote and, eventually, stand for office. Universal adult suffrage was granted in Jamaica in 1944 and in 1946 and 1950 in Trinidad and Tobago and Barbados, respectively. Even with the granting of universal adult suffrage in Trinidad and Tobago in 1946, women still were not eligible to stand as candidates until 1951 (Reddock, 2011).

Between 1944 and 1962, most Anglo-Caribbean countries attained universal adult suffrage, self-governance and independence. These countries were now free to conduct their elections and elect their representatives. While women were also granted the right to vote, this did not alter the unequal gender power relations inherited from the colonial period regarding civil, social and economic liberties. Even after women gained the right to vote and stand for elections, they comprised a minority of candidates in general elections, and only a few were successful at the polls (Reddock, 2004). Using statistical data on voting patterns in the Caribbean between 1992 and 2005, Barrow-Giles and Joseph (2006) pointed out that, despite being able to vote, few women contested general elections across the region. Jamaica was the first

32 Barriers, Biases, Boys' Club

Table 2.1 Women's Entry to Formal Political Participation (Anglo-Caribbean)[2]

Country	Year Vote Obtained by Women (national level)	Year Women Given the Right to Stand for Election (national level)	Year First Woman Elected to Parliament
Antigua and Barbuda	1951	1951	1984
The Bahamas	1962	1962	1977
Barbados	1951	1951	1951
Belize	1954	1954	1961
Dominica	1951	1951	1980
Grenada	1951	1951	1961
Guyana	1953	1945[3]	1953
Jamaica	1944	1944	1944
St Kitts and Nevis	1951	1951	1984
St Lucia	1951	1951	1974
St Vincent and the Grenadines	1951	1951	1957
Trinidad and Tobago	1946	1951	1961

Sources: Inter-Parliamentary Union, 2023; Barrow-Giles and Joseph, 2006; Reddock, 2004; Buddan, 2004; ECLAC, 1999.

English-speaking Caribbean country to gain universal adult suffrage and granted women the right to vote. The first general elections under universal suffrage in Jamaica were held on December 14, 1944. Following this election, Iris Collins became the first woman elected to the House of Representatives, representing the Jamaica Labour Party in the St James North-Western constituency. In 1949, Rose Leon became the second woman elected to parliament since universal adult suffrage was granted. Women have since contested every national election in Jamaica, with 47 being elected to the House of Representatives.

Women were also nominated as candidates in Trinidad and Tobago and Barbados in their first general election following the granting of universal adult suffrage in 1950 and 1951, respectively. Between 1944 and 1987, very few women in the Caribbean were successful at the polls (Jamaica, 1944; Barbados, 1951; Guyana, 1953; Belize, 1961; St Vincent and the Grenadines, 1971; Anguilla, 1976; and Bahamas, 1982) (Barrow-Giles & Joseph, 2006). Political parties did not nominate women in St Vincent and the Grenadines, St Kitts and Nevis, the Bahamas, Anguilla, Antigua, and Barbuda until the 1970s and 1980s (Barrow-Giles & Joseph, 2006). By the 1980s, more women were running in elections and getting elected to national parliaments. Still, the numbers were dismal, with none of the independent countries in the region electing more than 15 per cent of women to parliament (Barriteau, 1998). It was not until 2004 that the first woman won a seat in a general election in Antigua and Barbuda.

Despite the dominance of patriarchy in the political system of most English-speaking countries in the Caribbean, several women have broken the glass ceiling, becoming heads of states in their respective countries. Other women across the Caribbean have passed the barriers to entry and become household names. In 1980, Dame Eugenia Charles became the first female to be elected Prime Minister in the Caribbean. She co-founded the Dominica Freedom Party in 1972 and became Leader of the Opposition in 1975 (CARICOM, 2022). Since then, female leaders have been elected in many Caribbean countries, including Barbados, Guyana, Jamaica, and Trinidad and Tobago. Barbados and Trinidad and Tobago also have a female President. Some of these women are Janet Jagan (Prime Minister of Guyana), Portia Simpson-Miller (Prime Minister of Jamaica), Kamla Persad-Bissessar (Prime Minister of Trinidad and Tobago), and Mia Mottley (Prime Minister of Barbados) (see Table 2.2). As depicted in Table 2.2, other Caribbean countries have also boasted women in political positions of power, such as Prime Ministers, Premiers, Presidents, Governors-General, Party Leaders and Leaders of the Opposition. These include non-English-speaking countries such as Haiti and non-independent or overseas territories such as Anguilla, Bermuda, Curacao and the Turks and Caicos Islands.

Recent years have seen an increase, albeit slow, in the number of women elected or appointed to political office in the Caribbean, but there is still a long way to go. Based on the Inter-Parliamentary Union's global ranking for women in executive and government positions, on average, women in the English-speaking Caribbean make up 40.9 per cent of members of lower chambers and unicameral parliaments, 31.2 per cent of upper chambers, and 39.5 per cent of all chambers (Inter-Parliamentary Union, 2023). The percentage of women in the lower houses of parliament in the Anglo-Caribbean ranges from 5.6 per cent in Antigua and Barbuda to 31 per cent in Grenada. In contrast, in the upper houses, the percentage varies from 18 per cent in the Bahamas to 52.9 per cent in Antigua and Barbuda. As of 2022, Dominica, Grenada and Guyana are the only countries in the English-speaking Caribbean where women comprise more than 30 per cent of the total MPs in the lower house (see Table 2.3). In Antigua and Barbuda, women occupy 52.9 per cent of the seats in the upper house—the highest in the English-speaking Caribbean (Inter-Parliamentary Union, 2023). At the executive level, Barbados is the only country with a female Prime Minister. It is also the only country in the history of the Caribbean to be governed by a female Prime Minister, a female Deputy Prime Minister and a female President simultaneously.

In Jamaica, female politicians now occupy a historic 28.6 per cent of the 63 seats in the House of Representatives (lower house) and 38.1 per cent of the seats in the Senate (upper house). Most of these women (14) are on the

34 Barriers, Biases, Boys' Club

Table 2.2 Caribbean Countries with Females in Political Positions of Power

Country	Female politician	Political position
Anguilla	Palmavon Webster	Leader of the Opposition
Aruba	Evelyn Weaver-Croes	Prime Minister
Antigua and Barbuda	Louise Lake-Tack	Governor-General
	Dame Yvonne Maginley	Deputy Governor-General
Belize	Dame Dr Elmira Gordon	Governor General
Bermuda	Pamela Gordon	Premier
	Dame Jennifer Smith	Premier
	Paula Cox	Premier, Party Leader
	Jeanne Atherden	Leader of the Opposition
The Bahamas	Marguerite Pindling	Deputy Governor-General
	Cynthia Pratt	Deputy Prime Minister
	Dame Dr Ivy Dumont	Acting Governor-General
Barbados	Mia Mottley	Prime Minister, Party Leader
	Sandra Mason	President
	Santia Bradshaw	Deputy Prime Minister
	Sandra Mason	Governor-General
Curacao	Lucile Geore-Wout	Governor
Dominica	Dame Eugenia Charles	Prime Minister
	Jesma Paul Victor	Opposition Leader
Grenada	Dame Cécile La Grenada	Governor-General
Guyana	Janet Jagan	Prime Minister, President
	Janet Jagan	Vice President
	Viola Harper Burnham	Vice President
Haiti	Claudette Werleigh	Prime Minister
	Michèle Pierre-Louis	Prime Minister
	Ertha Pascal Trouillot	President
Jamaica	Portia Simpson-Miller	Prime Minister, Party Leader
	Portia Simpson-Miller	Opposition Leader
St Lucia	Dame Pearlette Louisy	Governor-General
St Vincent and the Grenadines	Monica Dacon	Acting Governor-General
	Susan Dougan	Governor-General
Trinidad and Tobago	Kamla Persad-Bissessar	Prime Minister
	Paula-Mae Weekes	President
	Kamla Persad-Bissessar	Leader of the Opposition
The Turks and Caicos Islands	Sharlene Cartwright-Robinson	Premier

Source: created by the authors with data from Sekou, 2020; Williams, 2020.

Barriers, Biases, Boys' Club 35

Table 2.3 Women in National Parliaments in the Anglo-Caribbean

Country	Seats (Lower House)	Women	%	Seats (Upper House)	Women	%
Antigua and Barbuda	18	1	5.6	17	9	52.9
Belize	32	5	15.6	14	6	42.9
The Bahamas	39	7	18.0	16	4	25.0
Barbados	30	6	26.7	19	8	42.1
Dominica	32	12	37.5	–	–	–
Grenada	16	5	31.3	13	4	30.8
Guyana	71	36	36.6	–	–	–
Jamaica	63	18	28.6	21	8	38.1
St Kitts and Nevis	16	5	31.3	–	–	–
St Lucia	18	2	11.1	11	5	45.5
St Vincent and the Grenadines	22	4	18.2	–	–	–
Trinidad and Tobago	42	12	28.6	32	13	40.6

Source: created by the authors with data from Inter-Parliamentary Union, 2023.

JLP-led government bench. Before the September 2020 general elections, female politicians comprised no more than 18 per cent of the total number of MPs in the lower house and 5 to 8 per cent in the upper house. In 2006, Portia Simpson-Miller broke the proverbial "glass ceiling" for women when she became the first female President of the PNP and the first female Prime Minister of Jamaica (2006–2007 and 2011–2016). She also became the third female Prime Minister in the Anglophone Caribbean. Affectionately known as "Mama P" or "Sista P," Portia Simpson-Miller entered Jamaica's political scene in the early 1970s: first as a member of the Kingston and St Andrew Municipal Council as an elected council member, then as an MP with the People's National Party—a position she held since 1976 (Johnson-Myers, 2019). During her political career, she served as Minister of Labour, Welfare and Sports; Minister of Tourism; and Minister of Local Government and Sports. In 1978, she was appointed vice president of the PNP—a position she held until 2006. Simpson-Miller retired in 2019 as Leader of the Opposition.

Barbados has also seen an increase, with women occupying 26.7 per cent of the seats in the lower and 42.1 per cent in the upper house. Before the 2022 general elections in Barbados, women did not comprise more than 20 per cent of the elected members of parliament in the lower house. Following the 2022 general elections, women make up at least a quarter of Barbados's parliamentary composition. The legislature and judicature remain predominantly male, but for the first time in the country's history, both the state and executive are led by women. With Mia Mottley as

36 *Barriers, Biases, Boys' Club*

Prime Minister, Dame Sandra Mason as President, and Santia Bradshaw as Deputy Prime Minister, three of the top leadership positions in Barbados are occupied by women. In 2018, Mia Mottley became Barbados' first female Prime Minister. Mottley also etched her name in Barbados' history as the country's first female Attorney General, the first female Leader of the Opposition, and the country's second female Deputy Prime Minister. She also served in other ministerial portfolios, such as the Minister of Home Affairs, Minister of Education and Minister of Economic Affairs and Development. In November 2021, Barbados relinquished ties with the British monarchy, declaring itself a republic. Dame Sandra Mason was elected President of the Republic of Barbados, replacing the Queen as head of state.

Between 2015 and 2019, Trinidad and Tobago boasted a critical mass of at least 30 per cent of women in parliament. By 2020, this number fell to 26 per cent—below the threshold for political leadership and effective participation. Today, women in Trinidad and Tobago occupy 12 (28.6%) of the 42 seats in the lower house and 13 (40.6%) of the 32 seats in the upper house. Despite a decrease in the number of women elected to parliament after the 2020 general elections, it is worth noting that at least 30 per cent (45) of the 150 candidates who contested the elections were women. Also noteworthy is that three political parties contesting the election were women-led. Trinidad and Tobago also boast a former female Prime Minister, Kamla Persad-Bissessar, who was first elected to the post in 2010. Before her rise to political leadership, Persad-Bissessar rose through the ranks of her political party, first serving as an Alderman for the St Patrick County Council in 1987, then as a Senator in 1994, and as a Member of Parliament for the Siparia constituency (Skard, 2014). Throughout her political career, she has served in other ministerial portfolios and positions of leadership, such as Attorney General, Minister of Legal Affairs and Minister of Education (Skard, 2014). She was also the first woman in the history of the Republic of Trinidad and Tobago to have served as Leader of the Opposition. Trinidad and Tobago also rank among one of two countries in the English-speaking Caribbean with a female President. In 2018, Paula-Mae Weekes was appointed President of Trinidad and Tobago, becoming the first woman appointed to that role.

Results/Findings: Challenges and Deterrents for Female Politicians in the Caribbean

Double Bind: Domestic Roles/Responsibilities

An interesting finding from our study is that the underrepresentation of women in politics in the Anglo-Caribbean can be attributed in part to a lack of supply, with too few women standing as candidates for political office. This undersupply is, however, grounded in a larger set of intersecting and deep-rooted factors—patriarchal culture, gender discrimination and societal norms, bias within political parties and institutions, as well as cultural and social barriers—which prevent women from successfully contesting an election or remaining in politics if elected. The women interviewed for the study overwhelmingly cited family commitments, resulting from unequal domestic responsibilities, as an obstacle to political participation and leadership, placing them in a "double bind."

The women felt undue pressure to be successful in their public and civic roles as politicians and office-holders and their private lives as "mothers" and "wives." These expectations and requirements are not the same for men. In describing this barrier, the women expressed how they and other female politicians have to play the role of wife, mother and homemaker alongside the role of a politician; they were expected to perform all these roles efficiently. This supports claims in the literature on barriers to women in politics that women often face significant challenges in balancing their family and domestic responsibilities with their political careers, including a lack of support and resources to manage caregiving and household duties (Bianchi et al., 2012; Iversen & Rosenbluth, 2006). This can make it difficult for women to devote the necessary time and energy to their political work and can limit their ability to participate in key political events and activities. At the same time, gender-based stereotypes and expectations about women's roles as caregivers and nurturers can also create a "double bind" for women in politics, in which they are expected to fulfil traditional gender roles while also pursuing political careers and leadership positions. This can create a significant barrier to women's political participation, as well as limit their opportunities for advancement and leadership within political parties and institutions

In the Caribbean, women are considered the backbone of the family and have the responsibility of raising children and taking care of the home. This expectation can make it more difficult for women to pursue political careers and participate in leadership roles, as they may face significant challenges in balancing their family and domestic responsibilities with their political work. However, it is important to note that this expectation is not universal across the Caribbean region, and attitudes towards gender roles and responsibilities can vary significantly between and within countries. Furthermore, there have been significant efforts by women's rights activists and feminist scholars to challenge gender-based stereotypes and expectations and to promote greater gender equality and women's empowerment in the region. It is also worth noting that while women may be primarily responsible for caregiving and domestic duties, this is often a result of systemic gender-based discrimination and unequal distribution of resources and opportunities. The following quotes from the interviews highlight some of the challenges posed by family responsibilities/obligations:

For the women coming in, the biggest problem they have is family. When I entered politics, I would have had a grown son; therefore, it

38   *Barriers, Biases, Boys' Club*

did not impact me in the same way. [But] there are other women, who are powerful women, who are well steeped in knowledge and experience having been community workers and all that, and when they choose to come to parliament, they have children who are still at primary school or the middle level like community colleges and so on. Their commitment to their family is: I want to make sure that these children do homework, and that when I am at parliamentary sitting[s] there is somebody there taking that role as parent or guardian so that my children can do their homework.

(Participant 1)

Women tend to … I would say be the primary caregivers of their homes. Now, if you're the primary caregiver of your home, including perhaps being the primary earner of your house, being able to give up your primary income or your revenue-earning capacity to pursue a course of elective politics may be sacrificial to your entire family.

(Participant 3)

I don't know how I got here, but my obstacle on a personal level is family commitments. My only child, a daughter, she was about, probably almost three. So obviously, I started from the campaigning side of it, so, you know, the hours are long. A lot of times that night, I had to take her with me … And for those of us, especially those of us with children, the hours don't always suit you. Sometimes you leave early and come in late, even with the very partner outside of ministries. You come in at night; sometimes, they're sleeping or stay awake, killing themselves waiting for you … Although the family support on my end is good, it wouldn't always work that way for the average person because more people in Barbados historically are single parents. When I say single parents, I don't mean necessarily unmarried. I mean parents that are only supported by mothers, families that are only supported by mothers. So, then it becomes difficult for mothers to get up and say, let me try for elections.

(Participant 4)

To cope, some women hired outside help to manage the home and care for children but felt regret and guilt that they were not able to fulfil their responsibilities as caregivers. As one female politician from Jamaica explained:

Women have, subsequently, kind of regretted national politics because of the impact on their children, because there is hardly anybody there to take up the slack for them. Fortunately, I had very good domestic support. A lot of people don't. It's costly, and so they're doing multiple things at the same time—caring for old parents, doing this, doing that. So, its multiple layers of support that you need to be able to undertake this. Layers that men don't need because they don't do those things. They don't go to the supermarket and they don't make sure the helper is there, and if the helper is not there, you are going to find somebody to look after the children and that kind of thing, you know.

(Participant 11)

The sitting hours of parliament also proved problematic for female politicians with children and caregiving responsibilities. Many parliamentary sessions can extend late into the evening or even run through the night, which can make it difficult for women to balance their political responsibilities with their caregiving responsibilities. As one participant explained, a parliamentary sitting session in Barbados could begin as early as 7:30 a.m. and not end until late into the night. This is not an uncommon practice in other Anglo-Caribbean countries. Furthermore, parliamentary sessions can often be scheduled at short notice, making it difficult for women to make alternative caregiving arrangements or plan ahead for their family responsibilities. Women are then forced to find safe and affordable childcare for their children. Some resorted to taking their children to parliament with them.

I can tell you that the long hours are not conducive to motherhood and that sometimes it's not conducive to womanhood. Sometimes you are in parliament for extended periods ... you are there for ... I mean, I remember one sitting starting at 10:00 a.m. and finishing probably at midnight, and you are there all day without a break. So, for women, at certain times, that is not conducive but also, as a mother, it means that I have ... I am limited in how much attention I can pay to my son even when I do go home, you know.

(Participant 7)

Not all women face this challenge in the same way, with some women having more family support than others. At least two participants expressed how their ability to engage in political activities was largely due to the considerable support from family and friends. This, however, is not the norm for most women in politics.

In my home, my family's support allowed me to be a mother, and to be an elected person. So, for instance, my brother lives next door, and my mother lives next door. If I have to pick up my son from school and I run late, I could call on my brother to pick him up. So, over the years I have cultivated that relationship with my family, and it works vice-versa as well because when I have free time. So, family support is important. Having your sisters or cousins or aunties and parents involved in your life, your family life whether you are a caregiver for an elderly parent or you are a parent yourself and you have young children.

(Participant 7)

40   *Barriers, Biases, Boys' Club*

I entered in [*year deleted*]. And at the time, my daughter was only two months old when I entered. So, I had the challenges of, family, the commitments. And you know a young child, and another child going to school, and running a business, and at the same time walking through the community seeking votes and support. So, I say all of that to say, in that regard, family support was very critical because I had to depend on the members of my family to help with the younger children and all of that.

Family support is always critical because you need that support system. Because I'm very close to my family, very close … Their support was very, very, critical, and the support of my spouse as well.

(Participant 10)

Those with supportive partners still had a challenge in balancing the roles in their milieu: they had less time to spend with family, they could not vent to their partners because they were asked to separate work and family issues, and they had to spend personal savings on political ventures. As one female politician from Jamaica pointed out:

My husband gave me support, but it was more of a silent kind of support. Yes. I'm with you, but I don't want to talk about politics when you come home. I don't want to hear of your troubles. I am here to support you, but I don't want to hear anything. So, I had to keep a lot of things inside and work them out myself, work them through my brain the night before I go to bed and work them out on my own.

(Participant 5)

As the women recounted the dual burden of family responsibilities and maintaining a political career, it became apparent that while they recognised the undue pressure placed on women in politics, there also appeared to be a general acceptance that women are primarily responsible for family/domestic matters. This gendered expectation places an additional burden on women in politics, who must navigate the demands of their political careers while also fulfilling their caregiving responsibilities. This can create a significant conflict and may contribute to the underrepresentation of women in politics, as women may feel that they cannot commit fully to their political careers while also fulfilling their family responsibilities.

The Caribbean has an extensive history of female-headed households, dating back to slavery and colonialism, where nuclear family structures were discouraged, and domestic duties fell squarely at women's feet. Writing in 1982, Jocelyn Massiah found that approximately 30 to 50 per cent of African-Caribbean families were headed by a female (Jamaica: 33.8%; Barbados: 42.9%; Trinidad and Tobago: 27%) (Massiah, 1983, p. 18). Today, Caribbean households remain highly matriarchal, with women fulfilling domestic roles. The women often rely on female family members to assist

Barriers, Biases, Boys' Club 41

with caring for young ones or the elderly. This legacy of female-headed households has persisted to the present day, and women continue to bear the burden of domestic responsibilities in many households throughout the region. This can make it difficult for women to pursue careers, including political careers, as they may feel that they are not able to commit fully to their professional responsibilities while also fulfilling their caregiving responsibilities at home. As one female politician in Barbados explained during her interview, "Barbados is a matriarchal society. Our families depend on females. The female carries a disproportionate responsibility for children, caregiving for elderly parents, being expected in a pinch to help out relatives, neighbours, etc." (Participant 13). In some households, a father or a male figure may live in the home but are often absent. He may act as the breadwinner, and the spouse/partner will defer to his authority. Still, ultimately, the woman is primarily responsible for child-rearing and caring for the home.

Lack of Networks and Support

Another barrier for women in politics, in the view of the participants, is the lack of a support/network system and mentorship programmes to meet their political, training, emotional and financial needs. In Jamaica, for example, both the PNP and the JLP have women's arms, but male dominance remains prevalent. Coupled with this, the participants believe that women are being deliberately excluded from male-dominated network groups, or what they termed the "old boys' club." The old boys' club atmosphere can create significant barriers for women who are interested in entering politics. Women who do not have connections to this network may struggle to gain access to political power and resources, while men who are part of the old boys' club may receive preferential treatment and support.

The old boys' club atmosphere is also evident in Barbadian politics. One participant indicated that when her political party nominated her, she went up against an incumbent who naturally had his party's support. Although she thought he was not an excellent candidate, he had the support of many, especially from the old boys' club of the party. Men were also thought to have greater access to resources because of their corporate and political associates. Participant 11 expressed how, based on her experience in politics, it was easier for men to get things done, primarily because they have access to more resources and more avenues from which to get other support. They are also taken more seriously than women. Similar sentiments were expressed by Participant 3, who maintained that during the early stages of her political career, she had very little party support. She felt alienated during most of her election campaign. After she won her seat in the general election, she felt pressured by the party to perform in ways the average politician was not required to do. She noted, for example, that she was expected to be at everyone's "beck and call" in

42 Barriers, Biases, Boys' Club

an unreasonable manner, such as attending funerals or social gatherings in the middle of the day when she had other personal and career obligations.

Notably, some women reported that they received party support, and at some point in their careers, they had a good team, hence their success:

> From [year deleted], [the party leader] decided that he definitely wanted more women in politics ... and he did what I would call an affirmative action. Not only did he support them in terms of selection against much pushback, but he also provided financial support, right, because he recognized that there was a gap. And, actually, I think, that was the largest number of women who ever ran. I also think it was the largest number of women we ever had in Parliament.
>
> I got much support from the leadership. Not just the leader, but the member[s], but I wouldn't say everybody was fully supportive of me, but you know, you did get some currency.
>
> (Participant 11)

> The party, of course, supported me in a small way as I went along, and I had a great management team who tried their best to garner support for me, but they themselves put in funding that was needed. But for the big part of it, I funded myself. I funded myself.
>
> (Participant 5)

However, they declared this was not the case for the typical woman who wanted to enter politics. If support from family, friends, the party, the party leader and the constituency was not simultaneously available, it was a doomed undertaking.

Women were also seen as perpetuating the lack of support for women in politics. Respondents mentioned a lack of solidarity and support among women as another critical barrier to women's political representation. Women in politics, unlike men, are perceived as demonstrating no interest in uniting for the common good of supporting other women. They were reported to treat politics as a competition among women, prioritising their career and party needs above those of the country and the women therein, especially those viewed as opponents, even within their own party. This lack of support manifested in personal attacks, snubbing and spreading rumours. Due to this apparent disunity and lack of a network, the women felt unsupported and that they would always lag behind the men who had sustainable linkages. The absence of such a network was incredibly distressing to the women because their constituents expected more from them than they could deliver, making them appear inept and untrustworthy. Women were also accused of trying to play the same game as men played, which did not work for them because the expectations of women are different from those of men. The following extracts from the interviews highlight some of these views:

Barriers, Biases, Boys' Club 43

We don't have that old boys' club, and you find that a lot of women don't bond together. Women don't support each other in Jamaica. So even if there might be a business woman who is doing well, they do not readily come on-board and say, I want to support you, I'm going to help you because I believe in the process. So, you still find that old boys' club that will help the men; the women don't have that kind of network.

(Participant 9)

I think that we are socialized in political work to be more comfortable helping men than helping women. There's a lot of help for men in politics like natural kind of and a lot of it comes from women. Whereas, as a woman getting into politics you better find the help that you need … I've observed a lot over the last six years most of the people who work in political campaigns are women. But I find that we have socialized ourselves into a place where those women feel more comfortable helping men. And we also have a reality where more women vote in politics certainly, in Barbados and I dare say across the region. But women have to give women a reason to vote for them. Whereas, with man, it's like it's almost, like, Yes, Well.

(Participant 6)

Women are more likely to vote than men … you would think that automatically there would be female support for female candidates. That is not automatic. It is beginning to change now because people are now getting more custom to females actually in political leadership, and so on, so you're beginning to see a change in that trend … but certainly in the early years, women were not expected to be able to manage and handle the rumble tumble of politics.

(Participant 13)

There is a general belief that having more women in politics will automatically result in women acting for or representing the interest of females in politics or the wider society. This, however, is not always the case. As noted by some of the participants, female MPs do not always support each other, and this, too, plays a fundamental role in perpetuating the barriers they face in getting elected. Many voters, interest groups, and organisations, including those led by women, often do not take female candidates and politicians as seriously as they do male ones. Some women do not want to be perceived as a feminist or to advocate for women's issues, while others do not wish to be closely aligned with women's issues. Furthermore, being a woman does not automatically translate to being gender sensitive.

44 *Barriers, Biases, Boys' Club*

Political Financing/Funding

Money is an important factor in politics; without it, politicians cannot effectively carry out their duties or run for political office. Those with greater access to money can get in, even if they are not the best candidate. This can lead to different types and levels of corruption or malfeasance because of the monies exchanged. Irregularities and inequality in political funding can also make governance difficult. In the Caribbean, there is a paucity of information on political financing, especially for women. Still, from the interview responses, it was unequivocal that the personal costs of running for office can be prohibitive, and fundraising is harder for female challengers than for men. The women reported not having enough funding or financial support, hence, they struggled to enter politics, campaign and execute projects. Some participants related the personal expenses of being a politician, such as the maintenance of their vehicles or people expecting to receive money when they visit their constituencies. They also lacked mentorship and had a limited network and support system compared to men. The participants noted that there was no active, all-female cadre dedicated to supporting women in politics. Donors were also more likely to give monetary support to a male political candidate than they were to a woman. This is a manifestation of gender bias in politics which creates significant challenges for women seeking to run for office and compete on an equal footing with male candidates. The gender disparity in donor funding also stems from a general view that men are more successful at the polls and, once elected to parliament, can provide jobs, contracts and other perks that women may not have such authority over.

Without money, women could not campaign effectively or carry out their duties if elected. Participants 1 and 13 both explained they needed money to compensate the people who worked with them on the campaign trails and at the polling stations. Candidates also needed to cover the costs of meetings, door knockings and rallies or purchasing drinks for their supporters and potential voters on the campaign trails. As Participant 13 explained, "one of the traditions of Caribbean politics is that politicians, to win their supporters and win their constituencies, they will scatter largesse here and there." The participants also needed money to help the people in their constituencies. For Participant 12, "the expectation of the people is high, and it's not set up for that, so you have to find the people employment so that they can build their own future."

The financial burden female politicians face is also aggravated by established electoral rules and regulations that can disadvantage potential women candidates. Notable is the principle of political neutrality of the public service, which curtails the rights of public servants to engage in partisan political activities. In Barbados, for example, public sector workers are expected to relinquish their jobs if they wish to contest an election. According to General Order 3.18.1 of the General Orders of the Public Service 1970 of Barbados:

Officers and employees are expressly forbidden to participate actively in politics, including being adopted as a parliamentary candidate, canvassing on behalf of any party or candidate; acting as agents or sub-agents of any candidate for election; holding office in party political organizations, and speaking at political meetings.

(cited in Barbados Today, 2022)

The Public Service (Conduct and Ethics of Officers) Code also establishes rules for public service workers to engage in political activities. In Trinidad and Tobago, Part II, Section 10 of the Civil Service Act disqualifies a civil servant "for membership of the House of Representatives and the Senate, and a Municipality and a Council." They can participate in the general elections as candidates and return to their substantive jobs if unsuccessful but must resign from their posts if elected. The Staff Orders for the Public Service Officers (4.2.6) in Jamaica expressly forbid persons employed in the central government from "engaging in any type of partisan activity in any elections at any level." There is, however, no prohibition for persons employed in statutory bodies and government-owned companies. Teachers, for example, can hold an electoral post at the local level but must opt for one salary, as they cannot be compensated twice from the same source. Though these constitutional rules and regulations apply to all public/civil service workers (men and women), for at least one female politician from Barbados, these institutional barriers present additional hurdles that female political aspirants must overcome when trying to balance a family and political career.

> Women, for example, if you were civil servant and you wanted to run in politics you would have to give up your job in this country to run in politics. So, let's say a teacher desiring to run, she has to resign her job.
>
> (Participant 3)

The registration fee to participate in an election can further hinder women's political participation. In Barbados, the registration fee to run in an election is 250 BBD In 2021, discussions emerged that this amount should be increased to, at minimum, 1,000 BBD. Participant 3 expressed her disapproval, noting that:

> [this] is wrong, and it is wrong because every person with a voice and desire should be allowed to participate in elections. The people will determine whether they want to, but there should be no institutional hindrance to your participation in the election, and that's what's happening today.
>
> (Participant 3)

46 *Barriers, Biases, Boys' Club*

Role Congruency and Gender Stereotypes

The women interviewed for this study recognise that they are in a male-dominated field, and there is the implication that they are viewed as imposters who must work harder than men to maintain equal status in the public's eye. This view was proposed as an explanation for the difficulties women report in garnering support for their political ambitions. Like women elsewhere, female politicians in the Anglo-Caribbean are still perceived as unsuited for political office. Some women have reportedly bought into that notion. They are perceived to be emotional and irrational and, therefore, not suited for the rigours of public office (Johnson-Myers, 2019); ergo, they resign themselves to nurturing and support roles within the party, such as secretarial and campaign duties. The people who organise meetings, plan and execute political campaigns and be the information hub for their parties are usually the women. As one participant explained, some women did considerable work in their respective constituencies, many of whom held significant constituency positions. Still, they were unsuccessful when it came time for them to be elected through the party process.

The participants also explained that although their male counterparts faced challenges throughout their political careers, they were dissimilar to those faced by women or were of a lesser degree due to the gendered roles, expectations, buffers and support system that men had. Women in politics must do and offer more than men to prove their worth. As Participant 13 from Barbados explained, "it is true that you have to be able to offer more than a male counterpart in order to get the pick." The statements below express similar views on the struggle by women in politics to prove their worth:

> With respect to the cultural barriers, the country would essentially see a man presenting himself for political leadership or political consideration and almost subliminally feel that he is capable to do the job. If a woman presents herself in similar fashion, she will have to prove herself ... and the notion of a woman, proving herself is that she will now have to list her involvement in community, in society. She will have to list how she has been previously successful before she even gets a hearing or before she becomes what I call visible ... women are asked to prove themselves in a way that men are not asked to prove themselves and even when you prove yourself, you're not visible.
>
> (Participant 3)

> I do think that a woman has to be a better candidate on average to get even a toe in the door than a man has to be. A man can show up as he is, belly out, whatever. I feel a woman has to—it's almost like, well,

Barriers, Biases, Boys' Club 47

why should I vote for you? You are just a woman. That kind of thing, but if a woman has to present as a stronger candidate, period.

(Participant 6)

We [females] have to fight to get to the top. Really fight and that's one of the reasons why I am lacklustre when it comes on to campaigning for or going further in politics. It's too hard.

(Participant 10)

There also appears to be less tolerance for women being dominant or strident about something than for men. Where it would be readily accepted for a man to say or do the same thing, there is likely to be more offence if it comes from a woman. How do women then wield leadership effectively without necessarily imitating male behaviours to get the job done? Women are also judged more harshly than men, and this, one participant believes, is gender-related:

While we [women] exist in the political landscape, our gender will always be a central focus of everything that we do. And you see it, because of the questions as to how we arrive at decisions are all coloured by people looking at our gender and scrutinizing whether that decision was made that way because you are female.

(Participant 1)

Even in terms of appearance and deportment, women were held to a higher standard than men:

How a woman should [behave] ... it's quite different from how a man should behave. [Constituents] don't want no woman who drink, smoke, "manise," right, if there is such a word. They want somebody who knows what they're doing, somebody who cares. Somebody who listens, even how they dress is important. How they dress is important you know. Where as a man can go to a function and just have on a shirt and pants you know that a woman must be elegant. Elegantly attired, you know I always say it's very unreasonable.

(Participant 9)

Women are also socialised to doubt their abilities, leading many to believe that the political field is skewed in favour of their male counterparts, even if this was not necessarily the case. Not only are women not confident in their abilities to participate in the political process, but they have been led by society to believe that men are better leaders:

I believe that [men] believe that women leaders are not females, and it's just as simple as that. And you and I know that. You know why

48 *Barriers, Biases, Boys' Club*

men believe that no women should lead. I just think that's where the problem is and there's nothing deeper than that; it's nothing personal. It is just tradition. I think it's just traditional. I don't think we are totally grasping what, or how our society is changing. That women, in their own rights, are leaders too.

(Participant 10)

Men are seen as more aggressive persons than females. And because of that, men have a better way of doing things and getting things done. But the roughness of the politics, it really is for men.

(Participant 12)

As one participant from Trinidad and Tobago explained, women in politics must be exceptional to sit at the proverbial table. Men do not need to be outstanding; they only need to be present. She recounted that it was not unusual for men with no experiences or ideas to put their names forward for nomination, while qualified women shied away from the process. This supports arguments by scholars such as Darcy, Welch and Clark (1994), Matland (2005) and Shevdova (2005) that women and men are culturally socialised to view politics through varying lenses. During the early stages of the socialisation process, girls are taught to believe that they should be submissive and passive, while boys should be aggressive, assertive and in control. Ultimately, women are viewed as being mild-mannered, less intimidating, honest, friendly and caring (Barnes & Beaulieu, 2014), while men are viewed as assertive, confident and, overall, make better leaders (Kahn, 1996; Fox & Lawless, 2014). Women in politics are also assigned more "feminine" or "soft" portfolios in areas such as childcare, health or education (Goodyear-Grant, 2013; Shvedova, 2005), while men are associated with "hard" issue areas such as defence, trade, security and economics. Politics, therefore, becomes a male-dominated territory, a dirty game avoided by women.

Violence against Female Politicians in the Anglo-Caribbean

During the interviews, the women were asked to explain the extent to which they believed political violence is a barrier to women in politics in the Caribbean. The participants from Barbados and Trinidad and Tobago reported that they and other women experienced "subtle" and covert acts of political violence, the most prevalent being intimidation, harassment, character assassination and defamation via social media platforms. The women in Jamaica reported more severe, overt acts of violence, including physical attacks. Overall, at least 70 per cent of the respondents stated that they had been subjected to discrimination, harassment, verbal abuse and character assassination while in parliament. Two participants from Jamaica reported being physically abused. Those who have never experienced political violence or harassment know someone who had.

One female politician from Barbados explained that throughout her political career, she was victimised, alienated and intimidated by other members of her political party. She was eventually expelled from the party. She also noted that other women in politics faced similar experiences. She recounted a situation in which a female politician, who successfully maintained her seat in parliament, was asked by her political party to step aside for a male colleague. The party rewarded her for stepping aside, but this is usually not the case for most women who are shoved to the periphery by their political parties. Participant 1 indicated that she never experienced political violence while in parliament, but she was aware of verbal attacks on other female politicians. She provided an example, wherein in 2018, three or four persons from the Opposition used derogatory comments about Prime Minister Mottley.

Aggressive rhetoric and disparaging comments about women's appearance, private life and sexual morality were also typical, especially on the political campaign trails. An overwhelming majority of the respondents expressed how they and other women must constantly deal with stereotypical comments and assumptions about their appearance, their private life, how they behave and the role they play. One participant stated that, while Barbados has not had a history of physical violence, some women shy away from politics because of the comments or questions they get asked while on the campaign trail. Negative messages included questions such as "Why don't you have children?" "Why are you not married?" "Who did you sleep with?" or "How did you get here?" Participant 2, from Trinidad and Tobago, explained that because she is not yet married, questions were raised on a Facebook blog page about her sexuality and whether she is a lesbian. Her decision-making and leadership skills were also questioned because she does not have a husband. She recounted an incident where someone said to her: "The only thing you missing is a husband. If you don't have a husband, how are we going to know you can make good decisions?" She referred to similar incidents with female political colleagues, including former Prime Minister, Kamla Persad-Bissessar, who in 2015 faced relentless harassment and character assassination during her election campaigns. Another colleague had sexually explicit videos of her posted on social media.

Incidents like these are commonly experienced by female politicians, who are often measured and judged differently than their male counterparts. From Eugenia Charles to Mia Mottley female politicians and political leaders in the Caribbean are discredited in ways that men are not. For example, Jamaica's Portia Simpson-Miller, the country's first female Prime Minister, was constantly placed under the microscope. The media and members of both the PNP and the JLP questioned her leadership abilities. They relentlessly sought to remind her of her "place" in society—not in a position of power. In the media, she was often the subject of editorial cartoons that portrayed her as "unintelligent, emotionally weak, confrontational, erratic, hot-tempered, and vulgar" (Johnson-Myers, 2019, p. 12).

50   *Barriers, Biases, Boys' Club*

Most notable in the responses is that political violence was more commonly experienced by female politicians in Jamaica than it was for women in Barbados and Trinidad and Tobago. In her research on the effects of political violence on female politicians in Jamaica, Johnson-Myers found that violent politics posed a barrier to women's success and durability in politics. What's more, the problem is ubiquitous, affecting women at every stage of their political careers and both levels of politics: national and local. She concluded that:

> Female politicians in Jamaica are affected by political violence before, during, and after an election, and even when they are in political office. Most of the violence experienced is of a gendered nature and can be defined as VAWIP. It is driven by gender-specific motivations aimed at preventing women from pursuing a political career or entering politics. Women politicians are targeted not just because of politics but because they are women.
>
> (Johnson-Myers, 2021, p. 14)

Her findings support claims by the interviewees from Jamaica that during their political careers, they and other women in politics were threatened, verbally abused and had their characters assassinated. In more extreme cases, female politicians were physically attacked. One female politician was shot in the chest at point-blank range. An act she considered politically motivated, carried out by a member of the opposing People's National Party. According to the respondent:

> The guy who shoot me, him a walk up and down, and me never even lock him up. Because is not him do it, a them send him come to me. And me and his parents are so good, but if I was a wicked person, his community would have had it hard. But what's the sense when you can see that innocent people a guh dead [are going to die].
>
> (Participant 12)

Another noted that she is aware of a female candidate who, in a local government election, was locked in a polling station by supporters of the opposing party and only released after the police intervened. Participant 9 was pushed and verbally attacked by a party supporter.

> I was in an area where the opposition was strong, and one man felt the need to push me. A bridge was being repaired in that opposition stronghold and he felt that I was not the one who commissioned the repair, but the past MP did before he left office. Now that MP was gone two years and he felt strongly about it and as I explained that it was my project [but] he wanted to hear nothing I was saying.
>
> (Participant 9)

Perpetrators of acts of violence against female politicians included members of their political parties (both men and women), hired political thugs and party supporters. The women were under threat, and their families were also potential targets. This threat was viewed as key in dissuading women from entering representational politics. Johnson-Myers (2021) in her assessment of the effects of violence on women in politics in Jamaica, found that some female legislators in Jamaica left political office prematurely because of the spill-over effects of violence on their families. Those who were not intimidated were viewed as "dirty politicians" because the notion is that endurance is indicative of involvement in violence. The women were understandably frustrated and burned out by the intersecting barriers and hurdles they have had to overcome during their political careers. As one female politician from Jamaica indicated:

> Politics nuh [is not] attractive. Women nuh waan guh through dem stuff dere [women do not want to go through these things]. You have yuh [your] kids them, you have a family and there is a bit of uncertainty about yuh life and all of that. It nuh [doesn't] make nuh [any] sense. The honest truth, I am fed up of it. That is the honest truth. I am fed up of it. It's not something that I love.
>
> (Participant 12)

This supports the argument by Johnson-Myers that "violence against women in politics [in Jamaica] demotivates female politicians, making them less likely to stand for elections and more likely to leave office after fewer terms" (2021, p.14).

Solutions to Increasing Women's Political Participation in the Anglo-Caribbean

When asked in the interviews, "what needs to be done to increase the number of women in politics in the Anglo-Caribbean?" the women unanimously expressed the importance of having greater financial support/resources, as well as strong support and network systems for women. They explained that addressing the supply-side aspect of women's political underrepresentation in the Anglo-Caribbean requires a nuanced approach that addresses the intersectional and underlying barriers that prevent women from entering and remaining in the region's politics. Historically, efforts to promote inclusivity and diversity in politics have primarily focused on electoral reform and the implementation of affirmative action policies such as gender quotas and reserved seats. Electoral reform is often offered as a viable solution to women's political underrepresentation, with arguments that in countries using a proportional representation electoral system, women are twice as likely to get elected to political office compared to a winner-take-all system (Matland, 2005; Reynolds, Reilly & Ellis, 2005; Norris &

52 *Barriers, Biases, Boys' Club*

Lovenduski, 1995; Bakopanos, 2004; Ogai, 2001; Kenworthy & Malami, 1999; Paxton, 1997; Darcy, Welch & Clark, 1994). There is also the general argument that quotas result in an increased descriptive and substantive representation of women in countries where they are used (Clayton & Zetterberg, 2018; Franceschet & Piscopo, 2008; Krook, 2010; Piscopo, 2011; Tremblay, 1998; Tripp & Kang, 2008).

Lack of access to political funding presents an immense challenge to women entering political office in Anglo-Caribbean countries. It was emphasised throughout the interviews that funding is necessary and crucial to lessen the financial burden on women. In many regions, including the Caribbean, the cost of running in an election can be prohibitively high for most candidates, regardless of gender. But coupled with intersecting factors and barriers, such as gender norms and stereotypes and the unequal distribution of wealth, a lack of funding can make entrance into parliament even worse for women. So, what can be done to level the playing field so female politicians in the Caribbean can enjoy financial viability? According to one interviewee from Barbados, the state could offer aid in the form of a subvention to any political party that fields more than 50 per cent female candidates in a general election. In Barbados, there are no substantive rules or legislation around party financing, but "under the Parliament Administration Act 1989 (CAP. 10), parliament provides an annual subvention of BD \$300,000 … which is shared among the political parties that have a parliamentary presence" (cited in Griner & Zovatto, 2005). Barbados has a two-party system, meaning there are two dominant political parties. The subvention is, therefore, usually split between the Barbados Labour Party and the Democratic Labour Party. Having a party subvention would be especially useful for candidates who may not be able to fund an election with their own money or through donations. In Trinidad and Tobago and Jamaica, there are no such provisions governing political party financing in the constitution or otherwise. There is also no Anglo-Caribbean country with political party financing affirmation measures for increasing women's political representation and participation.

Political party financing affirmation measures have been carried out in countries such as Chile, Croatia, Haiti, Moldova and Georgia (Andia & Hamada, 2019, p. 18), where political parties are awarded funding based on the number of women nominated or elected to parliament. In Chile, "political parties receive a flat rate of additional public funding for each woman candidate from that party who is elected" (Andia & Hamada, 2019, p. 18). In countries such as Ireland, Albania, Italy and France, political parties can be sanctioned if their targets for gender balance are not met. Formal legislation, whether at the state or party level, can help to break down the barriers to equal participation and representation between men and women. It provides an incentive for political parties to recruit and select more women for election. It can also result in early recruiting, because women entering politics would not feel pressured to have lucrative careers as buffers.

Interviewees also expressed how more needs to be done to protect the livelihood of women who run for political office, especially those in the public sector. In Barbados, male and female political candidates must relinquish public sector jobs once they express an interest in running for political office. In Jamaica and Trinidad and Tobago, public service workers must resign their roles once elected to parliament. At least two respondents raised concerns that for women, especially those who are the heads of their households, it is not feasible to give up their sole and sure source of income to pursue a political career. There was also concern that women who leave their jobs to contest an election may find it challenging to re-integrate themselves into the workplace should they lose the election or retire prematurely from politics.

Beyond financial constraints, participants expressed the need for family-friendly policies, such as affordable childcare to address the unequal distribution of familial obligations, which severely undermine women's ability to run for political office. It was suggested that childcare services be provided for mothers sitting in parliament. Moreover, new mothers should be allowed to bring their infants to work, and there should be designated areas where nursing mothers can feed and change their babies. One respondent explained that when she entered parliament, she had a young child whom she was sometimes forced to take with her due to a lack of childcare, especially when she had to work late nights and evenings. These challenges are not unique to Anglo-Caribbean women but, instead, reflect the struggles of female politicians globally. Stella Creasy, a British legislator, and mother of a three-month-old child was asked to stop bringing her baby with her to the House of Commons in 2021. In 2019, Kenyan MP Zuleikha Hassan was removed from the floor of the National Assembly for bringing her baby with her to work. Hassan explained that she was forced to take her five-month-old baby with her because she did not have any childcare arrangements and did not want to miss work. These and other stories of women taking their children to work reignite the debate about the challenges working mothers face, including those in politics. Having childcare services, whether in-home or at parliament, would provide mothers in parliament a sense of relief and assurance that their children are safe and being taken care of while they fulfil their obligations and duty to the country.

Another solution to the challenges faced by female politicians in the Anglo-Caribbean is the creation of a robust network of women to aid women's transition into politics:

> So, have your own money, have your own career. Create your own network. Create a network that can support you and create a network from all strata of society.
>
> (Participant 3)

54 *Barriers, Biases, Boys' Club*

Any Advice? I would say that it's really about finding a network. A network. You cannot do this thing alone, and you cannot make it a fight at every step. You're going to have to make friends and influence people. Many, many different kinds of people. You cannot do this without a network everywhere, and that network has to start inside the party. It has to start inside because the whole country could love you, but if you don't have support within the political organization, you are going nowhere fast. So, find those networks. On the ground, in the constituency where you want to run … find those networks inside the party, go back to people who have done this before. Understand that you have to make friends in a very organic way … I think that is the way to do it. If you start it top-down, it's not going to work.

(Participant 6)

One of the most important aspects of politics, is networking. Charming other people, clapping them on the back, building relations from a practical strategic position … and men do this.

(Participant 13)

So, you need to build your foundation, in relation to finances … and then you have to start to build networking relationships. Don't wait until you're trying to get into politics. You have to pay attention to the people you go to school with, you have to pay attention to people that you work with, you have to pay attention to people in your community, you need to get involved in a number of organizations and be a part of serving and building relationships and you have to spend the time nurturing those, so that you have some to draw on.

(Participant 13)

Establishing a support system for women with an intersection of age, social status and political party was also deemed essential to recruiting more women into politics. In politics, women's networks are crucial to climbing the career ladder, as they serve both as a tool of empowerment and as a support system for female politicians. Through these networks, women might be able to share survival strategies, skills and expertise. They could also provide financial and emotional support for each other. An example of this type of support is a parliamentary women's caucus, with part of its mandate being the recruitment and maintenance of a cadre of potential women candidates. In Barbados, Jamaica and Trinidad and Tobago, there are no inter-parliamentary women's caucuses. Even if women were willing to collaborate across party lines, their respective parties might not allow it. In Jamaica, there is a Women's Political Caucus (NGO), which acts at a non-partisan level to support and facilitate the participation of women in politics. Grenada is one of few Anglo-Caribbean countries with a women's parliamentary caucus.

Assets: The Recipe to Survive Politics as a Woman

The participants acknowledged that women who enter politics often face unique challenges and barriers. Therefore, it is important for them to develop the necessary attributes and leadership skills to navigate these challenges and succeed in political leadership roles. To achieve increased representation, women need to build confidence in themselves, be empathetic, deal with rejection with a "thick skin," show assertiveness and, when necessary, demonstrate aggressiveness. Confidence was viewed as the most beneficial trait for a female politician. The participants explained that a woman entering politics must know herself and what she wants once elected. They argued that, unlike men, women often underestimate their abilities and assume they need to be more qualified and educated than men to run for the same office. Some of these women will wait until they are more qualified than men to run for the same office or not run at all. Even when recruited to run in safe seats or strongholds, women will express doubts about their ability to win an election. This self-doubt is one of the biggest hurdles women must overcome if they wish to enter or remain in politics. To become more confident in themselves and their performance, women were encouraged to prepare themselves for the rigors of political life.

> The advice I would have is that you need to put yourself in positions where you can work on your confidence. Women here, in my mind, traditionally are a little more timid. And not only women, the Barbadian society; we are more timid. You will see that when people come in from overseas, they grow up in the [United] States, and you can tell the difference. Yeah, but generally, we are a polite society. That's one of the things I would like to see more coming from women.
>
> (Participant 4)

Female political aspirants were also encouraged to engage in public speaking activities and to volunteer with political parties and in their communities, thus creating a voice and presence for themselves before they put themselves forward for political office. Confidence was also closely linked to social and financial stability. As explained by one respondent:

> You need to have your own source of money and you need to have a career that does not make you vulnerable to the challenges of being a politically interested person. So have your own money, have your own career.
>
> (Participant 3)

Women were also encouraged to build a career and a future in which they could sustain themselves once out of politics.

56 Barriers, Biases, Boys' Club

The second thing I would advise women to do who want to get into politics, you have to build a career, a pathway by which you're [going to] stabilize your finances. So, you need to focus on your basic education and be sure that you'll develop a career that will give you sufficient that you can build a sound enough financial platform for yourself. That you can stabilize your family and so on. While a lot of people love to talk about people who stole money or misuse public funds and try to paint everybody with that brush, most people leave politics and are worse off because of the heavy demands and because you've broken your career and being able to get back to that 10 years later, you may be older, you might not be as relevant, you have not kept up. You then find yourself spiralling into genteel poverty coming out of politics ... and you see this across the Caribbean.

(Participant 13)

Passion was also viewed as an essential trait for women in politics. A strong altruistic thrust, determination to execute tasks, love of service and desire to effect change were deemed motivations to endure the challenges. The belief in the capacity to generate change is highly useful, even amidst institutional challenges. Additionally, displaying passion could result in support from observers. As one respondent recounted:

Just find your passion wherever it may be, the environment, whatever sort of advocacy you'd like, and get involved because your voice is important, and your voice needs to be heard ... Don't think about it too much just do it, and we'll get more people involved.

(Participant 2)

Do it with passion and you will see the results. Once you believe strongly in what you're doing [and] that you're doing good for the people ... you will come out of this free.

(Participant 5)

Ensure that this is really what you want to do. You must have a passion for it. And that's where it starts ... It starts with a passion. If you don't want to do it, you are going to be lacklustre. You're not going to want to do it. So, you have to have that motivation from deep down within you; that this is what I want to do. This is what I want to be. You really must want to lead and have the ability to do so. It's not going to start with ability, it starts with a passion to do it. And then you can develop the attitude. You can develop the characteristics as you go along, and leaders grow, leaders are not born.

(Participant 10)

Barriers, Biases, Boys' Club 57

So, one of the first [questions] is, what is it I'm passionate about? More politicians just cannot come to government knowing nothing. When you come to government, you do have to bring something. So, you need to find those areas where you want to build some expertise, and then you need to start serving in that as early as you can. Whatever NGO is around, be their voice, be an advocate, you develop some expertise.

(Participant 13)

More importantly, female aspirants were encouraged to find their niche or create a "big idea" that could transform politics and the lives of people:

Find your niche, find your passion, and let that fuel you into the campaign trail. You can't push everything. You can't push agriculture; you can't push housing; you can't push everything, but at least choose one or two that you can handle.

(Participant 8)

You need to establish what I would call the big idea.

(Participant 3)

Empathy was another trait that women entering politics were encouraged to display. Unlike men, who are not expected to be empathetic and nurturing, women were required to demonstrate this in their constituencies. They were asked to show that they prioritised human relationships by sitting with families and bonding, listening to problems faced by residents, offering comfort, making appeals to the police if a resident was detained, paying keen attention to the needs of residents, and trying to meet them to prove reliability.

I think we have that motherly touch, even if we're not mothers to children, I think we still have that motherly touch. Something that the men—it is not that they don't have it, but they're different. I think we serve better because we listen, and we understand what's happening to the communities because it is just the nature of who we are.

(Participant 5)

So, women, we are the mothers. We are the ones who you go to, even in the political parties, it's a lot more women than men that are in the political parties. They are the ones in the communities making a difference. I think we do it best because we're more compassionate.

(Participant 11)

Women were also encouraged to keep their dignity intact and never to change who they were before they became involved in politics. They were also encouraged to engage the community consistently so they could feel a connection:

58   Barriers, Biases, Boys' Club

> My advice to women that aspire to enter politics, is that you have to stand your ground. You have to keep your integrity and also your dignity. Because in politics, if you're a female, especially if you are a beautiful woman. If you're very attractive. You'll come up against a lot of these men trying to. You know what.
>
> (Participant 10)

> Whether if people know you to be friendly, to be committed, to be helpful, to be a mentor, to be a good listener, to be an action person you don't throw that out the window when you get to parliament and when people call you, you look at them with scorn. What I find is that some people become very arrogant and haughty and then they become removed from the people and their needs and of course you make promises you can't always fulfil ... I must tell you that we must continue to keep in touch and when we make promises try to make sure that the promises that we make to people if we can't fulfil them, we get back to them and let them know.
>
> (Participant 1)

Another beneficial trait identified by participants is being "thick-skinned." With mounting criticism from the public, personal attacks from opponents and naysayers and scrutiny from the media, the women believed being indifferent to negativity was strategic as female politicians, because they were being judged for behaviour more sternly than men. Moreover, this was particularly important when they were not only pressured to work but, to a greater extent, compelled to dress well and always exhibit a genteel manner, an expectation their male counterparts did not share. Hence, they reported blocking negativity and suppressing personality to avoid backlash and further criticism. Dominance, assertiveness and aggression were also considered essential traits. Due to the pressure to ensure they were not perceived as weak women, they had to maintain a tough exterior by holding firm with decisions, being confrontational and asserting dominance. Interestingly, women were expected to display courteousness and compassion, but some situations required aggression for fear that they would not be taken seriously.

> For women ... they cannot ... You can't be intimidated. In other words, as I said, politics is a man's world. You cannot ... You cannot let that limit you in terms of trying to get involvement from it.
>
> (Participant 12)

> Politics is not for the faint of heart. Politics is a vehicle. As women, we must be very firm about our cause and how far we want to advance that cause; how much we want to contribute to policies that will affect our cause.
>
> (Participant 7)

Conclusion

A fundamental human right of women is to be directly involved in decision-making. It is, therefore, crucial that they enjoy full and equitable representation in politics and public life. When women are significantly underrepresented in politics, they may be seen as "tokens" or symbolic representatives rather than as full and equal members of the political system. This can be a problem because tokenism can perpetuate the marginalisation and exclusion of women in politics, and it can also limit the impact that women can have on policy and decision-making. Women are also less likely to feel free to fully participate in engendering a significant impact on the decision-making processes. Having more women (in equitable numbers) in political spaces can lead to greater accountability for women, encourage the entrance of women into politics and promote actions and policies that benefit women. It also encourages diversity and promotes gender equality. Having more women in political spaces also has wider benefits for society, such as reducing poverty, increasing economic growth, increasing educational opportunities and improving healthcare. Recent years have witnessed an increase, albeit slowly, in the number of women elected or appointed to political office in the Anglo-Caribbean. The region also boasts prominent female heads of state/government. Barbados is today governed by a female Prime Minister, a female Deputy Prime Minister, and a female President simultaneously. In Trinidad and Tobago, Paula Mae Weekes currently serves as President. Despite these achievements, women continue to be largely marginalised in the legislative branches of government in nearly every country in the region. Only about 22 per cent of ministerial portfolios/cabinet positions in the Anglo-Caribbean are held by women. Except for Grenada and Guyana, there is no country in the region today with a critical mass (30%) of women in the lower or single house. In Antigua and Barbuda, the Bahamas, St Lucia and St Vincent and the Grenadines, women comprise less than 20 per cent of the lower or single house.

This suggests that there are intersecting and deep-rooted challenges preventing women from successfully contesting an election or remaining in politics if elected. Most of the challenges we identified in the study can be categorised as supply-side barriers. These include (i) family obligations/commitment, (ii) a lack of network/support system for women, (iii) lack of financial support/political financing, (iv) role congruency and gender stereotypes and (v) violence against women in politics. In identifying the barriers to women's political participation in the Anglo-Caribbean, we highlighted at least two key solutions to these barriers: the provision of financial support/funding and strong support networks for female politicians. We also outlined critical attributes and traits that female political aspirants and women in politics are encouraged to possess if they are to survive in politics. These include empathy, having a "thick skin," confidence, assertiveness and, where appropriate, aggression.

Notes

1 Interviews were conducted with female politicians in Jamaica in 2019 and with female politicians in Barbados and Trinidad and Tobago between March and April 2022.
2 The data represents only women elected to parliaments in the respective countries. In some countries, women were appointed to legislative assemblies before the granting of independence, or before women gained the right to stand for election.
3 Some women were granted the right in 1945 to vote under the Legislature of British Guyana.

References

Abele, A. E. (2003). The dynamics of masculine-agentic and feminine-communal traits: Findings from a prospective study. *Journal of Personality and Social Psychology* 85(4), 768–776. Retrieved on October 2, 2022, from https://doi.org/ 10.1037/0022-3514.85.4.768.

Aday, S., & Devitt, J. (2001). Style over substance: Newspaper coverage of Elizabeth Dole's presidential bid. *Harvard International Journal of Press/Politics* 6(2), 52–73. Retrieved on October 2, 2022, from https://doi.org/10.1177/108118001129172134.

Andia, R. & Hamada, Y. (2019). *The Integrity of Political Finance Systems in Latin America: Tackling Political Corruption. International IDEA Policy Paper No. 21.* Strömsborg: International IDEA.

Ashe, J. (2020). Canada's political parties: Gatekeepers to parliament. In M. Tremblay & J. Everitt (Eds.), *The Palgrave Handbook of Gender, Sexuality, and Canadian Politics* (pp. 297–316). New York: Palgrave Macmillan.

Bakopanos, E. (2004). Political recruiting and women in the political process. *Canadian Parliamentary Review* 27(1), 11–14.

Ballington, J., & Kahane, M. (2014). Women in politics: Financing for gender equality, funding of political parties and election campaigns. In A. Falguera, S. Jones & M. Ohman (Eds.), *Introduction to Political Finance* (pp. 303–343). Stockholm: International IDEA.

Barbados Today(2022). *Overhaul of Regulations Governing Public Officers Needed.* Retrieved on June 11, 2023, from https://barbadostoday.bb/2022/04/13/overha ul-of-regulations-governing-public-officers-needed.

Barber, M. J., Canes-Wrone, B., & Thrower, S. (2017). Ideologically sophisticated donors: Which candidates do individual contributors finance? *American Journal of Political Science* 61(2), 271–288.

Bardall, G. (2011). *Breaking the Mold: Understanding Gender and Electoral Violence.* Washington DC: International Foundation for Electoral Systems.

Barnes, T. D., & Beaulieu, E. (2014). Gender stereotypes and corruption: How candidates affect perceptions of election fraud. *Politics & Gender* 10(3), 365–391. doi:10.1017/S1743923X14000221.

Barriteau, E. V. (1998). *Engendering Local Government in the Commonwealth Caribbean*, CGDS, The UWI, Cave Hill Campus, Working Paper no. 1. Retrieved on October 2, 2022, from https://sta.uwi.edu/crgs/september2015/ journals/CRGS_9_Pgs195-244_EngenderingLocalGovt_VEBarriteau.pdf.

Barrow-Giles, C., & Joseph, T. S. D. (2006). *General Elections and Voting in the English-Speaking Caribbean.* Kingston, Jamaica: Ian Randle.

Bianchi, S., Sayer, L., Milkie, M., & Robinson, J. (2012). Housework: Who did, does or will do it, and how much does it matter? *Social Forces* 91(1), 55–63.

Bissessar, A. (2014). Challenges to women's leadership in ex-colonial societies. *International Journal of Gender and Women's Studies* 2(3), 13–35.

Braden, M. (1996). *Women Politicians and the Media*. Lexington: University of Kentucky Press.

Bucchianeri, P. (2018). Is running enough? Reconsidering the conventional wisdom about women candidates, *Political Behavior* 40: 435–466. doi:10.1007/s11109-017-9407-7.

Buddan, R. (2004). Universal adult suffrage in Jamaica and the Caribbean since 1944. *Social and Economic Studies* 53(4),135–162.

Burns, C., & Kattelman, K. (2017). Women chief executives: The political catch-22 of counterterrorism. *Journal of Terrorism Research* 8(2), 22–43.

Bush, B. (1990). *Slave Women in Caribbean Society 1650–1838*. Bloomington: Indiana University Press.

Bystrom, D. G., Robertson, T. A., & Banwart, M. C. (2001). Framing the fight an analysis of media coverage of female and male candidates in primary races for governor and US senate in 2000. *American Behavioral Scientist* 44(12), 1999–2013.

Campbell, Y.(2020). *Citizenship on the Margins: State Power, Security and Precariousness in 21st-Century Jamaica*. Cham: Palgrave MacMillan.

Cappella, J. N., & Jamieson, K. H. (1997). *Spiral of Cynicism: The Press and the Public Good*. Chicago, IL: University of Chicago Press.

CARICOM (2022). *Dame Eugenia Charles*. Retrieved on March 5, 2022, from https://caricom.org/personalities/dame-mary-eugenia-charles.

CEDAW (1997). *CEDAW General Recommendation No. 23: Political and Public Life, A/52/38*. Retrieved on March 3, 2022, from https://www.refworld.org/docid/453882a622.html.

Cigane, L., & Ohman, M. (2014). *Political Finance and Gender Equality*, White Paper Series. Washington DC: International Foundation for Electoral Systems.

Clayton, A., & Zetterberg, P. (2018). Quota shocks: Electoral gender quotas and government spending priorities worldwide. *Journal of Politics* 80(3), 916–932.

Conroy, M., Oliver, S., Breckenridge-Jackson, I., & Heldman, C. (2015). From Ferraro to Palin: Sexism in media coverage of vice-presidential candidates. *Politics, Groups, and Identities* 3(4), 573–591.

Cross, W. (2006). Candidate nomination in Canada's political parties. In J. Pammett & C. Dornan (Eds.), *The Canadian General Election of 2006* (pp. 171–195). Toronto, ON: Dundurn Press.

Crowder-Meyer, M. (2018). Baker, bus driver, babysitter, candidate? Revealing the gendered development of political ambition among ordinary Americans. *Journal of Political Behaviour* 42(2), 359–384.

Dahlerup, D. (1988). From a small to a large minority: Women in Scandinavian politics. *Scandinavian Political Studies* 11(4), 275–298.

Darcy, R., Welch, S., & Clark, J. (1994). *Women, Elections & Representation*, Lincoln: University of Nebraska Press.

Devitt, J. (1999). *Framing Gender on the Campaign Trail: Women's Executive Leadership and the Press*. Washington DC: Women's Leadership Fund.

Dittmar, K. (2015). Encouragement is not enough: Addressing social and structural barriers to female recruitment. *Politics & Gender* 11(4), 759–765. Retrieved on September 20, 2022, from https://doi.org/10.1017/S1743923X15000495.

62 *Barriers, Biases, Boys' Club*

Dolan, K. (2004). *Voting for Women: How the Public Evaluates Women Candidates.* Boulder, CO: Westview Press.

Eagly, A. H., & Karau, S. (2002). Role congruity theory of prejudice toward female leaders. *Psychological Review* 109(3), 573–598.

ECLAC (1999). *Participation and Leadership in Latin America and the Caribbean: Gender Indicators.* Retrieved February 26, 2022, from https://repositorio.cepal.org/bitstream/handle/11362/2690/S9900676_en.pdf?sequence=1.

Fiske, S. T., & Stevens, L. E. (1993). What's so special about sex? Gender stereotyping and discrimination. In S. Oskamp & M. Costanzo (Eds.), *Gender Issues in Contemporary Society* (pp. 173–196). Thousand Oaks, CA: Sage.

Fox, R., & Lawless, J. L. (2011). Gendered perceptions and political candidacies: A central barrier to women's equality in electoral politics. *American Journal of Political Science* 55(1), 59–73. doi:10.1111/j.1540-5907.2010.00484.

Fox, R. L., & Lawless, J. L. (2014). Uncovering the origins of the gender gap in political ambition. *American Political Science Review* 108(3), 499–519. Retrieved on June 16, 2023, from http://www.jstor.org/stable/43654389.

Franceschet, S., & Piscopo J. M. (2008). Gender quotas and women's substantive representation: Lessons from Argentina. *Politics & Gender* 4(3), 393–425.

Garcia-Blanco, I., & Wahl-Jorgensen, K. (2011). The discursive construction of women politicians in the European press. *Feminist Media Studies* 12(3), 422–441.

Gilmartin, P. (2001). Still the angel in the household. *Women & Politics* 22(4), 51–67.

Githens, M., & Prestage, J. (Eds.) (1977). *A Portrait of Marginality: The Political Behavior of the American Women.* New York: David McKay.

Goodyear-Grant, E. (2013). *Gendered News: Media Coverage and Electoral Politics in Canada.* Vancouver: University of British Columbia Press.

Gothreau, C., & Sanbonmatsu, K. (2021). Women and unequal voice in governors' races: A study of campaign contributions. *Politics, Groups, and Identities* 11(1), 158–168. doi:10.1080/21565503.2021.1932531.

Gray, O. (2004). *Demeaned but Empowered: The Social Power of the Urban Poor in Jamaica.* Kingston, Jamaica: University of the West Indies Press.

Griner, S., & Zovatto, D. (Eds.) (2005). *From Grassroots to the Airwaves: Paying for Political Parties and Campaigns in the Caribbean.* Washington DC: International IDEA.

Haraldsson, A., & Wängnerud, L. (2019). The effect of media sexism on women's political ambition: Evidence from a worldwide study, *Feminist Media Studies* 19 (4), 525–541. doi:10.1080/14680777.2018.1468797.

Heron, T. (2008). Political advertising and the portrayal of gender, colour and class in Jamaica's general elections 2007. In L. Dunn and J. Wedderburn (Eds.), *Gender and Governance*, Institute of Gender and Development Studies Working Paper Series 5 (pp. 59–104). Kingston, Jamaica: CGDS.

Henry-Wilson, M. (1987). *Women in Politics in Jamaica: Some Preliminary Findings.* Paper presented at the Caribbean Studies Association Conference, Belize City.

iKnowPolitics (2015). *Funding for Women Candidates.* Retrieved on June 11, 2023, from https://www.iknowpolitics.org/fr/comment/19297.

Inter-Parliamentary Union (2008). *Equality in Politics: A Survey of Women and Men in Parliaments.* Retrieved on June 11, 2023, from http://archive.ipu.org/pdf/publications/equality08-e.pdf.

Inter-Parliamentary Union (2020). *Women in Parliament 1995–2020*. Retrieved on September 21, 2022, from https://www.ipu.org/resources/publications/reports/2020-03/women-in-parliament-1995-2020-25-years-in-review.

Inter-Parliamentary Union (2023). *Monthly Ranking of Women in National Parliaments*. Retrieved on April 27, 2022, from https://data.ipu.org/women-ranking?month=2&year=2023.

Iversen, T., & Rosenbluth, F. (2006). The political economy of gender: Explaining cross-national variation in the gender division of labor and the gender voting gap. *American Journal of Political Science* 50(1), 1–19.

Jamieson, K. (1995). *Beyond the Double Bind: Women and Leadership*. New York: Oxford University Press.

Johnson-Myers, T. (2019). Negative media frames and female politicians: A case study of Jamaica's first female prime minister, Portia Simpson-Miller. *Social Politics: International Studies in Gender, State & Society* 28(1), 193–214. Retrieved on June 6, 2023, from https://doi.org/10.1093/sp/jxz043.

Johnson-Myers, T. (2021). Violence against women in politics: Female politicians' experience with political violence in Jamaica. *Bulletin of Latin American Research* 42(1), 115–130. Retrieved on June 6, 2023, from https://doi.org/10.1111/blar.13314.

Kahn, K. F. (1992). Does being male help? An investigation of the effects of candidate gender and campaign coverage on evaluations of U.S. Senate candidates. *Journal of Politics* 54(2), 497–517.

Kahn, K. F. (1994). The distorted mirror: Press coverage of women candidates for statewide office. *Journal of Politics* 56(1), 154–173.

Kahn, K. F. (1996). *The Political Consequences of Being a Woman: How Stereotypes Influence the Conduct and Consequences of Political Campaigns*. New York: Columbia University Press.

Kalla, T. D., & Rosenbluth F. (2018). The ties that double bind: Social roles and women's underrepresentation in politics. *American Political Science Review* 112(3), 525–541.

Kanter, R. M. (1977). Some effects of proportions on group life: Skewed sex ratios and responses to token women. *American Journal of Sociology* 82(1), 965–990.

Kenworthy, L., & Malami, M. (1999). Gender inequality in political representation: A worldwide comparative analysis. *Social Forces* 78(1), 235–269.

Krook, M. L. (2004). Gender quotas as a global phenomenon: Actors and strategies in quota adoption. *European Political Science* 3(3), 59–65.

Krook, M. L. (2010). *Quotas for Women in Politics: Gender and Candidate Selection Reform Worldwide*. New York: Oxford University Press.

Krook, M. L. (2020). *Violence against Women in Politics*. New York: Oxford University Press.

Krook, M. L. & Restrepo Sanín, J. (2016). Violence against women in politics: Concepts, debates, and solutions. *Política y gobierno* 23(1), 125–157.

Krook, M. L. & Restrepo Sanín, J. (2020). The cost of doing politics? Analyzing violence and harassment against female politicians. *Perspectives on Politics* 18(3), 740–755.

Lawless, J. L. & Fox, R. L. (2005). To run or not to run for office: Explaining nascent political ambition. *American Journal of Political Science* 49(3), 642–659. Retrieved on June 6, 2023, from https://doi.org/10.2307/3647737.

64 Barriers, Biases, Boys' Club

Lawless, J. L. & Fox, R. L. (2008). Why are women still not running for public office? *Issues in Governance Studies* 16. Retrieved on September 20, 2022, from https://www.brookings.edu/wp-content/uploads/2016/06/05_women_lawless_fox.pdf.

Lijphart, A. (1994). *Electoral Systems and Party Systems: A Study of Twenty-Seven Democracies, 1945–1990.* Oxford: Oxford University Press.

Mair, L. M., Beckles, H., & Shepherd, V. (Eds.) (2006). *A Historical Study of Women in Jamaica: 1655–1844.* Kingston, Jamaica: University of the West Indies Press.

Mansbridge, J. (2005). Quota problems: Combating the dangers of essentialism. *Politics and Gender* 1(4), 622–638.

Massiah, J. (1983). *Women as Heads of Households in the Caribbean: Family Structure and Feminine Status.* Paris: UNESCO.

Mathurin-Mair, L. (2006). *A Historical Study of Women in Jamaica, 1655–1844.* Kingston, Jamaica: University of the West Indies Press.

Matland, R. E. (1998). Women's representation in national legislatures: Developed and developing countries. *Legislative Studies Quarterly* 23(1), 109–125.

Matland, R. E. (2005). Enhancing women's political participation: Legislative recruitment and electoral systems. In J. Ballington and A. Karam (Eds.), *Women in Parliament: Beyond Numbers* (pp. 93–111). Stockholm: International IDEA.

National Democratic Institute (2017). *#NotTheCost: Stopping Violence against Women in Politics: Program Guidance.* Retrieved on September 21, 2022, from https://www.ndi.org/sites/default/files/not-the-cost-program-guidance-final.pdf.

Norris, P. (1997). Introduction: Women, media, and politics. In P. Norris (Ed.), *Women, Media, and Politics* (pp. 1–18). New York: Oxford University Press.

Norris, P., & Lovenduski, J. (1995). *Political Recruitment: Gender, Race, and Class in the British Parliament.* Cambridge: Cambridge University Press.

Ogai, T. (2001). Japanese women and political institutions: Why are women politically underrepresented?*PS: Political Science & Politics* 34(2), 2007–2010.

O'Neill, D., & Savigny H. (2014). Female politicians in the British press: The exception to the 'masculine' norm? *Journalism Education* 3(1), 6–16.

Ouellet, V., Shiab, N., & Gilchrist, S. (2021). *White Men Make Up a Third of Canada's Population, but a Majority of MPs—Here's Why.* Retrieved on February 7, 2022, from https://ici.radio-canada.ca/info/2021/elections-federales/minorites-visibles-diversite-autochtones-racises-candidats-politique/en.

Paxton, P. (1997). Women in national legislatures: A cross-national analysis. *Social Science Research* 26(4), 442–464.

Piscopo, J. M. (2011). Rethinking descriptive representation: Rendering women in legislative debates. *Parliamentary Affairs*, 64(3), 448–472.

Pitre, S. (2003). Women's struggle for legislative power: The role of political parties. *Atlantis* 27(2), 102–109.

Reddock, R. E. (1994). *Women Labour and Politics in Trinidad and Tobago.* Kingston, Jamaica: Ian Randle.

Reddock, R. E. (2004). *Reflections on Gender and Democracy in the Anglophone Caribbean: Historical and Contemporary Considerations*, SEPHIS-CODESRIA Lecture. Amsterdam and Dakar: SEPHIS and CODESRIA.

Reddock, R. E. (2011). *Address to the Graduation Ceremony of the Women in Politics Programme (Cohort II) of the National Women's Commission, Belize.* Retrieved on October 2, 2022, from https://www.academia.edu/3353038/Address_to_the_Graduation_Ceremony_of_the_Women_in_Politics_Programme_Cohort_II_of_the_National_Womens_Commission_Belize1.

Reynolds, A. (1999). Women in the legislatures and executives of the world: Knocking at the highest glass ceiling. *World Politics* 51(4), 547–572.

Reynolds, A., Reilly, B., & Ellis, A. (2005). *Electoral System Design: The New International IDEA Handbook*. Stockholm: International IDEA.

Robinson, G., & Saint-Jean, A. (1991). Women politicians and their media coverage: A generational analysis. In K. Megyery (Ed.). *Women in Canadian Politics: Toward Equity in Representation*, Research Studies for the Royal Commission on Electoral Reform and Party Financing 6 (pp. 127–169). Toronto, ON: Dundurn Press.

Ross, K. (2002). *Women, Politics, Media: Uneasy Relations in Comparative Perspective*. Cresskill, NJ: Hampton Press.

Ross, K., & Comrie, M. (2012). The rules of the (leadership) game: Gender, politics, and news. *Journalism* 13(8), 969–984. Retrieved on October 2, 2022, from https://doi.org/10.1177/1464884911433255.

Rule, W. (1981). Why women don't run: The critical contextual factors in women's legislative recruitment. *Western Political Quarterly* 34(1), 60–77. Retrieved on October 2, 2022, from https://doi.org/10.1177/106591298103400106.

Rule, W. (1994). Women's underrepresentation and electoral systems. *PS: Political Science & Politics* 27(4), 689–692. Retrieved on June 6, 2023, from https://doi.org/10.2307/420369.

Sampert, S., & Trimble, L. (2003). Wham, bam, no thank you ma'am: Gender and the game frame in national newspaper coverage of election 2000. In M. Tremblay & L. Trimble (Eds.), *Women and Electoral Politics in Canada* (pp. 211–226). Toronto, ON: Oxford University Press.

Sekou, N. (2020). Caribbean women of consequence: New leadership for the 21st Century. In F. Mills (Ed.), *Female Leadership in the 20th and 21st Century Caribbean* (pp. 12–21). Caribbean Perspectives. St Thomas, Virgin Islands: University of the Virgin Islands, Eastern Caribbean Center.

Shepherd, V. A. (Ed.) (2011). *Engendering Caribbean History: Cross-Cultural Perspectives: A Reader*. Kingston, Jamaica: Ian Randle.

Shugart, M. (1994). Minorities, represented and unrepresented. In W. Rule & J. Zimmerman (Eds.), *Electoral Systems in Comparative Perspective: Their Impact on Women and Minorities* (pp.31–41). Westport, CT: Greenwood Press.

Shvedova, N. (2005). Obstacles to women's participation in parliament. In J. Ballington & A. Karam (Eds.), *Women in Parliament: Beyond Numbers* (pp. 33–50). Stockholm: International IDEA.

Sives, A. (2003). The Historical Roots of Violence in Jamaica. In A. Harriot (Ed.), *Understanding Crime in Jamaica: New Challenges of Public Policy* (pp. 70–83). Kingston, Jamaica: University of the West Indies Press.

Skard, T. (2014). *Women of Power: Half a Century of Female Presidents and Prime Ministers*. Bristol: UN Policy Press.

Swers, M., & Thomson, D. (2020). Building a campaign donor network. In S. L. Shames, R. I. Bernhard, M. R. Holman & D. L. Teele (Eds.), *Good Reasons to Run* (pp. 239–257). Philadelphia, PA: Temple University Press.

Tremblay, M. (1998). Do female MPs substantively represent women? A study of legislative behaviour in Canada's 35th parliament. *Canadian Journal of Political Science* 31(3), 435–465. doi:10.1017/S0008423900009082.

Tripp, A. M., & Kang, A. (2008). The global impact of quotas: On the fast track to increased female legislative representation. *Comparative Political Studies* 41 (3), 338–361.

66 *Barriers, Biases, Boys' Club*

UN Women (2018). *Women in Political Leadership in the Caribbean.* Retrieved on September 18, 2022, from https://parlamericas.org/uploads/documents/WomensPoliticalLeadershipUNWomen.pdf.

UN Women & UNDP (2017). *From Commitment to Action: Policies to End Violence against Women in Latin America and the Caribbean.* Panama City: UNDP Regional Center for Latin America and the Caribbean.

Vassell, L. (2003). Women, power, and decision-making in CARICOM countries: Moving forward from a post-Beijing assessment. In G. T. Nain & B. Bailey (Eds.), *Gender Equality in the Caribbean. Reality or Illusion?* (pp. 1–38). Kingston, Jamaica: Ian Randle.

Vassell, L. (2013). *Gender Politics and Political Parties: The People's National Party (PNP) and an Agenda for Enhancing Women's Participation and Leadership.* Kingston, Jamaica: Friedrich Ebert Stiftung.

Williams, M. (2020). Inspiring a new generation of female political leadership across the Caribbean. In Mills, F. (Ed.), *Female Leadership in the 20th and 21st Century Caribbean* (pp. 22–28). Caribbean Perspectives. St Thomas, US Virgin Islands: University of the Virgin Islands. Eastern Caribbean Center.

Wilmot, S. (2011). Females of abandoned characters? Women and protest in Jamaica, 1838–65. In V. Shepherd (Ed.), *Engendering Caribbean History: Cross-Cultural Perspectives: A Reader* (pp. 449–459). Kingston, Jamaica: Ian Randle.

World Bank (2020). *Population, Female (% of Total Population).* Retrieved on June 10, 2023, from https://data.worldbank.org/indicator/SP.POP.TOTL.FE.ZS.

3 Debating the Illegality of Abortion Rights in Jamaica
Challenges for Gender Equality and Collaborative Governance Approaches

Introduction

Abortion rights are a contentious and highly politicised issue in Jamaica, where an 1864 colonial law makes it illegal and where different groups hold sharply divergent views, evident in ongoing debates about whether the law should be repealed, amended or retained and what policies should accompany the law. Anti-abortion and pro-abortion groups have expressed different views about what constitutes a human and the role of religion and morality in decisions about women's bodies and their reproductive rights. There are contentious views about whether the specific reasons, such as rape, for terminating a pregnancy should factor into decisions about the legality or illegality of abortion. Public debates about, and interest in, abortion rights in the Caribbean have been renewed in light of the US Supreme Court's decision to overturn the landmark Roe v. Wade, which established a constitutional right to abortion. It has even raised fundamental questions about how to define abortion. In Jamaica, where abortion is illegal, Christian groups have also problematised the definition of abortion, but most have refused to support the legalisation of abortion in limited circumstances. Pro-choice advocates have continued to support women's autonomy, captured under the popular feminist slogan "my body, my choice."

Following the decision in the US to overturn Roe v. Wade, an editorial in the *Jamaica Gleaner*, the country's oldest newspaper, argued that "the revolt that has broken out across the United States over the apparent intention of the country's Supreme Court to strike down Roe v. Wade is a reminder that the Holness administration continues to tiptoe around the abortion question, two years after a parliamentary committee recommended a conscience vote over whether women should have an easier path to terminating their pregnancies" (*Jamaica Gleaner*, 2022a). However, even before Roe v. Wade, anti-abortion and pro-abortion groups have engaged in extensive public debates. Daniel Thomas, a medical doctor and president of the Love March Movement, a Christian NGO group in Jamaica, took issue with the newspaper's prior support of abortion, arguing that

DOI: 10.4324/9781003130987-3

68 The Illegality of Abortion Rights in Jamaica

it bases its pro-death argument on the illogical premise that a woman having control of her body is the same as her killing a human being inside her body. This position upholds the laughable thinking that women from time to time develop 20 fingers and 20 toes, two hearts and two brains—complete with two different types of DNA ... Most shocking of all is the blatant and open admission that The Gleaner would support the abortion of intrauterine children up to 22 weeks. This is commonly accomplished through dilatation and evacuation, which culminates in the dismemberment of the little one, piece by piece. By this time, the baby is some 0.5kg and around 28cm, crown to rump. He or she would have developed the ability to feel pain, the sense of hearing, and even his or her grip.

(Thomas, 2021)

Similar arguments have been made in submissions to Parliamentary Committees that have led and facilitated debates on the current abortion laws, many of them from members of the Christian lobby. These submissions usually condemn the practice of abortion as immoral, ungodly and unconscionable: in one submission, the writer stated that "life begins at conception and to carry out abortion violates God's holy law of taking a life. Abortion, therefore, can be seen as murder (Jeremiah 1: 5)" (Monteith, 2019). But submissions from groups and individuals in favour of abortion argue that women should have access to legal, regulated health services that allow safe termination of pregnancies when necessary, and women should have autonomy over their bodies. Some have also pointed to the ways in which abortion laws and debates reflect a colonial and patriarchal paradigm of denying black women the right to exercise control over their bodies. In her submission to the Joint Select Committee of Parliament, Professor Opal Palmer-Adisa argued that the anti-abortion position is succumbing to a racist, patriarchal ideology in which:

enslaved black people never owned or had the rights to their bodies. Black men were forced to breed with women, and black women were raped and impregnated, with no control over what happened to the children they bore ... those men who insist on policing women's bodies need to understand they are encouraging flagrant disrespect for women's autonomy.

(Palmer-Adisa, 2019)

In this chapter, we examine these contending debates and use the public policy concept of collaborative governance to highlight the complexities involved in mediating such sharply divergent views and achieving consensus. Although numerous statements have been made, one recently by Kamina Johnson Smith, Jamaica's Minister of Foreign Affairs, about the "use of a multi-sectoral lens to address cultural biases that impede the

The Illegality of Abortion Rights in Jamaica   69

advancement of gender equality" (*Jamaica Gleaner*, 2022b), there is a dearth of scholarly work on multi-sectoral or collaborative governance approaches in the Jamaican context. By examining one of the primary mechanisms (collaborative governance) through which debates on reproductive rights take place, we want to call attention to the contested nature of gender policies and the female body as a site of moral, religious and political conflict. We are also suggesting that despite the use of a collaborative approach, state inaction remains a defining characteristic of the political response to abortion. There was a realisation in the policy sciences as early as the 1970s that although governments were expected to pursue policy actions to solve "wicked" problems, in some cases, they deliberately did not (Bachrach & Baratz, 1963). Inaction is sometimes purposefully pursued and enacted for politically strategic reasons (McConnell & Hart, 2019).

Our main argument is that, although collaborative governance, which involves bringing different stakeholders—including the state, human rights organisations, women's groups and Christian groups—to the policy table to build consensus, is important for achieving change in controversial policy areas, it has failed to produce a shift in Jamaica's policy on abortion for several reasons. The reasons for this failure include governmental power that extends to regulating women's sexual and reproductive rights, the influence of religion and the Christian lobby, public opinion and the political cycle. Abortion debates take place in a contested, multi-actor and diverse space, in which the state and the Christian lobby exercise dominance and have successfully resisted women's desire for bodily autonomy. This raises the question of whether collaborative governance was always doomed to failure.

At the parliamentary level, attempts, which we discuss in this chapter, have been made as early as the mid-1970s to amend the laws prohibiting abortion. These efforts have been hobbled by failure to secure consensus among the political elite themselves and between the political elite and a wider group of stakeholders in Jamaican society. We argue that subsequent use of collaborative governance, as seen in the use of a policy advisory group and parliamentary committees, has reinforced the power of dominant groups and so far maintained the status quo rather than providing a basis for change. Collaboration and consensus-building mechanisms have become important political symbols that resonate with the public and are helpful in mediating highly politicised and polarising issues, but have not been successful in changing Jamaica's abortion laws. By contrast, collaborative governance is likely to be more successful where there is less polarisation and religious opposition (Huxam et al., 2000).

Choosing abortion policy as our site of analysis to understand how collaborative governance works allows us to probe questions of power, ideology, religion and how they intervene in and shape deliberations on women's reproductive issues. Our approach in this chapter is relational and takes into account the broader sociocultural and historical context, as

70   *The Illegality of Abortion Rights in Jamaica*

shown in previous chapters in this book and as seen in the work of Caribbean feminists who have explored larger historical, sociocultural and legal questions as well as the social relations of gender (Barattieu, 2001; Robinson, 2003). These studies have laid the foundation for critically exploring issues of power, women's citizenship and state politics that are of interest in this chapter.

This chapter is organised as follows: in the first section, we examine the issue of abortion rights in Jamaica. Next, we explore the concept of collaborative governance as a public policy tool for solving "wicked" public policy problems. In the third section, we question the use of collaborative governance to change abortion laws in Jamaica by exploring the use of policy advisory bodies, Joint Select and Special Select Committees of Parliament. We consider a number of shortcomings in using a collaborative, multi-sector governance approach and question why it has failed to achieve policy shifts in abortion laws in Jamaica.

The Illegality of Abortion in Jamaica and Its Consequences

Abortion is illegal in Jamaica, and a breach of the law carries a penalty of life imprisonment. Abortion is dealt with under Sections 72 (administering drugs or using instruments to procure abortion) and 73 (procuring drugs, etc., to procure abortion) of the Offences against the Person Act. Section 72 of the act provides that:

> Every woman, being with child who with intent to procure her own miscarriage, shall unlawfully administer to herself any poison or other noxious thing, or shall unlawfully use any instrument or other means whatsoever with the like intent; and whosoever with intent to procure this miscarriage of any woman whether she be or not be with child, shall unlawfully administer to her, or cause to be taken by her, any poison or other noxious thing, or shall unlawfully use any instrument or other means whatsoever with the like intent shall be guilty of felony and being convicted thereof shall be liable to imprisonment for life, with or without hard labour.
>
> (Offences against the Person Act (Jamaica), 1864)

Although abortion is illegal, there is a "don't ask don't tell" policy which can be implied from the lack of enforcement. Notably, the law has not prevented women from seeking abortions, as evident in the estimated 22,000 abortions carried out annually in Jamaica (Sedgh et al., 2016). This is similar to other countries in the Caribbean, such as Antigua and St Kitts and Nevis, where "an increasing number of women are self-inducing abortions with misoprostol to avoid doctors, high fees and the public exposure of institutional care" and where doctors are open to performing illegal abortions (Pheterson & Azize, 2005, p. 51). But there are risks. The

The Illegality of Abortion Rights in Jamaica 71

illegality of abortion has real consequences and poses risks to women's reproductive health (Maxwell, 2012). These risks have been documented and made visible through various committees and the stories of women. Many of the risks associated with the illegality of abortions are worse for poorer women. They include botched abortions, medical complications, stigma and discrimination. For example, a 2014 study carried out at the Victoria Jubilee Hospital revealed that over 40 per cent of expectant mothers who were admitted and had complications had attempted an abortion (Abortion Policy Review Advisory Group, 2007). In 2016, of the 1,177 patients admitted to the Victoria Jubilee Hospital for pregnancy complications, 4 per cent were admitted with complications of induced termination of pregnancy (Jamaica Information Service, 2018).

Maternal deaths have also been a real challenge and featured prominently in debates in Jamaica and elsewhere about sexual and reproductive rights and the importance of abortion rights. According to the WHO, "each year 4.7–13.2% of maternal deaths can be attributed to unsafe abortion," with estimates showing that 220 women die for every 100,000 unsafe abortions in developing countries compared to 30 for every 100,000 in developed countries. Additionally, seven million women per year were treated in hospital facilities for complications of unsafe abortions (WHO, 2021). In 2016, the maternal mortality ratio in Jamaica was 110.6 per 100,000 live births (*Jamaica Gleaner*, 2018). The WHO (2021) also notes that unsafe abortion is a leading but preventable cause of maternal deaths and morbidities, which can lead to physical and mental complications and socioeconomic burdens for women, communities and health systems.

Poor women who face various barriers and are unable to afford safe abortions are often most affected by unsafe abortions that are linked to restrictive laws (Latt, Milner & Kavanagh, 2019). Studies have shown that the legal status of abortion matters less than the risk of complications and deaths due to illegality (Cates, Grimes & Schulz, 2003; Faúndes & Shah, 2015; Fathalla, 2020). In other words, while abortion being legal does not affect the abortion rate, illegality can result in medical complications and death. Consequently, "the more restrictive the legal setting, the higher the proportion of abortions that are least safe—ranging from less than 1% in the least-restrictive countries to 31% in the most-restrictive countries. In developing regions, 49% of abortions are unsafe (less and least safe), compared with 12% in the developed world" (Singh et al., 2018). Using data from the US, Cates, Grimes and Schulz (2003) showed that the legalisation of induced abortion under Roe v. Wade led to lower morbidity and mortality, affected the time during pregnancy (earlier gestational periods) women sought an abortion, lowered cost for women and allowed more unmarried women of racial minorities to terminate unintended pregnancies safely. Other studies have found similar evidence supporting the benefits of access to safe and legal abortions in other countries (Latt, Milner

72 *The Illegality of Abortion Rights in Jamaica*

& Kavanagh, 2019; Oluseye, Waterhouse & Hoggart, 2022). Farin, Hoehn-Velasco and Pesko (2021) studied the impact of abortion on maternal mortality in the US over the period 1969 to 1973 and found that legal abortion substantially lowered non-white maternal mortality by 30 to 40 per cent.

Legalising abortion is a major step, but there are many challenges to overcome, including doctors expressing an unwillingness to legally perform abortions based on beliefs that promoting abstinence from pre-marital sex and contraceptive use were more effective strategies for reducing abortion-related deaths (Okanto et al., 2010). Alongside these conservative attitudes, a study on abortion in Jamaica found that medical students at the University of the West Indies had favourable attitudes toward abortion. Being non-religious along with personal experience was a strong predictor of favourable attitudes (Matthews et al., 2020).

Given the benefits of abortion rights to women's reproductive health, especially concerning maternal deaths, many countries (approximately 50) have recognised this and made safe and legal abortion accessible to women (Centre for Reproductive Rights, 2022). At the same time many countries including some in the Caribbean still have restrictive laws or total bans on abortion. Suriname, Haiti and Jamaica have total bans. Most other countries have laws stipulating limited circumstances under which an abortion can be legally performed. Barbados and St Vincent and the Grenadines have the most progressive laws in the Caribbean. In Barbados, abortion is legal under the 1983 Medical Termination of Pregnancy Act and allowed in circumstances where the mother's life is in danger and to preserve her physical and mental health. It is also legal in cases of rape, incest and foetal impairment and for social and economic reasons. The law has been credited with a significant decrease in Barbados' maternal mortality rate. Whilst abortion is legal in Trinidad and Tobago to preserve mental and physical health, and in cases where a woman's life is in danger, it is not allowed in cases of rape, incest or foetal impairment.

In addition to national laws that regulate abortion, international laws and agreements make provisions for women's reproductive rights and their right to safe abortion. There is the International Conference on Population and Development (ICPD) Programme of Action, which Jamaica has ratified, and the WHO Global Reproductive Health Strategy, which the World Health Assembly adopted in 2004. There is also the Report of the Fourth World Conference on Women, held in Beijing in 1995, and the 1994 Programme of Action. The Fourth World Conference on Women report notes that unsafe abortions endanger the lives of a large number of women, posing a severe public health problem because the poorest and youngest women are disproportionately affected. Action 16 of the Programme of Action of the United Nations International Conference on Population and Development states that all governments and relevant intergovernmental and non-governmental organisations are urged to strengthen their commitment to women's health, to deal with the health impact of unsafe abortion as a major public health concern and to reduce the recourse to abortion through expanded and improved family-planning services (UN Population Fund, 1994).

Although these international agreements exist, and despite studies establishing clear benefits from the legalisation of abortions, the state in Jamaica is yet to decriminalise abortion. Debates among various pro-choice and anti-abortion groups in Jamaican society have taken place through formal processes facilitated by the state, with established procedures including meetings, reports and presentations, suggesting that the state wishes to resolve the question of the illegality of abortion through a collaborative governance approach. It is to this concept of collaborative governance that we now turn.

Collaborative Governance

The policy space in the Caribbean is characterised by a multiplicity of actors and the adoption of new approaches to solving public problems. Traditional approaches to decision-making relied on top-down, heuristic models, such as those proposed by Easton (1965) and Hogwood and Dunn (1984). Collaborative governance is part of a suite of reforms that have taken place in the public sector in many countries, including many Caribbean countries. These reforms mainly stemmed from dissatisfaction with old modes of governing and paved the way for two shifts—first, a change from emphasising governing to emphasising governance. Second, and to achieve the first, a shift from relying on traditional policy actors such as bureaucrats and politicians to solve public policy problems to a broader network of actors drawn from government, business and civil society organisations. The first shift was characterised by a call for a more minimal, transparent, effective and accountable state guided by collective decision-making rules (Chhotray & Stoker, 2009; Kettl & Milward, 1996). For Rhodes (1996), governance refers to self-organising, inter-organisational networks that complement markets and hierarchies as governing structures for authoritatively allocating resources and exercising control and coordination (p. 652). The second shift, to a focus on collaborative governance, bears similarity to the first but emphasises multiple actors and establishes processes and goals. Ansell and Gash define collaborative governance as:

> A governing arrangement where one or more public agencies directly engage non-state stakeholders in a collective decision-making process that is formal, consensus-oriented, and deliberative and that aims to make or implement public policy or manage public programmes or assets.
>
> (Ansell & Gash, 2008, p. 544)

74 The Illegality of Abortion Rights in Jamaica

For Emerson, Nabatchi and Balogh (2012), "collaborative governance is a complex phenomenon that involves many moving parts in dynamic relationship over time, connecting different institutional structures, multiple leaders, diverse stakeholders, and complicated substantive policy challenges" (p. 62).

Collaborative governance is very much related to concepts such as network governance, polycentric governance and collaborative public management (Ostrom, Tiebout & Warren, 1961; Provan & Kenis, 2008; Agranoff & McGuire, 2003). To achieve the aims of collaborative governance, trust, power-sharing, consensus and capacity for joint action are essential (Emerson, Nabatchi & Balogh, 2012). Collaborative governance implies a diversity of actors, negotiation, co-design, co-production, co-delivery and co-analysis of policies (Bianchi, Nasi & Rivenbark, 2021). A number of studies has investigated the advantages of using a collaborative governance approach. In a study examining the benefits of collaborative governance, Ahn and Baldwin (2022) found that collaborative governance "can positively affect desired policy outcomes [equity in this case], but questions remain about who benefits" (p. 1). Other studies have shown that collaboration has a role in improving democracy and political legitimacy (Leach, 2006) as well as productivity and resource access (Donahue & Zeckhauser, 2011). It has also proven beneficial in reducing conflict and promoting innovative solutions to complex problems and is capable of producing agreements, actions and outputs. Ulibari (2015), in a comparative case study exploring the connection between collaborative processes and policy outputs found that "high collaboration resulted in jointly developed and highly implementable operating regimes designed to improve numerous resources, while low collaboration resulted in operating requirements that ignored environmental concerns raised by stakeholders and lacked implementation provisions" (p. 283).

Abortion and Collaborative Governance

Most, if not all attempts to address the question of legalising abortion in Jamaica, have involved different stakeholders working through government-led advisory groups and committees. Following a 1975 Ministerial Policy Paper seeking legal clarity on the circumstances, including rape, carnal abuse and incest, in which registered medical professionals could legally perform abortions, there have been three significant steps, all relying on some form of collaborative governance, to put the question of abortion rights on the policy and legislative agenda. The first was the development of the Abortion Policy Review Advisory Group in 2005 by the then Minister of Health. This group was established because of a concern with maternal deaths and Jamaica's objective of reducing maternal deaths by 75 per cent by 2015. This committee, chaired by Dr Wynante Patterson, cited evidence from the Victoria Jubilee Hospital to show that poor, black women faced real risks because of

The Illegality of Abortion Rights in Jamaica   75

their inability to legally access safe abortions (Abortion Policy Review Advisory Group, 2007). Members of this advisory group included the Nurses Council of Jamaica and a member of the clergy, both of whom did not sign the final report as was noted by the Chair in her letter to the Ministry of Health. Recognising that most women seeking illegal abortions were "young, poor, unemployed and lived in economically and socially deprived communities," the Policy Advisory Group submitted 13 recommendations. These included the repeal of Sections 72 and 73 of the Offences against the Person Act that makes abortion illegal and replacing it with a new civil law titled the Termination of Pregnancy act, developing, maintaining and staffing specified centres in each health region for the provision of therapeutic abortions and making provision through registered private offices for abortions for pregnancies that are less than 12 weeks. The advisory group also recommended that terminations of pregnancies over 12 weeks were to be performed in a public facility with supervision from a gynaecologist/obstetrician, while termination of pregnancies over 22 weeks is not recommended except under exceptional circumstances agreed by the woman and two authorised medical practitioners and performed in an appropriate setting authorised by the Ministry. It is clear from these recommendations that the Advisory Group was interested in a policy shift. The recommendations represent a clear departure from the status quo. The report containing these recommendations was tabled in the House in 2008 and referred to a Joint Select Committee of Parliament, another collaborative governance mechanism, with established rules and procedures allowing various groups to appear in front of the committee.

Given the failure of the political elite to debate, accept or reject the policy recommendations of the advisory group, this Joint Select Committee constitutes a second attempt at using a collaborative approach to making a decision on whether to continue with the status quo or to depart from it. The Joint Select Committee is provided for in the 1964 Standing Orders of the House of Representatives. It is clear that the drafters of these Orders were well aware that there would be issues that needed to be addressed through collaborative approaches with stakeholders beyond the political elite. Section 76 provides that the House may appoint for purposes of any Select Committee other than the Public Accounts Committee no more than six members to sit with members of the Senate as a Joint Select Committee. In addition to the composition of the Joint Select Committee, the procedures as outlined in the Standing Orders further reinforce a collaborative approach, by making provisions for the committee to send for persons, papers, records and witnesses. This is important, as this is what has allowed the two Joint Committees that have dealt with the question of abortion to invite organisations and individuals to make submissions and presentations to the committee. The Standing Orders also allow these sittings to be made public, thus ensuring that the general public is able to keep abreast of the debates and discussions. The Joint Select Committee deliberated for close to

76 *The Illegality of Abortion Rights in Jamaica*

two years, received submissions and heard various presentations. These included submissions from doctors, Christians and anti-abortion groups as well as pro-choice groups and individuals The committee recommended that Sections 72 and 73 of the Offences against the Person Act should be repealed and replaced with a Termination of Pregnancy Act. It is clear that the Joint Select Committee comprised of members of both sides of the political divide and which heard submissions from various group were in broad agreement with the Policy Advisory group's recommendation. However, the parliament as a whole including the ruling party at the time, the People's National Party, failed to debate the report and come to a final decision, leaving the status quo and the laws that make abortion illegal unchanged.

In light of continuing pressure from pro-abortion groups and at least two female members of parliament, Juliet Cuthbert-Flynn, who moved a private members motion, and Lisa Hanna, in 2018, a third attempt was made using another type of parliamentary committee. The Sessional Committee on Human Resources and Social Development was established by parliament to deliberate on Private Members Motion no. 61, to examine policy documents and statements related to abortion, examine legislative proposals, receive submissions and facilitate discussions among different groups. This committee was extraordinary in terms of the high level of participation from different stakeholders and ordinary in its singular recommendation. The committee received a total of 69 written submissions, 90 petitions rejecting abortion rights, 780 emails opposing abortion, 145 emails in support of abortion and four emails supporting limited abortion rights. The committee, in their report, made it clear that they did not use the Abortion Policy Review Advisory Group recommendations as a frame of reference. Despite the high level of interest and participation in the proceedings by various groups, the committee had one recommendation: "our committee, being cognisant of the contending views on the subject matter, recommends that a conscience vote be done by the Members of this Honourable House" (Henry, 2020). We further recommend that "pregnant women and fathers should be provided with the option to receive counselling on how to become parents" (Henry, 2020). The question remains: what explains the inaction on abortion rights in Jamaica, despite the attempts that have been made to forge collaborative governance approaches?

Failure of Collaborative Governance? Power, the Christian Lobby and the Election Cycle

Collaborative governance has been the preferred tool of both the Jamaica Labour Party and the People's National Party to deal with abortion rights; however, it has failed to bring any significant policy or legal shifts. Despite the matter being deliberated by at least three committees of parliament and a policy advisory body, abortions remain illegal, and the "don't ask

The Illegality of Abortion Rights in Jamaica 77

don't tell" policy, which often results in back alley, botched abortions, maternal deaths and stigma, has not changed for poor, underserved black women. The collaborative approach has yielded participation and allowed for debate and discussions. However, in terms of outcomes, it has merely reinforced unequal power relations, preserving an 1864 colonial law that denies women the right to have abortions even in restricted circumstances. Here we discuss a number of reasons why this is so. Power is at the core of the difficulties confronting collaborative governance in Jamaica. Despite this, "little theory exists to guide conveners, participants, and researchers in understanding how power shapes collaborative processes and outcomes" (Purdy, 2012, p. 174). Scott and Thomas (2017) concluded from their study of collaborative governance regimes (CGRs) that they can indeed deepen or "further existing imbalances rather than distribute benefits more equitably (p. 647)." They found that the same set of actors are able to benefit from participation in different regimes. Access to financial, human and technical resources in collaborative governance arrangements depends on principled engagement (increased face-to-face communication, development of common problem understanding and awareness of other network actors). Kallis, Kiparsky and Norgaard (2009) also concluded from their study of the use of collective governance arrangements that radical political options are usually passed up in favour of common ground positions. This is usually seen as a win–win position. Similarly, Lemos and Agrawal (2006) argue that while collaborative governance may produce agreement over techno-managerial solutions, promoting radical options is unlikely.

State Power

Power is fundamental to understanding governments' inaction on abortion rights. The 1864 abortion laws were made by a colonial state comprising white males, and these laws were preserved at the time of independence in 1962 by the independent nation's founding fathers. Men have historically made legal and policy decisions about women's reproductive rights, making women's bodies a site of moral contestation where "gendered mechanisms of state control are enforced and contested" (Calkin, 2019, p. 22). To change abortion laws means changing the power dynamic between men and women and affording women power over their bodies. It also means shifting from a system where governmental power is centralised in reproductive decisions to one where individuals can make these decisions. For this to happen, the state has to be willing to cede power. The state and various conservative groups have historically viewed demands for sexual and reproductive rights as "foreign" and as an encroachment on national power and national identity. Miller and Roseman argue that:

78   *The Illegality of Abortion Rights in Jamaica*

resistance by many state and non-state actors for sexual and reproductive rights is a reminder of the fact that sexuality, gender and reproduction joined to rights do indeed challenge and shift and potentially reconstitute the nature of the state and state power.

(Miller & Roseman, 2011, p. 116)

Power from below and women's agency also matter, but the Jamaican state has been equally adept at resisting pressure from below, often through co-optation (Gray, 2004). Although the law restricts women's reproductive autonomy, as a whole, it has particular impacts on poor, black women, who often lack the means to organise effectively against patriarchy and the power structures in society. The Abortion Policy Review Advisory Group noted that most women admitted to Ward 5 of the Victoria Jubilee Hospital had inner-city addresses. The social power of the poor and the agency of these poor women should not be downplayed. However, patriarchy and state power limit women's choices and their ability to challenge systems that have historically oppressed them. The ability of these women to politicise abortion is restricted by the spatial and political realities they face, which include living in politically homogeneous spaces loyal to a particular political party. These spaces are considered safe seats and usually deliver votes to the same political party, irrespective of their policies (Campbell & Clarke, 2019).

Although the state has sometimes mandated that the public be "consulted," few opportunities are created for poor, disadvantaged women to engage directly in the decision-making process. Given the nature of state power and the state's history of oppressing women during the period of colonialism (Beckles, 2003) and certainly after, the reluctance of the parliament to debate the reports produced by at least two committees of parliament and cast a vote in favour of abortion should not be surprising. State power comes with a deep paranoia that radical changes to the status quo could threaten political power. While at least two female MPs on opposite sides of the political divide have been open about their views on abortion, with one, Juliet Cuthbert-Flynn, taking the step to move a private members motion in the house in 2018 to amend Jamaica's abortion laws, no Prime Minister or Leader of the Opposition has shown public support for their position.

In a Westminster/Whitehall system of government where tremendous power is vested in the Prime Minister, it is unlikely that a public issue as controversial as abortion will get parliamentary buy-in without strong support from the Prime Minister. Caribbean scholars have pointed to the ways in which prime ministerial power and the fundamental principles of collective and individual ministerial responsibility in the inherited Westminster/Whitehall political system has affected governance in the Caribbean (Girvan, 2015; Wheatle & Campbell, 2020). It is rare in the Caribbean, where Prime Ministers have the power to hire and fire cabinet members, for Ministers of

The Illegality of Abortion Rights in Jamaica 79

government to openly express views that are contrary to the position of a Prime Minister and his party. Additionally, the principle of collective responsibility means that cabinet members are expected to publicly support government decisions even if their private views conflict with these decisions. Two things can be implied from this: without a prime ministerial and cabinet decision on abortion, it is extremely unlikely that senior members of the government will openly express their views on abortion. Ministers of Health whose portfolios deal with sexual and reproductive health have also been coy about their views on abortion, preferring not to declare their support for or against the current laws that make abortion illegal in Jamaica. In 2008, the Minister of Health Rudy Spence, in light of pressure from the Christian lobby, declared that the government was "neither pro nor against abortion," arguing that:

> I found it very discouraging when I heard on the radio yesterday (Thursday, February 7) that the government was trying to fast track this (abortion) Bill. What was laid in the House was a report, because a particular group of people wanted exhaustive discussion on the matter, and the Ministry of Health advised that we would facilitate those discussions. And so, after the report was tabled in Parliament, we asked for a committee comprising members from the Senate and the House.
>
> (Jamaica Information Service, 2008)

Other Ministers of Health have called for "compassion," "understanding" and more discussions, using ambiguous language to frame their arguments and provide a shield against criticisms from so-called pro-life groups who are strongly against changing Jamaica's policies and laws.

Another clear evidence of political reticence is the appointment of Ronald Thwaites, an ordained deacon of the Roman Catholic Church and former member of parliament, to chair the 2019 committee that examined the law and heard debates from a large number of Christian groups and leaders. Having a chairman of a parliamentary committee is not inconsequential. The Catholic Church forbids abortion. Importantly too, as provided for in the standing orders, the Chair gets to draft the final report containing recommendations. Civil society groups have noted that the Chair of these committees matters significantly in determining how proceedings are carried out and the results. Political hesitance is largely shaped by public opinion and the power of the Christian lobby, to which we now turn.

Public Opinion

Public opinion matters in a political democracy where politicians must face the electorate every five years to determine their political future. Public opinion is certainly not static, but the force of religion and morality, which informs most people's views on abortion, can be. A

80 *The Illegality of Abortion Rights in Jamaica*

recent (2022) RJR-Gleaner Don Anderson poll, showed that two-thirds of Jamaicans believe abortion should remain illegal. Most Jamaicans, however, believe that women should have the choice to terminate a pregnancy in cases of rape and incest or where a woman's life is threatened. This is consistent with another 2016 survey conducted by the National Family Planning Board that found that over 70 per cent of respondents supported abortion in these circumstances and one conducted in 2018 by Johnson Survey Research Ltd. The latter found that while 70 per cent of Jamaicans opposed "abortion on demand," most supported abortion in limited circumstances, and 82 per cent of women thought that women, not the government, should have the final say on termination. While public opinion has remained firmly against abortion, the public is obviously willing to concede on a limited set of circumstances in which a woman should be legally allowed to terminate her pregnancy. Despite this the Christian lobby in Jamaica is anti-abortion and against repealing the law, which makes a woman liable for life imprisonment.

The Christian Lobby

The power of the Christian lobby remains significant in determining the outcomes of policies and laws dealing with sexual and reproductive health (Wheatle & Campbell, 2020; Johns, 2020; Lazarus, 2020). The Christian lobby has always been invested in women's bodies as a site of morality, motherhood and purity. It continues to have an outsized influence in defining gender norms in Jamaican society. The Christian lobby in Jamaica also plays a crucial role in the law-making process. This is very much evident in the abortion debates that have taken place in the parliament. No law that deals with sexuality and gender has been passed in the Jamaican parliament without Christian groups exercising a sizable influence on the process (Wheatle & Campbell, 2020). This influence can be seen at different stages of the law-making process: the drafting, interpretation and direct participation in contentious proceedings (Johns, 2020). As noted by Johns, a significant problem is that the Christian lobby exerts a powerful enough ideological influence, especially at the drafting stage, "to stymie meaningful judicial intervention at the adjudication stage" (2020, p, 16). Although the Church certainly does not speak with one voice, and this has become more apparent over the last decade, the voices of those with more fundamentalist and patriarchal beliefs about women's sexual and reproductive rights remain more powerful than a group of dissenting voices. The dominant Christian voices have argued that Christian values and morals should be preserved. This forms the basis of their opposition to abortion laws, LGBTQ rights and the legal recognition of marital rape.

The Illegality of Abortion Rights in Jamaica   81

Most submissions received from the two committees of parliament that considered the question of repealing the abortion law came from members of the Church. They have argued, consistently that abortion is synonymous with murder and not consistent with biblical teaching.

My position and those of the group to which I belong is that human beings are made in the Image of God, the Imago Dei, and as a consequence the lives of all human beings are inherently valuable. This inherent value is not determined by the state or any other human being. It comes from God as Creator.
(Jamaica Coalition for Healthy Society, 2019)

I submit that it is only this inherent value of all human beings which originates in a transcendent Being that provides a coherent basis for any and all human rights, the most fundamental of which is the right to life. I further submit that any society that accepts this concept as a core and binding principle should organize itself to seek the best interests of all its citizens at all times. The philosophical and ideological position I hold is to be contrasted with the utilitarian position of others who hold that human value is assigned, not inherent. In this context, inevitably that value is determined by the powerful in the society. Though it is usually deliberately framed as a medical concern, the abortion debate is primarily a philosophical and ideological issue. Medical problems are addressed using standard medical approaches which are geared to saving lives not killing human beings, as required by those who advocate for abortion. If the abortion concern were a true medical problem, efforts would be directed at saving the lives of both mother and unborn child. It is not primarily a medical issue. It is a social, ideological and political issue which seeks to corrupt the practise of medicine. No country, and certainly not this country, should ever sanction medical professionals legally killing any human being. The "elephant in the room" is the liberal ideological position of pro-choice feminists and their supporters who are seeking to construct new human rights, not based on the inherent value of all human beings, but rather on utilitarianism and the desires of the powerful. In this context the life of the unborn is dispensable.
(Jamaica Coalition for a Healthy Society, 2019)

In and about 2005, these discussion began here in our country about legalizing abortion. In discussion after discussion, was it a baby, or not? But I can clearly tell you without a doubt that "foetus, tissue or a blob" whatever you what to call that little human being inside of its mother tummy, it is a human being that is just like me and you, will look just like you and I are even better because fertility and the stages of development of a baby and even the human body is a Mystery and a part of God's Plans. So I being a Jamaican young women, I thank God Greatly that this bill was not pass and all pro-lifers had taken a stand, and you our members of parliament had listen to the cry of our nation's people and didn't pass the bill I pray that you will also do the same and give me a listen ear.

(Holy Innocent Centre, 2019)

I do believe that the unborn child has a God given right to life and it cannot be left to a woman or a man to choose that unborn child's faith to live. No child is a mistake and we must recognize that fact. God's word tells us "that even before we were formed in our mothers' womb He had a plan for us" ... So what gives us the authority to determine who lives and who dies.

(Holness, 2019)

Departing from mainstream religious views on abortion, a group of Christians made a submission to the parliament noting that the abortion of an embryo up to 12 weeks should not be considered murder and disagreed with the position that God intervened in the created world to infuse a soul at the moment of conception into a fertilised egg.

We, as committed Christians, fully support the call for abortion or termination of pregnancy on the terms advocated by the Advisory Committee to the Parliamentary Select Committee of 2007–2009 and by the Partnership for Women's Health and Wellbeing. These terms include: the procedure being carried out within the Health System by a qualified medical practitioner, not recommended beyond 12 weeks, involving pre- and post-abortion counselling, and with special provisions for pregnant girls under 18 years of age. We recognise that terminating a pregnancy is never an easy decision but we hold out the compassion of Christ to all women faced with this decision. We also feel the pain of those sisters who have had miscarriages or are unable to conceive.

(Committed Christians in Support of Abortion up to 12 Weeks, 2019)

Feminist groups and organisations or individuals in support of abortion have challenged the position of the church on matters of abortion:

I ask you to demonstrate that the lives, physical, mental and emotional well-being of women and girls matter, and, to ensure that our lives and well-being not continue to be sacrificed for or relegated to second place after that of a foetus, nor sacrificed because of religious or moral opposition to matters to do with our existential needs and decisions.

(Narcisse, 2019)

The *Illegality of Abortion Rights in Jamaica* 83

Similarly, in a submission from Professor Opal Palmer-Adisa who likened current anti-abortion views and activism to debates about slavery, she noted that "those against abolition quoted the Bible and God in their defense of their right to protect their property and those for emancipation did the same as evidence of why there were entitled to be free, and in retrospect the majority would agree that emancipation was the morally correct stance" (Palmer-Adisa, 2019). Palmer-Adisa challenges the Church to place its gaze and power on precarious lives threatened by poverty, abuse, homelessness and "an unjust economic and religious system" (Palmer-Adisa, 2019).

The PNP Women's Movement in their submission also appealed to the Joint Select Committee to consider the consequences of denying women the right to an abortion and the social and economic circumstances faced by vulnerable women in Jamaica.

> We also know that a number of women from these segments of the society do become pregnant under circumstances over which they have no control—the don-man culture of some inner-city settlements, rape, incest, sex for economic survival (not prostitution), unplanned pregnancy arising from the choice between buying contraceptives and providing the bus fare to work or the lunch money to school. We know that there are religious beliefs which inhibit a woman's decision to take contraceptives and so she has not one or two but ten or twelve children and is at the point where her physical and mental health is severely compromised.
>
> We also know of the harrow stories of botched abortions. We hear of the women who use clothes hangers to induce abortions. We hear about the women who take damaging tablets—two up one down [swallow one, insert two] and then end up at KPH bleeding, many unto death. We hear how these women are often damaged for life. They are the ones who cannot have children in the future. They are the ones who will never forget the experience of trying and succeeding or worst, trying and failing to have an abortion. Abortion is not an easy choice for these women. It is a life or death decision. It is dammed if they do and dammed if they don't. They do not choose abortion because they are careless, and loose and promiscuous. For many of them, an abortion is their only hope. It is also the only sure way of bringing a child into the world who is likely to be a victim or a perpetrator of violence.
>
> (People's National Women's Movement, 2019)

The Church remains a powerful source of power and authority in Jamaica. Most Christians are opposed to abortion as reflected in public discourse and the many submissions to the parliamentary committees deliberating on Jamaica's laws prohibiting abortion. Their ability to mobilise Jamaicans

84 *The Illegality of Abortion Rights in Jamaica*

against new sexual and reproductive laws shows how influential the Church is even in the face of growing secularism and more open attitudes toward sexuality and reproductive rights. The Church has also been able to mobilise a young group of advocates, including professional doctors and lawyers, to oppose any suggestions that the Church's views are anachronistic and dominated by older men and women.

The Political Cycle

The political cycle also has some bearing on the success or lack thereof of collaborative governance, mainly because these efforts are led and facilitated by or through the government and members of the political elite. Every five years, a new government may take office, threatening the viability of discussions and governance arrangements effected under a previous political administration. Because "political parties determine policy and laws, changes in political parties can affect the outputs of collaborative governance regimes that deal with the policy and legal issues" (Gordon et al., 2020). This seems to have certainly affected the effectiveness of collaborative governance to produce an outcome on abortion laws in Jamaica and provides the government with an excuse and an opportunity to pass the baton rather than complete the process. The Policy Advisory Committee was established in 2005 under the People's National Party. However, by the time a report was submitted two years later, in 2007, a new party, the Jamaica Labour Party, had won the election. Although the final report of this group was tabled in parliament in 2008 and referred to a special select committee, which submitted its recommendations by 2012, there was a new administration in office. A new political administration might also change the composition of collaborative groups and committees, which can affect levels of commitment to the process, leadership style, institutional knowledge and gains from deliberate efforts to build consensus.

Conclusion

Jamaica retains a colonial 1864 law that prohibits abortion and denies women the freedom to make decisions about their bodies and reproductive health. In practice, many women still seek out abortions. The problem is that the illegality of abortion, which forces poor women to seek cheap or unsafe alternatives, impacts maternal and reproductive health. The government has generally responded to the demands of pro-choice groups by initiating colla- borative governance arrangements, which have allowed multiple actors to participate in debates and discussions. Anti-abortion groups base their opposition on religious and moral arguments while pro-choice groups argue for gender equality and women's freedom and autonomy over their bodies. These two groups hold sharply divergent views. Despite attempts to build

The Illegality of Abortion Rights in Jamaica 85

consensus through collaborative governance, neither a shift in policy nor a repeal of the law has been achieved. This has raised questions about the effectiveness of collaborative governance and multi-stakeholder groups. In this chapter, we have shown how state power, the Christian lobby, public opinion and the political cycle mediate the outcomes of collaborative governance and their ability to deliver radical changes in the interest of women and public health. Women continue to challenge abortion rights in the Caribbean, albeit in non-confrontational ways. This has mainly taken the form of subversion of the law, despite the consequences, and women's participation in Joint Select Committees of parliament and other state-led initiatives.

References

Abortion Policy Review Advisory Group (2007). *Abortion Policy Review Advisory Group Final Report*. Retrieved on June 2, 2023, from https://www.japarliament. gov.jm/attachments/375_Abortion%20Policy%20Review%20Advisory%20Group %20Final%20Report.pdf.

Agranoff, R., & McGuire, M. (2003). *Collaborative Public Management: New Strategies for Local Governments*. Washington DC: Georgetown University Press.

Ahn, M., & Baldwin, E. (2022). Who benefits from collaborative governance? An empirical study from the energy sector, *Public Management Review*. doi:10.1080/ 14719037.2022.2044505.

Ansell, C., & Gash, A. (2008). Collaborative governance in theory and practice. *Journal of Public Administration Research and Theory* 18(4), 543–571.

Bachrach, P., & Baratz, M. S. (1963). Decisions and nondecisions: An analytical framework. *American Political Science Review* 57(3), 632–642.

Barriteau, E. (2001). *The Political Economy of Gender in the Twentieth Century Caribbean*. New York: Palgrave.

Beckles, H. (2003). Perfect property: Enslaved black women in the Caribbean. In E. Barriteau (Ed.), *Confronting Power, Theorising Gender: Interdisciplinary Perspectives in the Caribbean* (pp. 142–158). Kingston, Jamaica: University of the West Indies Press.

Bianchi, C., Nasi, G., & Rivenbark, W.C. (2021) Implementing collaborative governance: Models, experiences, and challenges. *Public Management Review* 23(11), 1581–1589. doi:10.1080/14719037.2021.1878777.

Biholar, R. (2022). Discriminatory laws: The normalization of sexual violence in anglophone Caribbean sexual violence laws. In R. Biholar & D. Leslie (Eds.), *Critical Caribbean Perspectives on Preventing Gender-Based Violence* (pp. 44–64). London and New York: Routledge.

Calkin, S. (2019). Towards a political geography of abortion. *Political Geography* 69, 22–29.

Campbell, Y., & Clarke, C. (2017). The Garrison community in Kingston and its implications for violence: Policing, de facto rights, and security in Jamaica. In T. Hilgers & L. Macdonald (Eds.), *Violence in Latin America and the Caribbean: Subnational Structures, Institutions, and Clientelistic Networks* (pp. 93–111). Cambridge: Cambridge University Press.

86 *The Illegality of Abortion Rights in Jamaica*

Cates, W., Jr, Grimes, D. A., & Schulz, K. F. (2003). The public health impact of legal abortion: 30 years later. *Perspectives on Sexual and Reproductive Health* 35 (1), 25–28. Retrieved on June 2, 2023, from https://doi.org/10.1363/3502503.

Centre for Reproductive Rights (2022). *The World's Abortion Laws.* Retrieved on June 2, 2023, from https://reproductiverights.org/maps/worlds-abortion-laws/#block_618bf1ddfb8c3.

Chhotray, V., & Stoker, G. (2009). *Governance Theory and Practice: A Cross-Disciplinary approach.* Basingstoke, Hants.: Palgrave Macmillan.

Committed Christians in Support of Abortion up to 12 Weeks (2019). *Submission to Human Resources and Social Development Committee Private Members Motion no. 61/2018.* Kingston, Jamaica: Houses of Parliament.

Donahue, J. D., & Zeckhauser, R. J. (2011). *Collaborative Governance.* Princeton, NJ, and Oxford: Princeton University Press.

Easton, D. (1965). *A Framework for Political Analysis.* Englewood Cliffs, NJ: Prentice-Hall.

Emerson, K., & Nabatchi, T. (2015). Evaluating the productivity of collaborative governance regimes: A performance matrix. *Public Performance & Management Review* 38(4), 717–747. doi:10.1080/15309576.2015.1031016.

Emerson, K., Nabatchi, T., & Balogh, S. (2012). An integrative framework for collaborative governance. *Journal of Public Administration Research and Theory* 22(1), 1–29. Retrieved on June 2, 2023, from https://doi.org/10.1093/jopart/mur011.

Farin, S. M., Hoehn-Velasco, L., & Pesko, M. (2021). *The Impact of Legal Abortion on Maternal Health: Looking to the Past to Inform the Present.* Retrieved on June 2, 2023, from https://papers.ssrn.com/sol3/papers.cfm?abstract_id=3913899.

Fathalla, M. F. (2020). Safe abortion: The public health rationale. *Best Practice & Research Clinical Obstetrics & Gynaecology* 63, 2–12.

Faúndes, A., & Shah, I. H. (2015). Evidence supporting broader access to safe legal abortion. *International Journal of Gynecology & Obstetrics* 131 (Supp. 1), S56–S59.

Girvan, N. (2015). Assessing Westminster in the Caribbean: Then and now. *Commonwealth & Comparative Politics* 53(1), 95–107.

Gordon, D., McKay, S., Marchildon, G., Bhatia, R. S., & Shaw J. (2020). Collaborative governance for integrated care: Insights from a policy stakeholder dialogue. *International Journal of Integrated Care* 20(1), 1–11. doi:10.5334/ijic.4684.

Gray, O., (2004). *Demeaned but Empowered: The Social Power of the Urban Poor in Jamaica.* Kingston, Jamaica: University Press of the West Indies.

Henry, B.(2020). House committee recommends conscience vote on abortion. *Jamaica Observer.* Retrieved on June 14, 2023, from https://www.jamaicaobserver.com/news/house-committee-recommends-conscience-vote-on-abortion.

Hogwood, B. W., & Gunn, L. A. (1984). *Policy Analysis for the Real World.* New York: Oxford University Press.

Holness, N. (2019). *Submission to Human Resources and Social Development Committee Private Members Motion no. 61/2018.* Kingston, Jamaica: Houses of Parliament.

Holy Innocent Centre (2019). *Submission to Human Resources and Social Development Committee Private Members Motion no. 61/2018.* Kingston, Jamaica: Houses of Parliament.

Huxham, C., Vangen, S., Huxham, C., & Eden, C. (2000). The challenge of collaborative governance. *Public Management: An International Journal of Research and Theory* 2(3), 337–358.

Jamaica Coalition for a Healthy Society (2019). *Submission to Human Resources and Social Development Committee Private Members Motion no. 61/2018.* Kingston, Jamaica: Houses of Parliament.

Jamaica Gleaner (2018). *Abortion War Needs Dose of Compassion.* Retrieved on June 2, 2023, from https://jamaica-gleaner.com/article/focus/20181028/christopher-tufton-abortion-war-needs-dose-compassion.

Jamaica Gleaner (2022a). *Where's the Termination of Pregnancies Act?* Retrieved on June 2, 2023, from https://jamaicagleaner.com/article/commentary/20220509/editorial-wheres-termination-pregnancies-act.

Jamaica Gleaner (2022b). *I Will Remain a Champion for Gender Equality.* Retrieved on June 14, 2023, from https://jamaica-gleaner.com/article/letters/20220531/letter-day-i-will-remain-champion-gender-equality.

Jamaica Information Service (2008). *Health Minister Sets Record Straight on Abortion Issue.* Retrieved on June 2, 2023, from https://jis.gov.jm/health-minister-sets-record-straight-on-abortion-issue/.

Johns, A. (2020). Public morals versus private rights: examining the influence of Christian norms and institutions on the development of LGBT rights in Jamaica. *Commonwealth & Comparative Politics* 58(3), 387–405. doi:10.1080/14662043.2020.1773113.

Kallis, G., Kiparsky, M., & Norgaard, R. (2009). Collaborative governance and adaptive management: Lessons from California's CALFED Water Program. *Environmental Science & Policy* 12(6), 631–643.

Kettl, D. F., and Milward, H. B. (Eds.) (1996). *The State of Public Management.* Baltimore, MA: Johns Hopkins University Press.

Latt, S. M., Milner, A., & Kavanagh, A. (2019). Abortion laws reform may reduce maternal mortality: An ecological study in 162 countries. *BMC Women's Health* 19(1), 1–9.

Lazarus, L. (2020). Enacting citizenship, debating sex and sexuality: Conservative Christians' participation in legal processes in Jamaica and Belize. *Commonwealth & Comparative Politics* 58(3), 366–386.

Leach, W. D. (2006). Collaborative public management and democracy: Evidence from Western watershed partnerships. *Public Administration Review* 66(1), 100–110.

Lemos, M. C., & Agrawal, A. (2006). Environmental governance. *Annual Review of Environment and Resources* 31, 297–325.

McConnell, A., & Hart, P. (2019). Inaction and public policy: Understanding why policymakers "do nothing." *Policy Sciences* 52(4), 645–661.

Matthews, G., Atrio, J., Fletcher, H., Medley, N., Walker, L., & Benfield, N. (2020). Abortion attitudes, training, and experience among medical students in Jamaica, West Indies. *Contraception and Reproductive Medicine* 5(1), 1–7.

Maxwell, S. (2012). Fighting a losing battle? Defending women's reproductive rights in twenty-first-century Jamaica. *Social and Economic Studies* 61(3), 95–115.

Miller, A. M., & Roseman, M. J. (2011). Sexual and reproductive rights at the United Nations: frustration or fulfilment? *Reproductive Health Matters* 19(38), 102–118.

Monteith, P. (2019). *Submission to Human Resources and Social Development Committee Private Members Motion no. 61/2018.* Kingston, Jamaica: Houses of Parliament.

88   The Illegality of Abortion Rights in Jamaica

Narcisse, C. (2019). *Submission to Human Resources and Social Development Committee Private Members Motion no. 61/2018*. Kingston, Jamaica: Houses of Parliament.

Offences against the Person Act (Jamaica) (1864). Retrieved on June 2, 2023, from https://www.ilo.org/dyn/natlex/docs/ELECTRONIC/73502/104126/F639019451/JAM73502%202010.pdf.

Okonta, P. I., Ebeigbe, P. N., & Sunday-Adeoye, I. (2010). Liberalization of abortion and reduction of abortion related morbidity and mortality in Nigeria. *Acta Obstetricia et Gynecologica Scandinavica* 89(8), 1087–1090.

Oluseye, A., Waterhouse, P., & Hoggart, L. (2022). 'I really wanted to abort': Desire for abortion, failed abortion and forced motherhood in South-Western Nigeria. *Global Public Health* 17(8), 1564–1577. Retrieved on June 2, 2023, from https://doi.org/10.1080/17441692.2021.1944264.

Ostrom, V., Tiebout, C. C., & Warren, R. (1961). The organization of government in metropolitan areas: A theoretical inquiry. *American Political Review* 55, 831–842.

Palmer-Adisa, O. (2019). *The Right to Choose: A Historical Lens: Submission to the Joint Select Committee of Parliament*. Kingston, Jamaica: Houses of Parliament.

People's National Party Women's Movement (2019). *Submission to Human Resources and Social Development Committee Private Members Motion no. 61/2018*. Kingston, Jamaica: Houses of Parliament.

Pheterson, G., & Azize, Y. (2005). Abortion practice in the Northeast Caribbean: "Just write down stomach pain." *Reproductive Health Matters* 13(26), 44–53. doi:10.1016/S0968-8080(05)26201-8.

Provan, K. G., & Kenis, P. (2008). Modes of network governance: Structure, management, and effectiveness. *Journal of Public Administration Research and Theory* 18(2), 229–252. Retrieved on June 2, 2023, from https://doi.org/10.1093/jopart/mum015.

Purdy, J. M. (2012). A framework for assessing power in collaborative governance processes. *Public Administration Review* 72(3), 409–417.

Rhodes, R. A. W. (1996). The new governance: Governing without government. *Political Studies* 44(4), 652–667.

Robinson, T. (2003). Beyond the bill of rights. In E. Barriteau (Ed.), *Confronting Power, Theorizing Gender: Interdisciplinary Perspectives in the Caribbean* (pp. 231–261). Kingston, Jamaica: University of the West Indies Press.

Scott, T. A., & Thomas, C. W. (2017). Winners and losers in the ecology of games: Network position, connectivity, and the benefits of collaborative governance regimes. *Journal of Public Administration Research and Theory* 27(4), 647–660.

Sedgh, G., Bearak, J., Singh, S., Bankole, A., Popinchalk, A., Ganatra, B., Rossier, C., *et al.* (2016). Abortion incidence between 1990 and 2014: Global, regional, and subregional levels and trends. *The Lancet* 388(10041), 258–267. Retrieved on June 2, 2023, from https://doi.org/10.1016/S0140-6736(16)30380–30384.

Singh, S., Ramez, L., Sedgh, G., Kwork, L., & Onda, T. (2018). *Abortion Worldwide 2017: Uneven Progress and Unequal Access*. New York: Guttmacher Institute.

Thomas, D. (2021). The pathetic pro-abortion push. *Jamaica Gleaner*. Retrieved on June 2, 2023, from https://jamaica-gleaner.com/article/commentary/20210121/daniel-thomas-pathetic-pro-abortion-push.

Ulibarri, N. (2015). Tracing process to performance of collaborative governance: A comparative case study of federal hydropower licensing. *Policy Studies Journal* 43(2), 283–308.

UN Population Fund (1994). *Programme of Action Adopted at the International Conference on Population and Development, Cairo, 5–13 September 1994.* Retrieved on June 2, 2023, from https://www.unfpa.org/sites/default/files/pubpdf/programme_of_action_Web%20ENGLISH.pdf.

Wheatle, S., & Campbell, Y. (2020). Constitutional faith and identity in the Caribbean: Tradition, politics and the creolisation of Caribbean constitutional law. *Commonwealth & Comparative Politics* 58(3), 344–365. doi:10.1080/14662043.2020.1773637.

WHO (2021). *Abortion.* Retrieved on June 2, 2023, from https://www.who.int/news-room/fact-sheets/detail/abortion.

4 The Invisibility of LGBTQ Women in Violence against Women Legislation in the Anglo-Caribbean

An Intersectional Analysis

Introduction

Violence against women and girls (VAWG, used interchangeably with gender-based violence, GBV), is a gross violation of fundamental human rights. It is a form of discrimination "directed against a woman because she is a woman or that affects women disproportionately" (CEDAW n.d., para 6) and is "rooted in gender-based discrimination, social norms that accept violence, and gender stereotypes that continue cycles of violence" (UN Women, n.d. a). Intersectional definitions of gender-based violence acknowledge that other marginalised and vulnerable groups—boys, gay men, and transgender people—also experience violence related to their gender and sexuality. Both men and women are affected by gender-based violence, but women and girls face a higher risk of different forms of violence. Men are also more likely than women to perpetrate interpersonal violence (e.g., intimate partner violence, murder, assault, rape, stalking) (UN Women, 2022; WHO, 2021a; UNODC, 2019; Fleming et al., 2015; Hester, 2013; Kimmel, 2002). While violence affects everyone, those who exist at the intersection of multiple identities are at a higher risk of experiencing all forms of violence due to various forms of oppression, such as sexism, racism, colonialism, homophobia, transphobia, ageism and ableism (Government of Canada, 2022). Among the most disadvantaged minority groups in Anglo-Caribbean countries are LGBTQ women. They face particular challenges and disproportionately higher levels of discrimination and violence yet receive the least attention.

Violence against women occurs primarily because of the unequal power relations between men and women. This power dynamic is grounded in masculinity and patriarchy. However, power dynamics in same-sex relationships or among members of the LGBTQ community are less difficult to assess due to the intersection of gender identity and sexual identity. In the Anglo-Caribbean, the intersection of multiple oppressions and identities—colonialism, racism, classism, sexism and religion—adds more complexity to the experiences of LGBTQ people in the region. For example, racial dynamics in Jamaica, mixed with gender and sexual politics, have created "a

DOI: 10.4324/9781003130987-4

The Invisibility of LGBTQ Women 91

troubling caste system" (*Rainbow Times*, 2017). Jamaica's motto "Out of Many, One People" speaks to the cultural and ethnic diversity of the country, but there exists a class system in which lighter-skinned, mixed-race and non-black Jamaicans enjoy higher class status through race-based colonial structures (M. D. A. Kelly, 2020; M. D. A. Kelly & Bailey, 2018). The result is that dark-skinned Jamaicans are mistreated and can be the subjects of employment and healthcare discrimination and violence (Spencer, Urquhart & Whitely, 2020; M. D. A. Kelly & Bailey, 2018; *Rainbow Times*, 2017). In St Lucia, Couzens, Mahoney and Wilkinson found that central to St Lucian society is "pigmentocracy or socio-cultural hierarchy based on skin colour that systematically provides privilege based on the lightness of skin" (2017, p. 3).

In Anglo-Caribbean countries with a history of colonialism and plantocracy, the privileges afforded to lighter-skinned or wealthier people can ultimately result in intolerance toward dark-skinned people in the LGBTQ community. Darker-skinned LGBTQ people could experience higher levels of homophobic discrimination and hatred than their white or light-skinned counterparts. They could also be subjected to poorer psychological health and professional services than lighter-skinned people (Couzen, Mahoney & Wilkinson, 2017). When viewed through an intersectional lens, it becomes apparent that darker-skinned LGBTQ Caribbean people will face not only homophobia but also colourism and classism.

The experiences of LGBTQ persons in the Anglo-Caribbean are exacerbated by the existence of GBV laws which are grounded in patriarchy and heteronormativity. They offer minimal protection to LGBTQ people, rendering their experiences with domestic and sexual violence invisible. The multiple identities of victims of GBV complicate the violence they experience, the protection they receive and how the criminal justice system treats them. LGBTQ people who are attacked for their sexual orientation are often reluctant to report attacks or assaults to the police due to fear and the stigma around homosexuality. This fear is legitimised by the country's anti-gay buggery laws, which criminalise same-sex/same-gender relationships. Sexual minorities whose sexual orientation lies outside the heterosexual mainstream are not only vulnerable to GBV but are less likely than cis-women to be taken seriously by the legal system. In Jamaica, the Jamaica Forum for Lesbians, All-Sexuals and Gays (J-FLAG) has reported several incidents of LGBTQ victims failing to report acts of violence perpetrated against them due to legitimate fears that the police will further perpetuate the abuse or humiliate them (J-FLAG, 2013). Between January 2009 and March 2011, J-FLAG received 17 reports of homophobic incidents perpetrated by the police (J-FLAG, 2021). According to Human Rights Watch, "police abuse is … profoundly destructive because it creates an atmosphere of fear sending a message to other lesbian, gay, bisexual, and transgender people that they are without any protection from violence" (2004, p. 19). In a 2019

92 *The Invisibility of LGBTQ Women*

report, Human Dignity Trust (HDT) found that, though not confined to the Caribbean, there is a lack of trust and confidence in the police from the LGBTQ community. The report found that:

> In multiple studies from the Americas, Africa and Asia, overwhelming majorities of trans and gender-diverse people experience harassment, violence and abuse from state officials and identify them as the main perpetrators of their discrimination. The abuse reported by trans and gender-diverse people includes blackmail, extortion, public humiliation, and physical and sexual violence. This occurs both in countries where there are laws that are used to criminalise trans and gender-diverse people and in countries without such criminalizing provisions.
>
> (Human Dignity Trust, 2019)

Using an intersectional approach to analysing violence against women, we attempt in this chapter to highlight the visibility of multiple intersecting inequalities in policies on violence against women in the Anglo-Caribbean, with a focus on women in the LGBTQ community. Feminists and critical race theorists use the concept of intersectionality to explain how the current social order perpetuates discrimination and how certain groups within society face multiple forms of discrimination. While it was designed primarily to assess, address and explain the lives of black women, intersectionality is a useful conceptual tool for considering the experiences of violence and abuse in the LGBTQ community due to its focus on minority groups who face discrimination. We deconstruct the Domestic Violence Act and the Sexual Violence Act of selected Anglo-Caribbean countries to reveal the inequalities and discrimination inherent in them, ultimately demonstrating how these laws create burdens that flow along intersecting axes, creating *de jure* discrimination for LGBTQ women. We also explain how the complexity of different identity categories and their intersections create varying experiences of violence for LGBTQ women in Anglo-Caribbean countries.

The analysis begins with a discussion of gender-based violence, including violence against LGBTQ women, from a global and regional perspective. Following that, we shed light on the inherent inequalities and discrimination found within domestic violence and sexual violence laws in Anglo-Caribbean countries. These laws give rise to burdens that intersect along various axes, resulting in *de jure* discrimination against LGBTQ women.

Gender-Based Violence

The United Nations, through its Declaration on the Elimination of Violence against Women, defines the term violence against women as:

The Invisibility of LGBTQ Women 93

any act of gender-based violence that results in or is likely to result in, physical, sexual or psychological harm or suffering to women, including threats of such acts, coercion or arbitrary deprivation of liberty, whether occurring in public or in private life.

(United Nations, 1993)

In CEDAW's *General Recommendation no. 19* gender-based violence is defined as a "form of discrimination that seriously inhibits women's ability to enjoy rights and freedoms on the basis of equality with men and, as such, is a violation of their human rights" (CEDAW, n.d., para. 1). According to the Convention of Belém do Pará, "violence against women" refers to "any act or conduct based on gender, which causes death, harm or psychological suffering to women, both in the private and public domain" (Convention of Belém do Para, n.d., Ch. 1, art. 1). This definition pushes the boundary further, including death as a possible outcome of acts of violence against women.

Violence against women and girls can manifest in many ways but is generally categorised as physical, sexual, psychological or economic. Its forms include, among other things, sexual harassment, rape, femicide, female genital mutilation, forced marriage, withholding access to money, gaslighting, verbal abuse, hitting, shoving and slapping. These acts of violence can occur in a private space (family/home) or publicly (work, community, or by the state) (United Nations, 2012). The most common form of violence against women is intimate partner violence (IPV), defined as "any pattern of behaviour that is used to gain or maintain power and control over an intimate partner" (World Bank, 2023). Based on this definition, intimate partner violence occurs within a marriage, common-law relationship or in a same-sex/same-gender or opposite-sex relationship. It can also occur during any relationship stage (whether at the beginning or after it has ended or is ending). Victims of domestic violence may also include children or any family member living within a household. The WHO (2021a) also estimated that "worldwide, almost one-third (27%) of women aged 15 to 49 years who have been in a relationship report that they have been subjected to some form of physical and/or sexual violence by their intimate partner." IPV encompasses all physical, sexual, emotional, economic and psychological actions or threats of actions that influence another person (WHO, 2021a).

Research on associated risk factors has found several reasons for violence against women. These risk factors are commonly framed within the context of the historically unequal power relations between men and women, where men maintain dominance over women and assure their subordination and inferiority. The correlation between violence and power is articulated in the UN's Declaration on the Elimination of Violence against Women, which states that VAW "is a manifestation of historically unequal power relations between men and women, which have led to domination over and

94   *The Invisibility of LGBTQ Women*

discrimination against women by men and to the prevention of the full advancement of women" (United Nations, 1993). These risk factors are further manifested through structural systems—such as unequal access to education, lower access to paid employment and harmful masculine behaviour, reinforcing patriarchal ideologies of domination and subordination. Gender-based violence is also instrumental in maintaining control and is "one of the crucial social mechanisms by which women are forced into a subordinate position compared with men" (United Nations, 1993).

Violence against women transcends geography and culture, affecting women disproportionately in low- and lower-middle-income countries. Statistics by the World Health Organization indicate that globally, one in three (approximately 736 million) women have experienced physical or sexual intimate partner or non-partner violence at least once in their lifetime (WHO, 2021b). It is also estimated that "37% of women living in the poorest countries have experienced physical or sexual intimate partner violence in their lifetimes" (WHO, 2021a). Women from minority and marginalised groups, including trans-women, lesbians, bisexuals, indigenous women, refugee women, women with disabilities and older women, also face a higher risk of different forms of violence (WHO, 2022; UNHCHR, 2022; UNODC, 2019; United Nations, 1993), due to multiple intersecting factors and identities (Derose, Escarce & Lurie, 2007; Sabri & Granger, 2018). Variables such as age, socioeconomic background, sexual orientation, disability, caste, class and religion also intersect to compound gender discrimination and increase the risk of marginalised and minority women being killed or victimised.

Violence against Women in the Caribbean

Violence against women in the Caribbean remains a pervasive and systematic issue, affecting one out of every three women. The most common forms of violence against women in the region are intimate partner violence, domestic violence and sexual assault. The UN, in its 2020 report, *Intimate Partner Violence in Five CARICOM Countries: Findings from National Prevalence Surveys on Violence against Women*, found that in Grenada, Guyana, Jamaica, Suriname and Trinidad and Tobago, violence against women is endemic, with 46 per cent of women in these countries having experienced at least one form of violence. At least 14 per cent have experienced one or more of the three types of current IPV (physical, sexual and psychological violence). In Jamaica, one in four women is a victim of physical, emotional or sexual violence by an intimate male partner and by men who are not their intimate partners (Jamaica *Gleaner*, 2021; Watson Williams, 2016). In 2018, results from the first national survey on gender-based violence in Jamaica indicated that at least 27.8 per cent of women in Jamaica had been affected by violence. The study also found no differences in the severity of violence based on location, age, education level or employment status (Watson Williams, 2016).

The Invisibility of LGBTQ Women 95

Additionally, some Caribbean nations have high rates of crime and homicide. Women and children are often the victims of these crimes. Countries in the Caribbean and Latin America have higher homicide rates than any other region (InSight Crime, 2020). In the Anglo-Caribbean, Jamaica has the highest murder rate at 49.4 murders per 100,000 inhabitants. Kingston, the capital of Jamaica, is also ranked one of the most dangerous cities in the world, with a homicide rate of 54.1 per 100,000 inhabitants (Jamaica *Gleaner*, 2020; InSight Crime, 2020; Jamaica Constabulary Force, 2021). In 2021, the Jamaica Constabulary Force recorded 1463 killings, giving the country a homicide rate of nearly 50 per 100,000 people (Jamaica Constabulary Force, 2021). The COVID-19 pandemic increased brutal slayings, robberies and attacks; worsened unemployment rates; heightened health and safety risks and placed undue strain on countries' ability to protect their citizens. Other Caribbean countries also ranked high on the list, with Trinidad and Tobago in fourth place with a homicide rate of 32 per 100,000 people and Belize in fifth, with a homicide rate of 29 per 100,000 people (Statista, 2022). In Latin America, Venezuela recorded the highest homicide rate (40.9 per 100,000 people), and Honduras ranked second with 39 per 100,000 people (Statista, 2022). According to the Economic Commission for Latin America and the Caribbean (ECLAC), in 2018, at least 3,529 women were killed because of their gender in the region. In the Anglo-Caribbean, the countries with the highest rates of femicides per 100,000 women include Guyana (9), Saint Lucia (4), and Trinidad and Tobago (3) (ECLAC, 2019).

In 2020, "at least 4,091 women were the victims of femicide in 26 countries (17 in Latin America and 9 in the Caribbean)" (ECLAC, 2021), with an average of 12 women murdered per day across the region. Between 2019 and 2020, several countries in the English-speaking Caribbean also reported an increase in the rate of femicides. The countries reporting the highest growth were Grenada, with an increase from 1.9 to 5.5 per 100,000 women; St Vincent and the Grenadines, from 0 to 5.5 per 100,000; Suriname, from 1.1 to 2.8 per 100,000 and Trinidad and Tobago, from 2.9 to 3.1 per 100,000 (ECLAC, 2021).

The Caribbean has one of the highest incidences of rape per capita globally. In 2022, the US-based World Population Review ranked Grenada (31%) and St Kitts and Nevis (29%) among the ten countries with the highest rape rates in the world. This makes them the two Caribbean islands with the highest incidents of rape per capita. Other countries with high rape rates per capita include St Vincent and the Grenadines (26%), Barbados (25%), Jamaica (24%), the Bahamas (23%) and Trinidad and Tobago (19%) (World Population Review, 2022). An Inter-American Development Bank (IADB) survey of 1,079 women in Trinidad and Tobago found that 30 per cent of ever-partnered women had experienced physical and/or sexual violence and 7 per cent of all respondents had been forced into sexual intercourse by a non-partner (Pemberton & Joseph, 2018). The prevalence of violence against women in the Caribbean stems

96   *The Invisibility of LGBTQ Women*

from the region's colonial past, and "was present from the time of conquest, colonization and the start of the decolonization movement" (Shepherd, 2017). According to Shepherd:

> Under African enslavement, women's bodies became the site of power contestation. Indeed, any honour or esteem attached to being an enslaver arose only from the power that he or she could exercise over the bodies of his/her chattel enslaved; and this was sanctioned by laws which allowed white men and women to exercise intimate power through punishment, torture and control.
>
> (Shepherd, 2017)

Bean supports this argument, noting that during slavery in the Caribbean:

> Enslaved women were faced with brutal lust and inhumane punishments as the order of the day for hundreds of years from both male and female perpetrators. Enslavers seized control of their reproductive lives by declaring their children as property using their blackness as justification for making them reproduce the status of enslavement, unlike white women who could only reproduce free children regardless of the race or status of the father. White women too found themselves bearing the brunt of (un)natural IPV from husbands with little or no recourse from the law which viewed them as second-class citizens.
>
> (Bean, 2022, p. 11)

Other possible explanations for the prevalence of violence against women in the Caribbean are "sexism, power and hegemonic masculinity, combined with notions of a gender, class and race hierarchy, religious orthodoxy, the lack of education around gender relations and the economic situation in which many men and women find themselves" (Shepherd, 2017). Violence against women and girls is also perpetuated by the culture of acceptance and silence around GBV in the Caribbean (UNFPA, 2022; Le Franc et al., 2008). It is "not uncommon for the blame to be placed on the survivor rather than the perpetrator, increasing the stigma surrounding the topic and presenting a barrier for survivors to access GBV response services" (UNFPA, 2022).

Violence against LGBTQ Women Globally

Gender-based violence research often focuses on violence in heterosexual relationships and against cis-women and cis-men, thus neglecting members of the LGBTQ community. Studies have shown, however, that people who identify as gay, lesbian, bisexual or of another sexual orientation that is not heterosexual are more likely to experience all forms of abuse than heterosexual people (Bayrakdar & King, 2021; Statistics Canada, 2020; Messinger

The Invisibility of LGBTQ Women 97

& Koon-Magnin, 2019; Messinger, 2011; Eaton et al., 2013; Guasp, 2012; B. C. Kelly et al., 2011; Murray et al., 2007). Using data from the 2010 National Intimate Partner and Sexual Violence Survey, Walters, Chen and Brieding found that in the US:

> the lifetime prevalence of rape, physical violence and/or stalking by an intimate partner is extremely high in the lesbian, gay and bisexual community with lesbians (43.8%), gay men (26%), bisexual women (61.1%), and bisexual men (37.3%) reporting experiencing this violence, compared to heterosexual women (35%) and heterosexual men (29%).
>
> (Walters, Chen & Brieding, 2013, p. 2)

Bisexual women also experience significantly higher rates of rape, physical violence, and/or stalking by an intimate partner than lesbians and heterosexual women (Walters, Chen & Breiding, 2013). A study by the Williams Institute at UCLA School of Law found that "LGBTQ people are nearly four times more likely than non-LGBT people to experience violent victimization, including rape, sexual assault, and aggravated or simple assault" (Williams Institute, 2020).

Acts of violence against LGBTQ are "particularly brutal and in some instances characterised by levels of cruelty exceeding that of other hate crimes" (UNHCHR, 2011, para. 23). Victims of transphobic violence are targeted "based on the perception that their sexual orientation, and/or gender identity or gender expression defy traditional gender norms and roles, or because their bodies differ from those of the standard concepts of female and male" (IACHR, 2015, p. 27). Abusive partners in LGBTQ relationships use all the same tactics to gain power and control as abusive partners in heterosexual relationships—physical, sexual or emotional abuse; financial control; isolation and more. Transphobic violence may be physical (including murder, beatings, kidnappings, rape and sexual assault) or psychological (including threats, coercion and arbitrary deprivations of liberty). These attacks constitute a form of gender-based violence, driven by a desire to punish those seen as defying gender norms (UNHCHR, 2011, para. 20). Transphobic violence can also manifest itself in the use of force by law enforcement agents pursuant to norms of "public morals" (IACHR, 2015). Another manifestation of violence, unique to the LGBTQ community, is the practice of "outing." The "outing" of the survivor's sexual/gender identity is often used as a tool of abuse and a barrier to seeking help. According to Serra:

> society's fear and hatred of homosexuality causes isolation and increases the vulnerability of gay men and lesbians to domestic abuse ... The batterer may threaten "to out" the victim to family, friends, co-workers, and ex-spouses who are not aware of and will not accept his or her sexuality.
>
> (Serra, 2013, p. 587)

98 The Invisibility of LGBTQ Women

Outing can have severe consequences for LGBTQ victims of violence, many of whom "may lose child custody, prestigious careers, and valued personal relationships" (Serra, 2013, p. 587). It can also prevent victims from accessing care or legal protection due to stigma and bias. The perpetrators of violence may also take advantage of the victim's fear, guilt or internal homophobia to convince them to stay in abusive relationships or convince them that they do not deserve better because of their sexual preferences. Other types of abuse unique to people in the LGBTQ community include telling offensive jokes, using banter or words that make fun of LGBTQ people, hate speech and hate crimes and forcing gays and lesbians to undergo therapy or punishments for being gay (IACHR, 2015). Ultimately, forms of violence against LGBTQ women "is based on the desire of the perpetrator to 'punish' those identities, expressions, behaviours or bodies that transgress traditional gender norms and roles, or that run contrary to the binary system of male/female."

Violence against LGBTQ People in the Anglo-Caribbean

Violence against LGBTQ people in the Caribbean is fuelled by the existence of discriminatory colonial-era anti-sodomy provisions known as "buggery"[1] laws, which facilitate abuse by public and state actors (Human Rights Watch, 2014; Gaskins, 2013; Gupta, 2008; Han & O'Mahoney, 2014). While these laws "do not specifically address sexual acts between women, rampant homophobia puts women who do have sex with women or women who do not conform to more feminine gender identity at risk" (IACHR, 2012). Grounded in British imperialism, patriarchy and Christianity (Gaskins, 2013; Gutzmore, 2004), these laws have played a significant role in attitudes to sexual orientation and gender identity in the region. Anglo-Caribbean countries, once colonised by Britain, were subjected to the 1861 Offences to the People Act, which penalized "the abominable crime of buggery," and the 1885 Criminal Law Amendment Act, which introduced penalties for "gross indecency" between men. The term "gross indecency" is generally taken to mean intimate acts between men other than anal sex. Despite gaining independence from Britain several decades ago, most of these countries retained these Acts in statute, though they are largely unenforced. Table 4.1 below provides an overview of homosexuality laws in seven Anglo-Caribbean countries. Five Anglo-Caribbean countries have decriminalised homosexuality. They are Antigua and Barbuda, the Bahamas, Belize, Trinidad and Tobago and St Kitts and Nevis.

In Jamaica, Sections 76 and 77 of the Offences against the Person Act make "the abominable crime of buggery" punishable by "imprisonment and hard labour for a maximum of ten years," while an "attempt" to commit buggery is punishable by seven years imprisonment. Article 76 of the Offences against the Person Act, entitled the "Unnatural Crime," states, "whosoever shall be convicted of the abominable crime of buggery

The Invisibility of LGBTQ Women 99

Table 4.1 Homophobic Laws in the Anglo Caribbean

Country	Law
Barbados	Section 9 of the Sexual Offenses Act (2002) imposes a sentence of up to life imprisonment for "buggery."
Dominica	The law in Dominica criminalises all forms of same sex conduct under the Sexual Offences Act 1998. The Act imposes criminal sanctions for "gross indecency" with sentences up to five years and for "buggery" with sentences ranging from five to 25 years.
Grenada	Same-sex/same-gender sexual activity is prohibited under the Criminal Code 1987, which criminalises "grossly indecent acts" and acts of "unnatural connexion." This provision carries a maximum penalty of ten years' imprisonment. Only men are criminalised under this law.
Guyana	Same-sex/same-gender sexual activity is prohibited under the Criminal Law (Offences) Act 1893, which criminalises acts of "buggery" and "gross indecency." These provisions carry a maximum penalty of life imprisonment. Only men are criminalised under this law. Transgender people were previously criminalised under a "cross-dressing" law which was actively enforced until 2018 when it was struck down.
Jamaica	Same-sex/same-gender sexual activity is prohibited under the Offences against the Person Act 1864, which criminalises acts of "buggery" and "gross indecency." This law carries a maximum penalty of ten years' imprisonment with hard labour. Only men are criminalised under this law.
St Lucia	Same-sex/same-gender sexual activity is prohibited under the Criminal Code 2004, which criminalises acts of "buggery" and "gross indecency." These provisions carry a maximum penalty of ten years' imprisonment. Both men and women are criminalised under this law.
St Vincent and the Grenadines	Same-sex/same-gender sexual activity is prohibited under the Criminal Code 1988, which criminalises acts of "buggery" and "gross indecency." These provisions carry a maximum penalty of ten years' imprisonment. Both men and women are criminalised under the law.

Source: created by the authors using data from Equality Network n.d.

committed either with mankind or with any animal, shall be liable to be imprisoned and kept to hard labour for a term not exceeding ten years" (Offences against the Person Act, 1864). The Act also requires men convicted of the "abominable crime of buggery" to register as sex offenders. Article 77 makes the attempt to engage in "buggery" or "indecent assault" on a male punishable by seven years with or without hard labour:

100 *The Invisibility of LGBTQ Women*

> Whosoever shall attempt to commit the said abominable crime or shall be guilty of any assault with intent to commit the same, or of any indecent assault upon any male person, shall be guilty of a misdemeanour, and being convicted thereof shall be liable to be imprisoned for a term not exceeding seven years, with or without hard labour.
>
> (Offences against the Person Act, 1864)

Similar Acts and laws can be found in other Anglo-Caribbean countries such as Antigua and Barbuda, Barbados, Dominica, Grenada, Guyana and St Vincent and the Grenadines, where consensual sexual acts between adults of the same sex are categorised either as "buggery" or "gross indecency," and homosexuality remains illegal (Statista, 2020; Equality Network, n.d.). In Barbados, consensual sex between people of the same sex can result in life imprisonment. Though unenforced, Barbados imposes the most severe punishment for "buggery" or "gross indecency," life imprisonment. In Barbados, The Sexual Offences Act (1992) Section 9 criminalises the act of "buggery" between men with life imprisonment. Further to this, Section 12 of the same Act punishes "serious indecency" with imprisonment of up to ten years and is defined as any "act, whether natural or unnatural, by a person involving the use of the genital organs for the purpose of arousing or gratifying sexual desire." It is applicable to such acts between men and between women and is punishable with imprisonment of up to ten years. While the "buggery law" is often not enforced in many countries, keeping it in the statute book marginalises LGBTQ people and legitimises harassment, discrimination and violence against them. These laws:

> invade privacy and create inequality. They relegate people to inferior status because of how they look or whom they love. They degrade people's dignity by declaring their most intimate feelings "unnatural" or illegal. They can be used to discredit enemies and destroy careers and lives. They promote violence and give it impunity. They hand police and others the power to arrest, blackmail, and abuse. They drive people underground to live in invisibility and fear.
>
> (Gupta, 2008)

The existence of the buggery laws also influences public opinion and attitude towards the LGBTQ community. In 2014, a *Jamaica Gleaner*-commissioned Bill Johnson poll found that a significant majority (91%) of Jamaicans believe lawmakers should not attempt to repeal the buggery law (*Jamaica Gleaner*, 2014). In Barbados, a Caribbean Development Research Services study found that most Barbadians were either tolerant or accepting of homosexuals. At least 17 per cent of the population could be "genuinely described as 'homophobic.'" Most Barbadians, however, supported the retention of the "buggery law" (58 per cent), down from 87 per cent in 2004 (Barbados

The Invisibility of LGBTQ Women 101

Today, 2014). Violence against LGBTQ people in the Caribbean is also grounded in the adherence to traditional gender roles, hyper-masculinity and the privileging of heterosexual normativity (Hope, 2001; Lewis, 2003). This is further exacerbated by "the dissemination of 'hate speech' targeted at this community in different contexts, including through public debate, manifestations against events organised by LGBTI persons, such as pride parades, the media, and the internet" (IACHR, 2015, p. 361).

In some Caribbean countries, violence against the LGBTQ community is insidious, while for others, acts of physical threats and violence are more explicit. Victims, and survivors of homophobic and transphobic violence in the Anglo-Caribbean, have reported being excluded from their families, churches and schools. Others, according to Human Rights Watch (2014), were "taunted; threatened; fired from their jobs; thrown out of their homes; beaten, stoned; raped and even killed." Some victims have reported "being stabbed, struck, pelted with bottles and bricks, beaten, slapped, choked and, in one instance, chased with a harpoon" (Human Rights Watch, 2018). In a 2014 UNAIDS-commissioned survey of men who have sex with men in the Caribbean, it was found that within the past month, one-third (33%) of respondents had been stared at or intimidated, while almost a quarter (23%) experienced verbal abuse. About one in ten (11%) reported being physically assaulted in the past five years (UNAIDS, 2022). Those who are poor and unable to live in safer, more affluent areas are especially vulnerable to violence. Trans-women are particularly vulnerable to attacks by their partners and strangers (Human Rights Watch, 2018).

Between 2006 and 2008, J-FLAG received 150 reports of homophobic assaults and murders (J-FLAG, 2013). From 2009 to 2012, another 231 incidents of attacks against LGBTQ people in Jamaica, including home invasions, physical assaults and mob attacks, were reported (J-FLAG, 2013). The perpetrators of violence against LGBTQ people include strangers, neighbours, acquaintances and intimate partners, emboldened by the stigma surrounding homosexuality in the Caribbean and the unlikeliness of victims reporting their abuse to the police. Oppressive and discriminatory laws also perpetuate harmful societal norms and "inhibit LGBT people from reporting abuse and strengthen the hand of abusers" (Human Rights Watch, 2018). The perpetrators of violence against LGBTQ people are rarely arrested or held responsible. Discriminatory laws also mean that LGBTQ people are "perceived as less credible by law enforcement agencies, or not fully entitled to an equal standard of protection, including protection against violence carried out by non-State agents" (UN Human Rights Council, 2001, para. 17). It is also not uncommon for "members of sexual minorities, when arrested for other alleged offences or when complaining of harassment by third parties, to be further victimised by the police—verbally, sexually and physically" (UN Human Rights Council, 2001, para. 17).

102 *The Invisibility of LGBTQ Women*

Gender-Based Violence Laws in the Anglo-Caribbean

Most countries in the Anglo-Caribbean are signatories to international laws and conventions preventing violence against women and girls. All have ratified the Convention on the Elimination of All Forms of Discrimination against Women. Other vital human rights instruments at the international level protecting the rights of women in the Caribbean are the Universal Declaration of Human Rights; the Beijing Declaration and Platform Action (1995); the Convention on the Elimination of All Forms of Discrimination against Women (CEDAW) (1979) and *General Recommendation no. 19* (1992) and the Convention on the Rights of the Child 1989 and its Optional Protocol on the Sale of Children, Child Prostitution and Child Pornography 2008. At the regional level, there is the Inter-American Convention on the Prevention, Punishment, and Eradication of Violence Against Women, "The Convention of Belém do Pará" (1994), and the CARICOM Charter of Civil Society (1997) (which is not legally binding).

By ratifying these conventions, Caribbean countries commit themselves to implement policies to fully realise women's rights as set out in the conventions. Among them are measures to prevent and punish acts of violence against women; improving access to justice through establishing fair and effective legal procedures for victims and setting up the necessary legal and administrative infrastructures to ensure that victims of GBV have access to just and effective remedies. Each country also has a clause in its constitution that protects its people against discrimination. For example:

> Section 23 of the Barbados Constitution explicitly states that "no law shall make any provision that is discriminatory either of itself or in its effect" and that "no person shall be treated in a discriminatory manner by any person by virtue of any written law or in performance of the functions of any public office or any public authority."
>
> (Constitution of Barbados, 2002)

> Article 149(1) of the Guyanese Constitution states that (a) no law shall make any provision that is discriminatory either of itself or in its effect and that (b) no person shall be treated in a discriminatory manner by any person acting by virtue of any written law or in the performance of the functions of any public office or any public authority.
>
> (Constitution of the Co-operative Republic of Guyana Act, 1980)

> Section 15 of St Kitts and Nevis's Constitution states that: (1) Subject to subsections (4), (5) and (7), no law shall make any provision that is discriminatory either of itself or in its effect. (2) Subject to subsections (6), (7), (8) and (9), a person shall not be treated in a discriminatory manner by any person acting by virtue

of any written law or in the performance of the functions of any public office or any public authority.

(Federation of Saint Kitts and Nevis Constitutional Order, 1983)

Section 13 of Grenada's Constitution states: "(1) Subject to the provisions of subsections (4), (5) and (7) of this section, no law shall make any provision that is discriminatory either of itself or in its effect. (2) Subject to the provisions of subsections (6), (7) and (8) of this section, no person shall be treated in a discriminatory manner by any person acting by virtue of any written law or in the performance of the functions of any public office or any public authority."

(Grenada Constitution Order, 1973)

Additionally, each country has comprehensive laws on domestic violence and sexual violence. Table 4.2 below shows a list of country-specific legislation governing gender-based violence in the Anglo-Caribbean.

Domestic Violence Legislation in the Caribbean

All English-speaking countries in the Caribbean have enacted domestic violence legislation, though with essential nuances among them. The "first generation" of domestic violence legislation in the region commenced in the 1990s (UN Women, n.d. b; UNDP & UN Women, 2017) but was vague and limited in scope. The Bahamas and Barbados were among the first countries to enact these laws, with the Sexual Offences and Domestic Violence Act 1991 and the Domestic Violence (Protection Orders) Act 1992, respectively. These acts, however, "provide no definition of domestic violence, and the scope of persons who could seek relief was very limited" (UN Women, n.d. b), protecting only the rights of victims/survivors of domestic or intra-family violence. As part of its intervention measures to address issues affecting women in the Caribbean, CARICOM, in 1997, developed the Model Legislation on Domestic Violence, also known as the Family (Protection against Domestic Violence) Act, to address domestic violence and provide remedies to mitigate the effects of such violence (CARICOM, 2015). This initiative was influential in the revision of existing legislation on VAW and in the drafting of new national legislation across the region. It, however, had its weaknesses, as, although it allows for the making of protection orders, tenancy orders and occupation orders, it does not adequately define domestic violence (UN Women, n.d. b; UNDP, 2012; Bailey, 2022).

Some countries in the region have since made progress in their violence against women legislation, in what is known as "second-generation" legislation on violence against women. Examples include Trinidad and Tobago (Domestic Violence Act 1999), Belize (Domestic Violence Act 2007), Bermuda (Domestic Violence (Protection Orders) Act 1997), and

104   *The Invisibility of LGBTQ Women*

Table 4.2. Legislation Governing Gender-Based Violence in the Anglo-Caribbean

Country	Domestic Violence	Sexual Violence	Sexual Harassment
Antigua and Barbuda	Domestic Violence (Summary) Act 1999	Sexual Offences Act of 1995	–
The Bahamas	The Domestic Violence (Protection Orders) Act 2007	Sexual Offences and Domestic Violence Act 1991	Sexual Offences and Domestic Violence Act 1991
Barbados	Domestic Violence (Protection Orders) 1992	Sexual Offences and Act 1992	–
Belize	Domestic Violence Act 2007	Criminal Code "2000 Rev"	Protection against Sexual Harassment Act 1996 "2000 Rev"
Dominica	Protection against Domestic Violence Act 2001	Sexual Offences Act 1998	–
Grenada	Domestic Violence Act 2010	Criminal Code Cap.1 (Continuous Revised Edition) Criminal Code Amendment Act (2012)	–
Guyana	Domestic Violence Act 1996	Sexual Offenses Act 2010	Prevention of Discrimination Act 1997
Jamaica	Domestic Violence Act (1995)	a) Sexual Offenses Act 2009 b) Child (Pornography) Prevention Act 2009	Sexual Harassment (Protection and Prevention) Act 2021
St Kitts and Nevis	The Domestic Violence Act (2000)	a) Offences against the Person Act CAP 4.21 21 (Amended by The Offences against the Person (Amendment) Act 2008) "2002 Rev" b) Criminal Law Amendment Act Cap 4.05 "2002 Rev"	–
St Lucia	Domestic Violence (Summary Proceedings) Act Chapter 4.04 "2005 Rev"	Criminal Code Chapter 3.01 "2005 Rev"	a.Criminal Code Chapter 3.01 "2005 Rev" b.Equality of Opportunity and Treatment in Employment and Occupation Act 2000

Country	Domestic Violence	Sexual Violence	Sexual Harassment
St Vincent and the Grenadines	Domestic Violence (Summary Proceedings) Act 1995	Criminal Code Cap. 124 "1990 Rev"	–
Trinidad and Tobago	Domestic Violence Act 1999	Sexual Offences Act Chap. 11:28 "2006 Rev"	Offences against the Person (Amendment) (Harassment) Act 2005

Source: created by the authors using data from UN Women, n.d. b.

the Bahamas (Domestic Violence (Protection Orders) Act 2007) (UN Women, n.d b; Bailey, 2022). Unlike the first-generation legislation, these laws refined the definition of domestic violence. They expanded the forms of violence against women and the range of persons who could seek redress under these laws. Domestic violence was also expanded to include "any controlling or abusive behaviour that harms the health, safety or well-being of the applicant or any child in the care of the applicant" (Bailey, 2022, p. 74). These acts of violence can take place both in a public or private sphere and include, among others, physical abuse or threat; sexual abuse or threat; emotional/psychological abuse; economic abuse; intimidation; stalking; destruction of property (Bailey, 2022; UNDP & UN Women, 2017; UN Women, n.d. b). Some countries, through second-generation laws, also adopted approaches that consider the diverse groups of women in the region and their multiple intersecting identities—age, class, socioeconomic status, sexual orientation, marital status and so on. As explained in earlier sections of the chapter, not all women experience violence or protection from such violence in the same way; some women are at higher risk of violence due to unique circumstances and vulnerabilities.

Sexual Offences Legislation in the Anglo-Caribbean

Currently, only seven countries in the Anglo-Caribbean have enacted laws prohibiting sexual violence offences, and fewer still have enacted laws that provide legal recourse for victims of sexual harassment (UN Women, n.d. b). As it relates to sexual offences, Trinidad and Tobago (Sexual Offences Act, Chap. 11:28 "2006 Rev") and Guyana (Sexual Offences Act 2010) now serve as models for the rest of the English-speaking Caribbean (UN Women, n.d. b). When compared with the CARICOM model legislation on sexual offences and sexual harassment, both countries have:

widened the range of offences, increased penalties, removed all exemptions from marital rape prosecution, improved measures to protect victims during police investigation and court proceedings and

106 *The Invisibility of LGBTQ Women*

have provisions in place to keep track of sex offenders after they have served their sentence.

(UN Women, n.d. b)

Developments in second-generation legislation resulted in the protection of persons in non-cohabiting intimate relationships to seek redress. First-generation legislation only protected married or formerly married people and men and women in common-law relationships (living together but not married to each other) (Bailey, 2022). Rape is also included in second-generation legislation, even though only in Barbados, Guyana and St Lucia is the law governing rape gender neutral. The scope of persons protected has also widened to include men and boys. New sexual offences and categories of victims were also added, and these include grievous sexual assault (Jamaica, Trinidad and Tobago); unlawful sexual connection (Dominica) and sexual assault (Grenada); sexual touching and sexual grooming of a child (Jamaica); sexual activity with a child, causing a child to watch a sexual act (Guyana); sexual exploitation of a child (Bermuda); child pornography (Jamaica, Bermuda); caregiver facilitating sexual abuse of persons suffering from mental disorders (Guyana) (UN Women, n.d. b). The definition of rape has also been widened to include:

a forced anal sex (Barbados, the Bahamas)
b forced oral sex (the Bahamas)
c husband forcing his wife to have sexual intercourse with him while suffering from a sexually transmitted infection (Jamaica).

(UN Women, n.d. b)

In 2021, the Sexual Harassment (Protection and Prevention) Act 2021 was passed in Jamaica to address concerns about sexual harassment that are employment-related, occurring in institutions or arising in a landlord–tenant relationship.

It is worth noting, however, that none of this legislation provide a comprehensive framework that would consider the intersectional experiences of LGBTQ women. Domestic violence and sexual offences policies in Anglo-Caribbean countries ignore many of the nuances surrounding violence against LGBTQ women and their vulnerabilities. The emphasis is frequently on the shared experiences of cis-men and cis-women and heterosexuals, without acknowledging that not everyone self-identifies as a cis-man, cis-woman or heterosexual. There are also Anglo-Caribbean countries that do not prohibit discrimination on the basis of sexual orientation, gender identity and expression and sex characteristics (SOGIESC).

In Jamaica, for example, anti-discrimination laws do not prohibit discrimination on the basis of sexual orientation or gender identity. The Charter of Fundamental Rights and Freedoms guarantees protection against discrimination, but it is limited in scope. Section 13(3) (i) of the

Charter prohibits discrimination on the ground of being male or female, race, place of origin, social class, colour, religion or political opinion. There is also piecemeal legislation in place, such as the 2014 Disabilities Act, to protect persons with disabilities. Similarly, in Dominica, there are no laws prohibiting discrimination based on sexual orientation, gender identity or gender expression in any aspect of society. In Guyana, the Prevention of Discrimination Act of 1997 makes no mention of sexual orientation or gender identity. The result is that only persons who identify as biologically male or female can be protected from discrimination. This leaves transgender people who experience violence based on their sexual orientation without protection. People in same-sex relationships are also at heightened risk of violence in these countries. Failure to recognise the intersection of gender and sexuality in these women's experiences of domestic and sexual violence contributes to their exclusion and invisibility, as well as weakening their right to protection. For GBV policies to be inclusive, marginalised groups and their specific challenges must be considered.

The Invisibility of LGBTQ Women in Domestic Violence Laws in the Anglo-Caribbean

While there are a number of international human rights conventions and legislation which protect all persons from discrimination, LGBTQ people are not recognised under any legislation in many Anglo-Caribbean countries. Most countries in the region expanded their domestic violence laws to include a wide range of victims, including persons who are married; persons who were married; man and woman living together as husband and wife although not married to each other; man and woman who lived together as husband and wife although not married to each other (UN Women, n.d. b). Despite these expansions, no Anglo-Caribbean country has a domestic violence statute that explicitly covers gay and lesbian couples, raising serious equal-rights concerns. Women in same-sex relationships are excluded from the institution of marriage or common-law relationships and the protection that comes with them. Countries in the region also limit protective orders to opposite-sex couples or interpret the law to apply only to opposite-sex couples. So, while women in same-sex/same-gender relationships might face gender-based violence, the domestic violence laws do not recognise their unions and specific experiences. Those who identify as non-binary and transgender also find it challenging to seek relief under this legislation. They are also not accommodative of transgendered people as the victims of domestic violence. For instance, transmen and trans-women are not allowed a change of sex or gender marks on official state identification documents. These constitutional and legislative barriers prevent the recognition of trans- and non-binary people and can adversely affect their ability to access health care, jobs, education and their personal security.

108 *The Invisibility of LGBTQ Women*

Using exclusionary and gendered language to validate certain types of relationships while excluding others from legal protection is a common feature of Anglo-Caribbean domestic violence legislation. Some statutes implicitly exclude gays and lesbians, either through a requirement of marriage or connection as biological parents, whereas others require that both victim and abuser be of opposite sexes. In Jamaica, for example, the term "spouse" is defined in Part 1, Section 2 of the Domestic Violence Act as:

a a woman who cohabits with a man as if she were in law his wife
b a man who cohabits with a woman as if he were in law her husband
c a former spouse

(Ministry of Justice, Jamaica, 1995)

Based on this definition, only persons in relationships with someone of the opposite sex can seek legal recourse under the Act. Similarly, in Antigua and Barbuda, for example, the Domestic Violence Act defines "domestic relationship" as:

a relationship between an applicant and a respondent in any of the following ways:
  a they are or were married to each other, including marriage according to any law, custom, or religion
  b they cohabit or cohabited with each other in a relationship of some permanence
  c they are the parents of a child or are persons who have or had parental responsibility for that child, whether or not at the same time
  d they are family members related by consanguinity, affinity or adoption
  e they would be family members related by affinity if the persons referred to in paragraph (b) were or were able to be married to each other; or
  f they share or shared household or residence.

(Government of Antigua and Barbuda, 2016)

The language used in clause b of the definition suggests that women in same-sex relationships may seek relief from domestic violence or abuse because they "cohabit or cohabited with each other in a relationship of some permanence." This is, however, made impossible by the definition of "cohabitant," which, in the Act, is "a person who is living or has lived with a person of the opposite sex as a husband or wife although not legally married to each other." In Trinidad and Tobago, where homosexuality has been decriminalised, the Domestic Violence Act (2006) does not recognise same-sex relationships in its definitions of "domestic violence" or "spouse." In the Act, "domestic violence" is defined as "physical, sexual, emotional, or psychological or financial abuse committed by a person

The Invisibility of LGBTQ Women   109

against a spouse, child, any other person who is a member of the household or dependent" (Ministry of Attorney General and Legal Affairs, Trinidad and Tobago, 1999). A "spouse" is defined as "a former spouse, a cohabitant or former cohabitant", who should be "a person of the opposite sex" or "husband and wife" (Ministry of Attorney General and Legal Affairs, Trinidad and Tobago, 1999). Domestic Violence Acts in these countries make it difficult for women in same-sex relationships to seek protection by restricting protection to cohabitants of the opposite sex.

Saint Lucia is the only Anglo-Caribbean country that provides legal protection to "explicitly prohibit discrimination based on sexual orientation and gender identity in the implementation of such laws" (Thompson, 2022). In March 2022, St Lucia's parliament passed the Domestic Violence Act 2022, which expanded the definition of domestic violence to include "economic and sexual abuse, harassment and cyber-stalking, coercion, threats, intimidation and a wide range of harmful behaviours" (Thompson, 2022). It also widened the scope of persons accessing legal redress under the Act, including those in same-sex/same-gender relationships. The Act further defines, in a gender-neutral way, terms such as "domestic relationship," "spouse," "cohabitant," "visiting relationship," "applicant" and "respondent." Prior to 2022, there were no provisions in the Domestic Violence Act for same-sex partners.

In January 2016, the Barbados parliament passed an Act to amend the Domestic Violence (Protection Orders) Act 1992, Cap. 130A. This amendment changed the definitions of "domestic violence," "spouse," and other pertinent terms to be gender-neutral. Among other things, the amended Act:

a makes provision for a comprehensive definition of the term "domestic violence"
b extends the classes of persons who are considered to be victims of domestic violence
c and ensures that victims of domestic violence receive the appropriate counselling or therapy

The altered definitions are:

a "domestic violence"—is the wilful infliction or threat of infliction of harm by one person in a domestic relationship upon another person in that relationship and includes child abuse, emotional abuse, financial abuse, physical abuse and sexual abuse
b "domestic relationship"—the relationship between a perpetrator of domestic violence and victim who is a spouse, former spouse, child, dependant or other person who is considered to be a relative
c "spouse" means a party to a marriage or cohabitation relationship

110   *The Invisibility of LGBTQ Women*

d "visiting relationship"—a relationship where the parties do not live together in the same household, but in which there are romantic, intimate or sexual relations.

(Barbados Parliament, 2016).

In July 2021, the parliament passed a law that prohibits employment discrimination on the basis of age, skin colour, creed, disability, domestic partnership status, marital status, medical condition, physical features, political opinion, pregnancy, race, trade, sex, sexual orientation, social status or union affiliation. Prior to Barbados' transition to a republic in November of 2021, Prime Minister Mia Mottley presented a new Charter of Rights to parliament, which states in Article 1 that "Barbadians are born free and are equal in human dignity and rights regardless of age, race, ethnicity, faith, class, cultural and educational background, ability, sex, gender or sexual orientation" (Barbados Today, 2021). Though homosexuality is still criminalised in Barbados and St Lucia, these advances in GBV and discrimination laws may influence future legislation that promotes LGBTQ rights.

The exclusion of same-sex couples from domestic violence legislation in the Anglo-Caribbean is based in part on the societal assumption that domestic violence occurs only in cis-gender relationships and that same-sex domestic violence is not a crime at all. There is also the misconception that "LGBT people deserve what they get (e.g., to be assaulted, abused and victimised) because they are abnormal, criminal and/or immoral" (Morrison, 2003, p. 124). The criminal justice system in the Anglo-Caribbean, by criminalising homosexual behaviour and barring members of the same sex or same gender from marrying, has "rendered the identities of LGBT persons invisible or has spotlighted those identities by deeming LGBT persons immoral, criminal and/or pathological" (Morrison, 2003, p. 124).

In many Caribbean countries where the country's domestic violence statute may potentially cover same-sex couples, the victim would have to confess to a criminal act to prove the existence of a domestic relationship with her abuser. They might also face threats from law enforcement officials to publicly disclose their birth sex or sexual orientation. This could cause most victims to abstain from reporting abuses (UN Human Rights Council, 2001). This means that a woman in an abusive same-sex relationship would be hesitant to seek protection under these Acts, both for fear of persecution and because she does not qualify for protection. The invisibility of same-sex relationships in legislation in the Anglo-Caribbean is also perpetuated by its omission from international and national laws regarding domestic violence. A number of international human rights conventions exist to protect everyone, regardless of sexual orientation or gender identity. There is, however, no single international human rights treaty that specifically protects the rights of LGBTQ people. Although CEDAW acknowledges that women have intersecting identities and discriminations, the discourse on domestic violence is grounded in hetero-normativity and cis-normativity, in which violence occurs between males (perpetrators) and their female partners (victims).

Transgender women, too, are rendered invisible by domestic violence laws in the Anglo-Caribbean. In some Caribbean countries—Antigua and Barbuda, the Bahamas, Barbados, Belize, Guyana, Jamaica and Trinidad and Tobago—transgender people can change their names on some documents but not their gender marker. The result is that their sex and gender do not align in the way that it does for cisgender people. It also means that the photographs and gender markers on official documents do not reflect the gender identity of trans-people. Unless a trans-woman can change her gender marker to match her name, there will be no legal proof of her existence, hindering the full exercise of her constitutional rights and rendering them invisible. Not only are they vulnerable to domestic violence, because there is no gender recognition from the state of their affirmed gender identity, but they also experience pervasive discrimination due to a mismatch of their gender and identity documents. If an individual does not have documents matching their gender identity, they may be denied health services, face travel restrictions, be bullied, humiliated and experience gender-based violence. By denying transgender women identification documents, the state also inadvertently or intentionally denies them access to protection from violence. It "creates a legal vacuum and a climate that tacitly fosters stigma and prejudice against them" (UNHCHR, 2022).

The Invisibility of LGBTQ Women in Sexual Offences Legislation in the Anglo-Caribbean

Gender-based violence, including sexual violence and assaults against women in the Anglo-Caribbean, remains prevalent. Many Anglo-Caribbean countries still rely heavily on "first-generation" sexual violence legislation to protect victims of abuse. And in many cases, even the legislation that was expanded as part of the "second-generation" is still grounded in hetero-normativity, cis-normativity and androcentrism. Some countries have attempted to constitutionally reform their legislation on sexual violence, but, due to public pressure or other cultural factors, these attempts proved futile. Guyana is one such example. In 2003, the "Sexual Orientation" Amendment Bill was introduced in Guyana's parliament to be voted on as a constitutional amendment that would include "sexual orientation" as a ground for discrimination. The bill was voted on but was withdrawn due to significant opposition from the religious community.

We agree with Biholar's assessment of sexual violence legislation in the Anglo-Caribbean:

> Narrow, heteronormative definitions of rape, constructions of grievous sexual assault, and the conditional criminalization of marital rape in a

112 *The Invisibility of LGBTQ Women*

number of the region's laws preserve gender codes of femininity and masculinity and ensuing gender relations that help perpetuate biased models of sexual violence victimization and perpetration, by which heterosexual sexual violence in marital relations or against cis men, as well as same-sex/same-gender sexual violence, are undervalued or rendered invisible by the law.

(Biholar, 2022, p. 44)

We further argue that sexual violence laws in the Anglo-Caribbean do not reflect the realities of victims who exist at the point of "intersections between inequalities." This renders the experiences of marginalised and underrepresented women invisible in sexual assault and sexual violence legislation. For the purpose of discussion in this section of the chapter, we focus our arguments on the definition and conception of rape and gross indecency in Anglo-Caribbean Sexual Violence Acts to determine how they exclude or discriminate against LGBTQ women.

Definition of Rape in the Anglo-Caribbean

LGBTQ people in the Anglo-Caribbean are especially vulnerable to sexual violence, including rape. There is, however, no legislation in the region that explicitly protects them. While the law governing rape in countries such as Barbados, Guyana, Grenada, St Lucia and Trinidad and Tobago, is gender-neutral, for others, like Jamaica, Antigua and Barbuda, and St Vincent and the Grenadines, the definition of rape or forms of rape often applies to specific sexes (male or female) and to particular acts—that is, non-consensual penile–vaginal sex. No law protects men or women against forced anal or oral sex (Human Rights Watch, 2018). It, therefore, implies that rape cannot take place in same-sex relationships and that only those with a penis can be a per-petrator of rape, and only those with a vagina can be victims. In Jamaica, a man commits the offence of rape, if he has sexual intercourse with a woman:

a without the woman's consent; and
b knowing that the woman does not consent to sexual intercourse or recklessly not caring whether the woman consents or not.
(Jamaica Sexual Offences Act, 2009, s. 3)

Based on this definition, rape is limited to non-consensual penetration of a vagina (female) by a penis (male). Similarly, in Antigua and Barbuda, rape is defined as non-consensual penile to vaginal penetration. A male person commits the offence of rape when he has sexual intercourse with a female person who is not his wife either:

a without her consent where he knows that she does not consent to the intercourse, or he is reckless as to whether she consents to it; or

The Invisibility of LGBTQ Women 113

b with her consent where the consent –
  i. is extorted by threats or fear of bodily harm to her or to another; or
  ii. is obtained by impersonating her husband; or
  iii. is obtained by false and fraudulent representations as to the nature of the act.
  (Antigua and Barbuda Sexual Offences Act, 1995, s. 3 (1))

Saint Vincent and the Grenadines Criminal Code also defines rape in gender-specific terms:

1. A man who rapes a woman is guilty of an offence and liable to imprisonment for life.
2. A man commits rape if—
   a he has unlawful sexual intercourse with a woman who at the time of intercourse did not consent to it; and
   b at that time, he knew that she did not consent to the intercourse, or he was reckless as to whether she consented or not.
   (Saint Vincent and the Grenadines Criminal Code, 1988,
   Cap. 171, s. 123(2) (a))

In Barbados, the law governing rape is mostly gender-neutral, except when speaking about marital rape. Barbados' Sexual Offences Act of 1992 addresses spousal rape as follows:

A husband commits the offence of rape where he has sexual intercourse with his wife without her consent by force or fear where there is in existence in relation to them
a a *decree nisi* of divorce.
b a separation order within the meaning of section 2 of the *Family Law Act*
c a separation agreement; or
d an order for the husband not to molest his wife or have sexual intercourse with her.
(Barbados Sexual Offences Act, 1992, Pt. 1, Sec. 3)

Based on this definition, spousal rape is only possible between a cis-woman and a cis-man, leaving men and women in same-sex relationships vulnerable and unprotected. One might argue that because same-sex marriages and common-law partnerships are not legally recognised in the Anglo-Caribbean, it is not prudent for countries like Barbados to expand the definition of marital rape to include same-sex couples. By defining perpetrators of rape as males and victims as females, gender-specific definitions of rape exclude acts committed against LGBTQ women/people, particularly those in same-sex relationships. Furthermore, male victims

114 *The Invisibility of LGBTQ Women*

and female victims of rape who are not vaginally raped or penetrated with objects or body parts other than the penis are not protected (Biholar, 2022). Non-consensual sexual acts between women are also rendered invisible in the context of rape, according to Biholar (2022). These definitions of rape also do not take into consideration the diversity of trans- and intersex bodies.

When we juxtapose the definition of rape with "buggery," we also see how GBV laws in the Anglo-Caribbean fail to protect women who do not meet heteronormative standards. Rape is often defined or explained in narrow and heteronormative terms (Biholar, 2022), while sexual activities between consenting same-sex couples are criminalised and labelled "buggery." In most Anglo-Caribbean countries, rape is defined as an offence committed in a heterosexual relationship, while buggery is an offence committed in a same-sex relationship. The difference between these two acts is that "buggery" is a consensual sexual activity between same-sex adults, while rape is a non-consensual sexual activity. By criminalising and likening consensual sex between members of the same sex to rape, the law is "encroaching on the rights to non-discrimination and the right to privacy of individuals engaging in consensual same-sex activity" (Human Rights Watch, 2018). It also contradicts the principle of equality. Biholar explains that "gay, transgender, as well as cis men's experiences of sexual violence that could qualify as rape are diminished and do not benefit from law's full protection commensurate with the severity of the harm experienced" (2022, p. 55).

Gross Indecency

In Anglo-Caribbean countries where homosexuality is still criminalised, consensual sex between same-sex people is often described as "unnatural," "gross indecency," "abominable," and "serious indecency." Heterosexuality, on the other hand, is described as "good, normal, natural, blessed" (IAHCR, 2015). Other sexual violence crimes, including rape, incest and heterosexual sex, are usually not described as "unnatural" or "indecent." In essence, "heterosexuality is seen as the natural sexuality," and "penile–vaginal intercourse as the exclusive or more important sexual act" (Karkazis, 2008, p. 139). It would, therefore, seem that sexual violence is only unnatural or indecent when it occurs between persons of the same sex.

Similar to the buggery laws, laws against indecency "vary in specificity and scope, and in many cases, they discriminate against LGBT persons, whether by their intent or through their impact" (IAHCR, 2015). In countries like the Bahamas, sexual contact between same-sex couples, prior to 2018, was deemed unnatural and could be punishable, if done in public. In St Vincent and the Grenadines for example:

> any person, who in public or private, commits an act of gross indecency with another person of the same sex, or procures or attempts to

procure another person of the same sex to commit an act of gross indecency with him or her, is guilty of an offence and liable to imprisonment for five years.

(Saint Vincent and the Grenadines Criminal Code, 1988, Cap. 171, s. 148)

Similarly, in Barbados, Section 12 of the Sexual Offences Act punishes "serious indecency" with imprisonment of up to 10 years. Serious indecency is defined as "any act, whether natural or unnatural by a person involving the use of genital organs for the purpose of arousing or gratifying sexual desire" (Barbados Sexual Offences Act, 1992, Pt. 1, Sec. 12). It is applicable to acts between men and between women. Gross indecency is also punishable under the penal law in Dominica. Under Section 14 of the Sexual Offences Act of 1998, in Dominica, "gross indecency" between persons of the same sex is punishable for imprisonment of up to five years. An amendment in 2016 increased this to up to 12 years. Prior to the decriminalisation of homosexuality in Trinidad and Tobago, "acts of serious indecency" was understood as "an act, other than sexual intercourse (whether natural or unnatural), by a person involving the use of the genital organ for the purpose of arousing or gratifying sexual desire" (Ministry of Attorney General and Legal Affairs, Trinidad and Tobago, 1986). It also stipulated that sexual intimacy between persons of the same sex could result in imprisonment for up to five years. A commonality in the Sexual Offences Act of most Anglo-Caribbean countries is that acts of serious indecency cannot occur in heterosexual relationships.

Unique to Trinidad and Tobago, when compared to countries such as Jamaica, Barbados, Dominica and St Vincent and the Grenadines, is Article 8 (18/1) of the Immigration Act which prohibits certain classes of people from entering the country. Included in this list are "persons who are idiots, imbeciles, feebleminded persons, persons suffering from dementia and insane persons"; "persons who are dumb, blind or otherwise physically defective, or physically handicapped"; persons who have been convicted of or admit having committed any crime"; and "prostitutes, homosexuals or persons living on the earnings of prostitutes or homosexuals" (Ministry of Attorney General and Legal Affairs, Trinidad and Tobago, 1974).

While the Sexual Offences Act and the Offences against the Person Act in Anglo-Caribbean countries explicitly criminalise male-to-male sexual contact, female-to-female sexual contact and relationships are also not legal. Anti-homosexuality laws, though generally unenforced, can have serious consequences for the LGBTQ community. We agree with Leslie, in his assessment of sodomy laws in the United States, that "sodomy laws exist to brand gay men and women as criminals" (2000, p. 112). Furthermore, "gay citizens are treated and punished as criminals, but without any of the procedural safeguards afforded criminal defendants" (Leslie, 2000, p. 116).

116 *The Invisibility of LGBTQ Women*

The effects of anti-homosexual laws on LGBTQ people in the Anglo-Caribbean are numerous. The mere existence of these laws creates a criminal class of sexual minorities, who are targeted for violence or discriminated against because of their criminal status (Leslie, 2000). In Trinidad and Tobago, the Immigration Act helps to criminalise and ostracise a group of people based on their gender identity and sexuality, by conflating homosexuals into a prohibited class with drug addicts, prostitutes and alcoholics. It also violates the rights of LGBTQ people to live free from fear or want. The social ordering effects of sodomy laws in the Anglo-Caribbean can be likened to the Jim Crow laws that were implemented in the United States of America to segregate people on the basis of race. As Leslie aptly sums it up:

> By inflicting the taint of criminality on homosexuals, sodomy laws have produced the following effects: (1) creating a social hierarchy that diminishes the value of the lives of gay men and lesbians, imposing severe psychological injury on many gay men and lesbians; (2) encouraging physical violence and police harassment against gay men and lesbians; (3) justifying employment discrimination against gay and lesbian employees and job applicants; (4) separating children from their gay or lesbian parent; (5) stifling the development of gay organizations; (6) squelching speech rights of gay citizens; and (7) facilitating immigration discrimination against homosexuals.
>
> (Leslie 2000, p. 116)

In short, vaguely defined and gendered terms such as "rape," "buggery" and "gross indecency" criminalise people in same-sex relationships, bisexuals and trans-people, making them susceptible to violence, arrest and persecution for consensual and or unconventional sexual acts such as oral sex or public displays of affection. Buggery and gross indecency laws also "provide a means to harass, arrest, and in some cases imprison individuals. They also perpetuate social prejudices" (Human Rights Watch, 2004, p. 24). Or, as Gaskins explains, "anti-homosexual laws stigmatize non-heterosexual subjects and this stigmatization is used to rationalize sexual prejudice" (2013, p. 436).

Conclusion

LGBTQ women in the Anglo-Caribbean experience multiple and intersecting forms of violence and systems of oppression. Their experiences with gender-based violence differ from cisgendered women, as does the protection they receive from the state. Due to their inability to fit into stereotypical societal roles, individuals of multiple identities may be overlooked and marginalised, thus rendering them metaphorically invisible. They also suffer from institutionalised discrimination and social stigma, which are legitimised by antiquated laws criminalising same-sex/same-gender relationships and

The Invisibility of LGBTQ Women 117

maintaining negative stereotypes. Gender-based violence laws in the Anglo-Caribbean do not protect the LGBTQ community. There is also no single human rights law or policy in the region which specifically protects the rights of LGBTQ persons. The exclusion of LGBTQ women from state protection and intervention increases their risk and vulnerability to violence and other life-threatening exclusions and discriminations:

> These victims cannot receive protection orders and they remain vulnerable and disempowered. Furthermore, because gay men and lesbians are not protected by these statutes, police are not encouraged or mandated to respond to same-sex/same-gender partner abuse incidents, report these incidents, to arrest the abusive partners or to inform the victims of their civil and criminal remedies ... Without intervention, the abuse may continue unnoticed and unchallenged. Victims may be fatally abused or may kill their batterers in a final effort to end the violence.
>
> (Da Luz, 1994, p. 274)

Generally, lesbians, bisexuals, and (some) transgender women in most Anglo-Caribbean countries can claim protection from GBV as women (gender identity), but they cannot claim protection as lesbians, bisexuals or trans-women (sexuality plus gender identity). Additionally, due to the lack of legal protections for LGBTQ people in the Caribbean, women cannot seek protection based solely on their sexual orientation. This reiterates the importance of considering the intersecting elements of victims' identities—race, gender, sexuality and religion—in mitigating gender-based violence. The invisibility of LGBTQ women from gender-based legislation in the Anglo-Caribbean reinforces the argument that gender-based violence prevention measures that do not include an intersectional dimension will undoubtedly exclude victims of violence who exist at the point of "intersections between inequalities." Gender and sexuality are overlapping rather than competing inequalities. It means that one cannot be assessed in isolation from the other. It is also counter-productive to view abuse or violence in same-sex/same-gender relationships as similar to abuse in heterosexual relationships. Unlike violence in heterosexual relationships, there are additional factors, such as homophobia, which compound discrimination faced by women in same-sex/same-gender relationships. In other words, if we are to start simply by taking domestic abuse in heterosexual relationships as the norm against which we measure that of same-sex/same-gender relationships, we will fail to develop an understanding of the dynamics that shape that abuse.

Note

1 The term "buggery," also known as "sodomy," describes anal or oral copulation between a man and another man, a woman or an animal.

118 *The Invisibility of LGBTQ Women*

References

Antigua and Barbuda Sexual Offences Act (1995). Retrieved on November 10, 2022, from https://www.oas.org/dil/The_Sexual_Offences_Act_Antigua_and_Barbuda.pdf.

Bailey, B. (2022). Gender-based violence against Caribbean women, femicide: A major gap in the legislative framework. In R. Biholar, and D. Leslie (Eds.), *Critical Caribbean Perspectives on Preventing Gender-Based Violence* (pp. 65–86). London and New York: Routledge.

Barbados Parliament (2016). *Domestic Violence (Protection Orders) (Amendment) Bill 2016: Explanatory Memorandum.* Retrieved on November 10, 2022, from https://www.barbadosparliament.com/uploads/bill_resolution/907d022cc76d0c58b3353e80836ba3e6.pdf.

Barbados Sexual Offences Act (1992). Retrieved on November 10, 2022, from https://evaw-global-database.unwomen.org/-/media/files/un%20women/vaw/full%20text/americas/barbados%20-%20sexual%20offences%20act%202002%20(1).pdf?vs=4355.

Barbados Today (2014). *Confusion over Buggery Laws.* Retrieved on July 14, 2022, from https://dev.barbadostoday.bb/focus/confusion-over-buggery-laws/?amp.

Barbados Today (2021). *Charter of Barbados "Promotes Active Citizenship."* Retrieved on July 14, 2022, from https://barbadostoday.bb/2021/11/24/pm-charter-of-barbados-promotes-active-citizenship/.

Bayrakdar, S., & King A. (2021). LGBT discrimination, harassment, and violence in Germany, Portugal and the UK: A quantitative comparative approach. *Current Sociology* 17(1), 152–172. doi:10.1177/00113921211039271.

Bean, D. (2022). Looking back to move forward: A historical reflection of gender-based violence and intimate partner violence in Jamaica during slavery. In R. Biholar, and D. Leslie (Eds.), *Critical Caribbean Perspectives on Preventing Gender-Based Violence* (pp. 10–26). London and New York: Routledge.

Biholar, R. (2022). Discriminatory laws: The normalization of sexual violence in Anglophone Caribbean sexual violence laws. In R. Biholar & D. Leslie (Eds.), *Critical Caribbean Perspectives on Preventing Gender-Based Violence* (pp. 44–64). London and New York: Routledge.

CARICOM (2015). *CARICOM Model Legislation on Domestic Violence.* Retrieved on June 12, 2023, from https://drupal.caricom.org/documents/caricom-model-legislation-domestic-violence.

CEDAW (n.d.). *General Recommendation no. 19,* Retrieved on October 19, 2022, from https://www.un.org/womenwatch/daw/cedaw/recommendations/recomm.htm#recom 19.

Constitution of Barbados (2002). Retrieved on July 11, 2022, from https://www.oas.org/dil/the_constitution_of_barbados.pdf.

Constitution of the Co-operative Republic of Guyana Act (1980). Retrieved on November 10, 2022, from https://www.oas.org/juridico/spanish/mesicic2_guy_constitution.pdf.

Convention of Belém do Pará (n.d.). Retrieved on October 20, 2022, from https://www.oas.org/juridico/english/treaties/a-61.html.

Couzens J., Mahoney B., & Wilkinson D. (2017). It's just more acceptable to be white or mixed race and gay than black and gay: The perceptions and experiences of homophobia in St. Lucia. *Frontiers in Psychology* 8, 1–16.

The Invisibility of LGBTQ Women   119

Da Luz, C. M. (1994). A legal and social comparison of heterosexual and same-sex/same-gender domestic violence: Similar inadequacies in legal recognition and response. *Southern California Review of Law & Women's Studies* 4, 251–294.

Derose K. P., Escarce J. J., & Lurie, N. (2007). Immigrants and health care: Sources of vulnerability. *Health Affairs* 26(5), 1258–1268.

Eaton, L. A., Pitpitan, E. V., Kalichman, S. C., Sikkema, K. J., Skinner, D., Watt, M. H., & Pieterse, D. (2013). Men who report recent male and female sex partners in Cape Town, South Africa: An understudied and underserved population. *Archives of Sexual Behavior* 42(7), 1299–1308. Retrieved on June 3, 2023 from https://doi.org/10.1007/s10508-013-0077-1.

ECLAC (2019). *In 2018, at Least 3,529 Women were Victims of Femicide in 25 Latin American and Caribbean countries.* Retrieved on June 3, 2023 from https://www.cepal.org/en/pressreleases/2018-least-3529-women-were-victims-femicide-25-latin-america n-and-caribbean-countries.

ECLAC (2021). *At Least 4,091 Women were Victims of Femicide in 2020 in Latin America and the Caribbean, despite Greater Visibility and Social Condemnation.* Retrieved on June 16, 2022, from https://www.cepal.org/en/pressreleases/eclac-lea st-4091-women-were-victims-femicide-2020-latin-america-and-caribbean-despite.

Equality Network (n.d.). *Caribbean and the Americas.* Retrieved on June 12, 2023, from https://www.equality-network.org/campaigns/caribbean-and-americas.

Federation of Saint Kitts and Nevis Constitutional Order (1983). Retrieved on June 16, 2022, from https://pdba.georgetown.edu/Constitutions/Kitts/kitts83.html.

Fleming, P. J., Gruskin, S., Rojo, F., & Dworkin, S. L. (2015). Men's violence against women and men are inter-related: Recommendations for simultaneous intervention. *Social Science & Medicine* 146, 249–256. Retrieved on June 2, 2023, fromhttps://doi.org/10.1016/j.socscimed.2015.10.021.

Gaskins J. (2013). "Buggery" and the Commonwealth Caribbean: A comparative examination of the Bahamas, Jamaica, and Trinidad and Tobago. In C. Lennox & M. Waites (Eds.), *Human Rights, Sexual Orientation and Gender Identity in the Commonwealth: Struggles for Decriminalisation and Change* (pp. 429–454). London: School of Advanced Study, University of London.

Government of Antigua and Barbuda (2016). *Domestic Violence Act (2015), No. 27 of 2015. (Published in the Official Gazette Vol. XXXVI No. 18 dated 17th March, 2016).* Antigua and Barbuda: Government Printing Office. Retrieved on July 4, 2022, from https://www.ilo.org/dyn/natlex/docs/ELECTRONIC/102698/124269/F-477110290/ATG102698.pdf.

Government of Canada (2022). *What is Gender-Based Violence?* Retrieved on June 12, 2023, from https://women-gender-equality.canada.ca/en/gender-based-violence/about -gender-based-violence.html.

Grenada Constitution Order (1973). Retrieved on July 4, 2022, from https://www.cpahq.org/media/gq5dtcj5/gre_constitution.pdf.

Guasp, A. (2012). *Gay and Bisexual Men's Health Survey.* London: Stonewall.

Gupta A. (2008). *This Alien Legacy: The Origins of Sodomy Laws in British Colonialism.* New York: Human Rights Watch.

Gutzmore, C. (2004). Casting the first stone! Policing of homo/sexuality in Jamaican popular culture. *Interventions* 6(1), 118–134. doi:10.1080/1369801042000185697.

Han, E., & O'Mahoney, J. (2014). British colonialism and the criminalization of homosexuality. *Cambridge Review of International Affairs* 27(2), 268–288. doi:10.1080/09557571.2013.867298.

120 *The Invisibility of LGBTQ Women*

Hester, M. (2013). Who does what to whom? Gender and domestic violence perpetrators in English police records. *European Journal of Criminology* 10(5), 623–637.

Hope, D. P. (2001). *Of "Chi-Chi" Men: The Threat of Male Homosexuality to Afro-Jamaican Masculine Identity*. Paper presented at the 26th Annual Caribbean Studies Association Conference, Maho Bay, St. Marteen, May 27 to June 2, 2001.

Human Dignity Trust (2019). *Transgender People Say Law Enforcement Officials are Main Perpetrators of Harassment, Violence, and Abuse Against Them*. Retrieved on June 3, 2023 from https://www.humandignitytrust.org/news/transgender-people-say-law-enforcement-officials-are-main-perpetrators-of-harassment-violence-and-abuse-against-them.

Human Rights Watch (2004). *Hated to Death: Homophobia, Violence and Jamaica's HIV/AIDS Epidemic*. Retrieved on July 14, 2022, from https://www.hrw.org/reports/2004/jamaica1104/jamaica1104.pdf.

Human Rights Watch (2014). *Not Safe at Home: Violence and Discrimination against LGBT people in Jamaica*. Retrieved on July 14, 2022, from https://www.hrw.org/report/2014/10/21/not-safe-home/violence-and-discrimination-against-lgbt-people-jamaica.

Human Rights Watch (2018). *"I Have to Leave to be Me": Discriminatory Laws Against LGBTQ People in the Eastern Caribbean*. Retrieved on July 14, 2022, from https://www.hrw.org/report/2018/03/21/i-have-leave-be-me/discriminatory-laws-against-lgbt-people-eastern-caribbean#_ftn51.

IACHR (2012). *Report on the Situation of Human Rights in Jamaica*. Retrieved on July 28, 2022, from https://www.oas.org/en/iachr/docs/pdf/Jamaica2012eng.pdf.

IACHR (2015). *Violence against LGBTI Persons*. Organization of American States. OAS/Ser.L/V/II.rev.1 Doc. 36. Retrieved on October 20, 2022, from https://www.oas.org/en/iachr/reports/pdfs/ViolenceLGBTIPersons.pdf.

InSight Crime (2020). *InSight Crime's 2020 Homicide Roundup*. Retrieved on August 17, 2022, from https://insightcrime.org/news/analysis/2020-homicide-round-up.

Jamaica Constabulary Force (2021). *Crime Statistics*. Retrieved on August 17, 2022, from https://jcf.gov.jm/stats.

Jamaica Gleaner (2014). *Majority of Jamaicans Resolute on Keeping Buggery Law Intact*. Retrieved on August 17, 2022, from https://jamaica-gleaner.com/article/lead-stories/20141006/majority-jamaicans-resolute-keeping-buggery-law-intact.

Jamaica Gleaner (2020). *Jamaica Tops Homicides in Latin America and the Caribbean*. Retrieved on August 17, 2022, from https://jamaica-gleaner.com/article/lead-stories/20210131/jamaica-tops-homicides-latin-america-and-caribbean.

Jamaica Gleaner (2021). *Violence against Women an Urgent National Problem*. Retrieved on October 22, 2022, from https://jamaica-gleaner.com/article/news/20210127/violence-against-women-urgent-national-problem.

Jamaica Sexual Offences Act (2009). Retrieved on November 10, 2022, from https://japarliament.gov.jm/attachments/341_The%20Sexual%20Offences%20Act,%202009.pdf.

J-FLAG (2013). *Human Rights Violations against Lesbian, Gay, Bisexual, and Transgender (LGBT) People in Jamaica: A Shadow Report*. Retrieved on July 12, 2022, from https://tbinternet.ohchr.org/Treaties/CCPR/Shared%20Documents/JAM/INT_CCPR_ICO_JAM_22756_E.pdf.

J-FLAG (2021). *J-FLAG's Report on Human Rights Violations, January 2011–March 2017*. Kingston, Jamaica: J-FLAG and Equality Jamaica.

The Invisibility of LGBTQ Women   121

Karkazis, K. (2008). *Fixing Sex: Intersex, Medical Authority, and Lived Experience.* Durnham, NC: Duke University Press.

Kelly, B. C., Izienicki, H., Bimbi, D. S., & Parsons, J. T. (2011). The intersection of mutual partner violence and substance use among urban gays, lesbians, and bisexuals. *Deviant Behavior* 32(5), 379–404. Retrieved on June 3, 2023, from https://doi.org/10.1080/01639621003800158.

Kelly, M. D. A. (2020). Examining race in Jamaica: How racial category and skin color structure social inequality. *Race and Race Problems* 12, 300–312. Retrieved on June 3, 2023, from https://doi.org/10.1007/s12552-020-09287-z.

Kelly, M. D. A., & Bailey, S. R. (2018). Racial inequality and the recognition of racial discrimination in Jamaica. *Social Identities* 24, 688–706.

Kimmel, M. S. (2002). Gender symmetry in domestic violence: A substantive and methodological research review. *Violence Against Women* 8(11), 1332–1363.

Le Franc, E., Samms-Vaughan, M., Hambleton, I., Fox, K., & Brown, D. (2008). Interpersonal violence in three Caribbean countries: Barbados, Jamaica, and Trinidad and Tobago. *Revista Panamericana de Salud Pública* 24(6), 409–421.

Leslie, C. R. (2000). Creating criminals: The injuries inflicted by unenforced sodomy laws. *Harvard Civil Rights-Civil Liberties Law Review* 35(1), 103–182.

Lewis, L. (2003). Caribbean masculinity: Unpacking the narrative. In L. Lewis, (Ed.), *The Culture of Gender and Sexuality in the Caribbean* (pp. 94–125). Gainesville: University of Florida Press.

Messinger, A. M. (2011). Invisible victims: Same-sex IPV in the national violence against women survey. *Journal of Interpersonal Violence* 26(11), 2228–2243. Retrieved on June 3, 2023, from https://doi.org/10.1177/0886260510383023.

Messinger, A. M., & Koon-Magnin, S. (2019). Sexual violence in LGBTQ communities. In: W. O'Donohue & P. Schewe (Eds.), *Handbook of Sexual Assault and Sexual Assault Prevention* (661–674). Cham: Springer.

Ministry of Attorney General and Legal Affairs, Trinidad and Tobago (1974). *Immigration Act.* Retrieved on June 13, 2023, from https://www.ilo.org/dyn/na tlex/docs/ELECTRONIC/62136/128626/F-418782335/TTO62136.pdf.

Ministry of Attorney General and Legal Affairs, Trinidad and Tobago (1986). *Sexual Offence Act.* Retrieved on June 3, 2023, from https://rgd.legalaffairs.gov. tt/laws2/alphabetical_list/lawspdfs/11.28.pdf.

Ministry of Attorney General and Legal Affairs, Trinidad and Tobago (1999). *Domestic Violence Act.* Retrieved on June 3, 2023, from https://www.ilo.org/dyn/ natlex/docs/ELECTRONIC/105242/128670/F-141848199/TTO105242.pdf.

Ministry of Justice, Jamaica(1995). *Domestic Violence Act.* Retrieved onJune 13, 2023, fromhttps://laws.moj.gov.jm/library/statute/the-domestic-violence-act.

Morrison, A. M. (2003). Queering domestic violence to straighten out criminal law: What might happen when queer theory and practice meet criminal law's conventional responses to domestic violence. *Southern California Review & Women's Studies* 81(162), 8–160.

Murray C. E., Mobley A. K., Buford A. P., Seaman-DeJohn M. M. (2007). Same-sex intimate partner violence: Dynamics, social context, and counseling implications. *Journal of LGBT Issues in Counseling* 1(4), 7–30. Retrieved on June 3, 2023, from https://doi.org/10.1300/J462v01n04_03.

Offences against the Person Act (Jamaica) (1864). Retrieved on June 2, 2023, from https://www.ilo.org/dyn/natlex/docs/ELECTRONIC/73502/104126/F639019451/ JAM73502%202010.pdf.

122 *The Invisibility of LGBTQ Women*

Pemberton, C., & Joseph, J. (2018). *National Women's Health Survey for Trinidad and Tobago*. Washington DC: Inter-American Development Bank. Retrieved on July 3, 2023, from https://publications.iadb.org/publications/english/document/National-Women-Health-Survey-for-Trinidad-and-Tobago-Final-Report.pdf.

Rainbow Times (2017). *TRT Exclusive: Queer and Caribbean: LGBTQ+ Culture & The Island Identity*. Retrieved on June 12, 2023, from http://www.therainbowtimesmass.com/queer-and-caribbean-lgbtq-culture-the-island-identity.

Sabri, B., & Granger, D. A. (2018). Gender-based violence and trauma in marginalized populations of women: Role of biological embedding and toxic stress. *Health Care for Women International* 39(9), 1038–1055. Retrieved on July 3, 2023, from https://doi.org/10.1080/07399332.2018.1491046.

Saint Vincent and the Grenadines Criminal Code (1988). Retrieved on November 10, 2022, from https://www.oas.org/en/sla/dlc/mesicic/docs/mesicic5_svg_annex8.pdf.

Serra, N. E. (2013). Queering international human rights: LGBT access to domestic violence remedies. *American University Journal of Gender Social Policy and Law* 21(3),583–607.

Shepherd, V. (2017). *The History of Gender-Based Violence in the Caribbean*. Retrieved on October 22, 2022, from http://digjamaica.com/m/blog/the-history-of-gender-based-violence-in-the-caribbean/2.

Spencer, N., Urquhart, M.A., & Whitely, P. (2020). Class discrimination? Evidence from Jamaica: A racially homogeneous labor market. *Review of Radical Political Economics* 52(1), 77–95. doi:10.1177/0486613419832674.

Statista (2020). *Legal Status of Same-Sex/Same-Gender Sexual Acts in Latin America and the Caribbean as of December 2020, by Country and Year of Regulation*. Retrieved on June 20, 2022, from https://www.statista.com/statistics/1021330/being-lgbti-legal-latin-america-caribbean.

Statista (2022). *Homicide Rates in Selected Latin American and Caribbean Countries in 2021*. Retrieved on June 14, 2022, from https://www.statista.com/statistics/947781/homicide-rates-latin-america-caribbean-country/#statisticContainer.

Statistics Canada (2020). *Sexual Minority People almost Three Times as Likely to Experience Violent Victimization than Heterosexual People*. Retrieved on June 3, 2023 from https://www150.statcan.gc.ca/n1/en/daily-quotidien/200909/dq200909a-eng.pdf?st=PgGDeCv_.

Thompson, L. (2022). St. Lucia "breaks the bias" with new LGBTQ-inclusive Domestic Violence Act. *Outright Action International*. Retrieved on June 29, 2022, from https://outrightinternational.org/StLucia-LGBTIQ-InclusiveAct.

UN Human Rights Council (2001). *Report of the Special Rapporteur on Torture and Other Cruel, Inhuman or Degrading Treatment or Punishment*, A/56/156. New York: United Nations.

UN Women (2021). *Measuring the Shadow Pandemic: Violence against Women during COVID-19*. Retrieved on June 21, 2022, from https://data.unwomen.org/sites/default/files/documents/Publications/Measuring-shadow-pandemic.pdf.

UN Women (2022). *Facts and Figures: Ending Violence against Women*. Retrieved on June 12, 2022, from https://www.unwomen.org/en/what-we-do/ending-violence-against-women/facts-and-figures#notes.

UN Women (n.d. a). *Focusing on Prevention: Ending Violence against Women*. Retrieved on October 19, 2022, from https://www.unwomen.org/en/what-we-do/ending-violence-against-women/prevention#:~:text=Violence%20against%20women%20and%20girls,services%20for%20survivors%20of%20violence.

The Invisibility of LGBTQ Women   123

UN Women (n.d. b). *GBV Developments in the Law*. Retrieved on June 12, 2022, from https://caribbean.unwomen.org/en/caribbean-gender-portal/caribbean-gbv-law-portal/gbv-developments-in-the-law.

UNAIDS (2022). *Justice is Never Given, It is Won: How Eastern Caribbean Activists Developed the Successful Strategy to Defeat the Laws which Criminalised LGBT people*. Retrieved on June 29, 2022, from https://www.unaids.org/en/keywords/human-rights.

UNDP (2012). *Caribbean Human Development Report 2012: Human Development and the Shift to Better Citizen Security*. Retrieved on June 27, 2022, from https://caricom.org/documents/13919-c_bean_hdr_jan25_2012_3mb.pdf.

UNDP & UN Women (2017). *From Commitment to Action: Policies to End Violence against Women in Latin America and the Caribbean*. Panama City: UNDP Regional Center for Latin America and the Caribbean.

UNFPA (2018). *Young Persons with Disabilities: Global Study on Ending Gender-Based Violence and Realizing Sexual Reproductive Health and Rights*. Retrieved on June 20, 2022, from https://www.unfpa.org/sites/default/files/pub-pdf/Final_Global_Study_English_3_Oct.pdf.

UNHCHR (2011). *Discriminatory Laws and Practices and Acts of Violence against Individuals Based on Their Sexual Orientation and Gender Identity*. HRC/19/41. Geneva: United Nations Human Rights Council. Retrieved on October 20, 2022, from https://www.ohchr.org/sites/default/files/Documents/Issues/Discrimination/A.HRC.19.41_English.pdf.

UNHCHR (2015). *Discrimination and Violence against Individuals Based on Their Sexual Orientation and Gender Identity*. A/HRC/29/23. Geneva: United Nations Human Rights Council.

UNHCHR (2022). *The Struggle of Trans and Gender-Diverse Persons: Independent Expert on Sexual Orientation and Gender Identity*. Retrieved on June 3, 2023 from https://www.ohchr.org/en/special-procedures/ie-sexual-orientation-and-gender-identity/struggle-trans-and-gender-diverse-persons.

United Nations (1993). *Declaration on the Elimination of Violence Against Women*. Retrieved on June 12, 2022, from https://www.ohchr.org/sites/default/files/eliminationvaw.pdf.

United Nations (2012). *Handbook for National Action Plans on Violence Against Women*. Retrieved on June 20, 2022, from https://www.unwomen.org/sites/default/files/Headquarters/Attachments/Sections/Library/Publications/2012/7/HandbookNationalActionPlansOnVAW-en%20pdf.pdf.

UNODC (2019). *Global Study on Homicide: Gender-Related Killing of Women and Girls*. Retrieved on October 20, 2022, from https://www.unodc.org/documents/data-and-analysis/gsh/Booklet_5.pdf.

Walters, M. L., Chen J., & Breiding, M. J. (2013). *The National Intimate Partner and Sexual Violence Survey (NISVS), 2010 Findings on Victimization by Sexual Orientation*. Atlanta, GA: National Center for Injury Prevention and Control, Centers for Disease Control and Prevention. Retrieved on June 21, 2022, from https://www.cdc.gov/violenceprevention/pdf/nisvs_sofindings.pdf.

Watson Williams, C. (2016). *Women's Health Survey: 2016: Jamaica: Final Report*. Retrieved on June 13, 2023, from https://caribbean.unwomen.org/sites/default/files/Field%20Office%20Caribbean/Attachments/Publications/2018/AF%2020180618%20Jamaica%20Health%20Report%20for%20web.pdf.

124 *The Invisibility of LGBTQ Women*

WHO (2021a). *Devastatingly Pervasive: 1 in 3 Women Globally Experience Violence.* Retrieved on June 12, 2022, from https://www.who.int/news/item/09-03-2021-deva statingly-pervasive-1-in-3-women-globally-experience-violence.

WHO (2021b). *Violence Against Women Prevalence Estimates, 2018.* Retrieved on June 15, 2022, from https://apps.who.int/iris/bitstream/handle/10665/341338/9789240026681-eng.pdf.

WHO (2022). *Violence against Women.* Retrieved on October 20, 2022, from https://www.who.int/health-topics/violence-against-women#tab=tab_1.

Williams Institute (2020). *LGBT People Nearly Four Times More Likely than Non-LGBT People to be Victims of Violent Crime.* Retrieved on October 20, 2022, from https://williamsinstitute.law.ucla.edu/press/ncvs-lgbt-violence-press-release.

World Bank (2023). *What is Domestic Abuse?* Retrieved on June 12, 2023, from https://www.worldbank.org/en/work-with-us/hsd/home/hsd_dapp_what_is_abuse.

World Population Review (2022). *Rape Statistics by Country 2022.* Retrieved on October 22, 2022, from https://worldpopulationreview.com/country-rankings/rape-sta tistics-by-country.

5 Health Inequalities and the Gendered Impact of COVID-19 on Women

Introduction

COVID-19 has significantly affected women in the Caribbean and exposed pre-existing inequalities in health and across social and economic systems. The pandemic has shown how a health crisis can morph into a gender crisis in the absence of sufficient protection for women. From mental health to socioeconomic challenges and the impacts on healthcare workers (HCWs), women have been disproportionately affected by COVID-19 (Brysk, 2022; Burki, 2020). Although the mortality rate has been higher for men in several Caribbean countries, women have been severely and disproportionately affected by the social and economic consequences of the pandemic (Kabeer, Razavi & Rodgers, 2021). Response measures such as stay-at-home orders, curfews and the closure of schools affected women in adverse ways. The gendered impact of the pandemic has proved especially challenging in the Caribbean because of high levels of gender-based violence, social inequality, poor healthcare systems, labour market challenges, women's low economic status relative to men's and a patriarchal culture that places the burden of childcare on women. COVID-19 intensified these challenges and created new ones.

In this chapter, we combine secondary and primary data to examine the ways in which Caribbean women have been affected by the COVID-19 pandemic. We draw on evidence from four Caribbean countries: Jamaica, Guyana, Trinidad and Tobago and Barbados. Using snowball sampling, we conducted an online survey between January and June 2022. It was important to design open-ended questions to allow women to describe their pandemic experiences. We used qualitative content analysis methods to analyse these questions. Most of the respondents surveyed for the study were between the ages of 36 and 41. Approximately 78 per cent of respondents were employed, and out of that number, 15.7 per cent were self-employed. Most were employed in the public sector (56.2 %), while another 34.2 per cent were employed in the private sector.

Our findings show that the pandemic significantly impacted women's physical and mental health, financial circumstances, income and childcare

DOI: 10.4324/9781003130987-5

responsibilities. The COVID-19 measures imposed by the state which posed the most significant challenge for Caribbean women were lockdowns, curfews and vaccine requirements. Poor, uneducated women who work in the informal sector were significantly affected. In most countries, the government response was inadequate to allow women to cope effectively. The public sector in most Caribbean countries retained their employees at full salary and allowed them to work from home, while informal workers had no such option. The women in our study also reported that their mental health had worsened during the pandemic due to financial worries, loneliness from social isolation and increased childcare responsibilities.

These findings and the pandemic experiences of women shed light on gendered social relations in the Caribbean, women's unequal citizenship and the intersectional forces and disadvantages women face. The time spent on unpaid domestic work and caregiving increased substantially (ECLAC, 2021), and women who had no choice but to shelter in place with abusive partners were increasingly at risk of experiencing gender-based violence. Caused mainly by the economic downturn and labour market disruptions in the Caribbean, women's employment, especially in the service sector where they are overrepresented, was severely impacted, especially in the first year of the pandemic (Campbell & Connell, 2021; ECLAC, 2021). Latin America and the Caribbean also experienced the highest levels of service disruption in healthcare during the first year of the pandemic. This reduced access to reproductive and sexual health services for women and services for mental health, NCDs and HIV (WHO, 2021a).

These findings are consistent with global studies showing that women suffered disproportionately from the pandemic in many ways. A higher number of women suffered from mental health issues (WHO, 2022). More women reported a loss of employment at the beginning of the pandemic (Bluedorn et al., 2021; Desai, Deshmukh & Pramanik, 2021; ILO, 2020a). More girls reported dropping out of school, and women were likely to report gender-based violence (Dlamini, 2021; Flor et al., 2022; Mittal & Singh, 2020). With at least three billion people sheltering in place (Hall & Tucker, 2020), this led to increases in the burden of childcare and unpaid employment for women and loss of income which accompanied the economic fall-out.

In the first section of this chapter, we examine health inequalities, looking closely at gendered differences in health outcomes and the role played by the social determinants of health in these outcomes. This is important because it helps us analyse the impact of COVID-19 on women side by side with these pre-existing equalities rather than seeing COVID-19 in isolation. The second section focuses on the socioeconomic impacts of COVID-19 on women. Again, we take a broad look at the literature. We then present and analyse our findings and provide a conclusion.

Health Inequalities and Social Determinants of Health

COVID-19 is one representation of how health inequality manifests during a pandemic and how it shapes women's experiences and their ability to cope. However, these inequalities predate the pandemic and have always been present, especially for women of low socioeconomic status with limited access to economic resources. According to the 2008 report of the WHO's Commission on the Social Determinants of Health, "health inequalities are differences in health status or in the distribution of health resources between different population groups, arising from the social conditions in which people are born, grow, live, work and age" (WHO, 2008). By this definition, health inequities are not inescapable. They can be addressed through a redistribution of health resources and policy interventions that target the social determinants of health. Similarly, health inequalities are "systematic, avoidable and unfair differences in health outcomes that can be observed between populations, between social groups within the same population or as a gradient across a population ranked by social position" (McCartney et al., 2019, p. 1). By contrast, health equity "means that everyone has a fair and just opportunity to be as healthy as possible" (Braveman et al., 2017, p. 35).

The social determinants of health are significant, accounting for 30 to 55 per cent of health outcomes globally (WHO, 2021a). They include housing and basic amenities, income and social protection, education, working conditions, affordable health access, social inclusion and food security. For many poor women in the Caribbean and globally, these social determinants have significantly impacted their access to healthcare.

Studies internationally have revealed the role these social determinants play in producing a "gender paradox," often captured in the maxim "women get sicker but men die younger." This is revealed in data which have shown gender inequalities across various health outcomes and disease burdens (WHO, 2021a). These studies have all confirmed that, although women have a greater life expectancy, they suffer from higher morbidity during those years. That is so, even though more women, usually from urban spaces, than men seek healthcare. There is a higher prevalence of non-fatal, debilitating diseases such as arthritis, asthma, depression, mental health challenges/ depression and morbidity, especially in middle- and old-aged women (Crimmins, Kim & Solé-Auró, 2011). In many countries, women are more likely to be obese than men. An 18-country Pan American Health Organization (PAHO) study found that over 70 per cent of women in Nicaragua and Belize are overweight or obese. On the contrary, cardiovascular diseases such as stroke are higher among men (Colafella & Denton, 2018).

Health Inequalities in the Caribbean

Women in the Caribbean are more likely than men to be affected by three of the most prevalent non-communicable diseases: diabetes, hypertension

128   *Health Inequalities and COVID-19*

and obesity. Data from the 2016/17 Jamaica Health and Lifestyle survey showed that one in two Jamaicans or 54 per cent were overweight or obese. It also revealed that women were more affected, with two-thirds of Jamaican women 15 years or older being overweight or obese (Ministry of Health and Wellness, Jamaica, 2018). In Barbados, over 35 per cent of girls aged between 13 and 15 years are also overweight or obese (WHO, 2019).

Diabetes, estimated to affect 10 to 15 per cent of the adult population in the Caribbean, affects a significant number of women. There is a statistically significant association between gender and diabetes in the Caribbean region, with women at more than one and a half times greater risk than men (Sobers-Grannum et al., 2015). A study of diabetes in Barbados, found that women had a higher age-specific prevalence of diabetes than men in all age groups, with self-reported cases showing an increase from 9.1 per cent at 40 to 49 years of age to 24 per cent at 70 to 79 years of age (Hennis et al., 2002). This is in contrast to what obtains in high-income countries.

The ethnicity and socioeconomic status of women matter in these disparities. In Trinidad and Tobago, diabetes is more prevalent among women from lower socioeconomic backgrounds and associated with older age and ethnicity (Gulliford & Mahabir, 1998). There is also a negative association of systolic blood pressure with increasing income or education in women in Trinidad and Tobago, for example (Guilliford, Mahabir & Rocke, 2004). Moreover, in Barbados, women's lower socioeconomic status is positively correlated with higher levels of obesity. A study in Barbados found that, for women, a higher educational level was related to higher fruit and vegetable intake, more physical activity, less diabetes and less hypercholesterolaemia (Howitt et al., 2015).

Among Caribbean populations, diabetes among black Afro-Caribbeans was higher than among Caucasians but lower compared to South Asian origin groups (Bennett et al., 2015). In Barbados, the prevalence of known diabetes was also higher among blacks, at 17.5 per cent, than among people of mixed race (black/white), at 12.5 per cent. In Jamaica, the prevalence of diabetes mellitus was significantly higher among women than men, diabetes control was more common in higher-income women, and persons without health insurance were less likely to control their diabetes. (Cunningham-Myrie et al., 2013)

In the Caribbean, certain mental health disorders are more prevalent among women. These include depression and anxiety which are twice as prevalent among women (Gaviria & Rondon, 2010). In Jamaica, for example, the 2016/17 Jamaica Health and Lifestyle Survey found that 14.3 per cent of persons have depression. It found that women (18.5%) were more likely to have depression, and the prevalence was highest among women in urban areas (19.2%) (Ministry of Health and Wellness, Jamaica, 2018). In Guyana, women make up 60 per cent of all those treated in mental-health outpatient facilities and approximately 50 per cent of users of mental hospitals (WHO-AIMS, 2008). Part of the reason for the gender difference in the diagnosis of anxiety and depression is the fact that women are more likely to internalise emotions (withdrawal) while men externalise stress and emotions (aggression and compliance) tending more towards substance abuse or antisocial disorders (Eaton et al., 2011). In a context where there is a persistent stigma associated with mental illness, this is even more challenging for women. For example, black Caribbean women in the UK "believe that it is inappropriate to discuss personal matters outside the home and that disclosure of mental health problems is considered a sign of moral weakness" (Nadeem et al., 2007, p. 1551).

Women living with HIV also experience higher rates of mental health conditions, such as depression, anxiety and post-traumatic disorder, than their HIV-unaffected male counterparts (Waldron et al., 2021). Caribbean women's experience with intimate partner violence also contributes (see Chapter 2) to the disproportionate ways women are affected by mental health (Lang & Stover, 2008). Women from a low socioeconomic status who experienced abuse were also more likely to experience mental disorders, as shown by a study among women who attended walk-in clinics in Trinidad and Tobago (Maharaj et al., 2010). It was found that abuse was common among 40 per cent of these women.

The Gendered Impact of COVID-19

The death rate from COVID-19 has generally been reported to be higher for men (Hawkes et al., 2022; Cook et al., 2020), while COVID-19 cases are either higher among women or equal across gender in many countries. These reports vary across time and space. Male deaths have been higher in at least 48 countries with sex-disaggregated data (Burki, 2020). This finding has been associated with men's higher appetite for risk-taking. Other studies have found that the balance of excess deaths affected more men early in the pandemic but changed to being higher among females later on (Kontis et al., 2020).

Aleksanyan found that gender played a role in explaining country-level disparities between recorded cases and death rates among men and women.

> In countries where women's rights are less protected and women do not have access to personal finance and education, the associated gap between men's and women's recorded case and death rates from COVID-19 are larger than expected. When women have less power in decision-making and less financial independence in such extreme health-related emergencies, they cannot afford tests and hospital stays and need to rely on family members' benevolence for help … Left with lower or no income, women will inevitably have lower access to healthcare and their cases of infection and deaths may largely go unreported.
>
> (Aleksanyan, 2022, p. 3)

130 *Health Inequalities and COVID-19*

In the Caribbean, confirmed cases of COVID-19 have been generally higher among women, while the mortality rate is higher among men. Cases among females in Jamaica were higher, as shown by data from 2020 to 2021. As of August 2021, confirmed cases for women were 38,124 compared to 29,275 for men in Jamaica, for example (Ministry of Health and Wellness, Jamaica, 2021). In Barbados, of the total number of confirmed cases, 42,880 were women, and 36,039 were men up to May 2022.

The gendered impact of COVID-19 on health outcomes was also evident among healthcare workers, 70 per cent of whom are women, mainly nurses and midwives, and who face inequities in the workforce (Boniol et al., 2019). Female HCWs experienced higher rates of COVID-19 infections than men and higher mental health challenges (Miyamoto, 2020). The pandemic widened the gender disparities in mental health, more generally (WHO, 2021a). Women suffered from higher rates of depression, anxiety and post-traumatic stress (Pappa et al., 2020), which resulted partly from measures implemented to contain the spread of the virus and the social and economic consequences. Research found that since the beginning of the pandemic, a quarter of parents reported worsening mental health for themselves and 14 per cent reported worsening of their children's behavioural health (Patrick et al., 2020). This was associated with the lack of child care due to school closures, reduced access to healthcare due to closures of health facilities and a decline in food security. Again not all women were affected in the same way. Women who were pregnant, postpartum, miscarrying or experiencing intimate partner violence were at high risk of developing mental health problems during the pandemic (Piquero et al., 2020).

In the Caribbean, most healthcare workers are women, and they, too, were adversely affected by the pandemic. They suffered from stigma, discrimination, fear of infection, and mental health challenges (Xavier, 2021). Some were even refused passage on public transport because of the early stigma associated with and fear of the disease. One nurse in St Lucia explained how some healthcare workers were affected:

> They should have allowed the nurses counselling session ... because we went through a lot of distress, disrespect. A lot. So the trauma that was there, if you weren't strong you would have broken down from all the disrespect, the vulgarity, all ... Everything that came with it.
>
> (Xavier, 2021)

In Barbados, more adverse mental health outcomes and severity of COVID-19 infection were reported among younger and unemployed Barbadian women (King & Devonish, 2022). In another study conducted in Trinidad and Tobago, there was a high prevalence of depression, anxiety and stress among HCWs (mainly women) during the pandemic (Nayak et al., 2021). The gender and marital status of HCWs were considered to be

Health Inequalities and COVID-19 131

correlated with anxiety. Our findings also confirmed that women's mental health worsened due to financial worries, loneliness from social isolation and increased childcare responsibilities.

Social and Economic Impacts

COVID-19 disrupted economic activity and labour markets and led to an economic downturn globally (Lee, Schmidt-Klau & Verick, 2020). The pandemic intensified numerous socioeconomic crises in small-island developing states, such as unemployment, debt, exhaustion of remittances and savings by family members, domestic violence, food insecurity, inadequate infrastructure (including housing) and access to services (such as clean water), political tensions, digital and rural–urban divides (Campbell & Connell, 2021).

This resulted in major socioeconomic troubles for women not just in the Caribbean but in other small-island developing states and even in developed countries. While women's employment and income declined, many women's hours spent on unpaid care in the household increased (Seedat & Rondon, 2020; UN Women, 2021). Poor women and racial minorities, especially black women and those with less education and low-income jobs, tended to suffer more. Women with children and single mothers were also likely to suffer disproportionately.

Because women are overrepresented in the service sector and industries mainly affected by COVID-19, they tend to face major economic disadvantages. According to UN Women (2021), women's job loss exceeded men's by 22.5, 6.0 and 10.2 percentage points in the arts, tourism, and trade industries, respectively. These were the sectors that experienced the most significant declines. These impacts were also evident in the Caribbean, where many women are employed in the informal sector and the sectors most affected by COVID. In most Caribbean countries, the tourism sector accounts for over 30 per cent of the GDP and employs between 40 and 50 per cent of women (ILO, 2020b). Not only are women overrepresented in the tourism sector in the Caribbean, but their employment tends to have a high measure of informality. A staggering 40 per cent are hired on a part-time basis and fixed-term contracts and are mainly employed in service and sales (59%) and medium-skill occupation categories (75%). The Statistical Institutes of Jamaica, in their 2020 report entitled *The Jamaican Labour Market: Impact of COVID-19* revealed the disproportionate employment impacts on women:

> Supporting the findings from ILO and UNWOMEN that youth, women and persons residing in rural areas as some of the most vulnerable, the employment numbers reveal that these groups were disproportionately impacted by the virus. For females, the largest declines in employment were in the industries that were classified by the ILO as medium to

high-risk industries as it relates to job security. There was an increase in youth unemployment of which the largest proportion resided in rural areas. Similarly, levels of engagement in educational activities since the closure of schools showed that children in rural areas were less likely to participate in online classes.

(STATIN, 2020, p. 7)

Because of the nature of their jobs, domestic workers belong to another category of workers severely affected by COVID-19. A very high number of all domestic workers in Jamaica are women (STATIN, 2020). A significant number faced disruptions in employment owing to lockdown measures, stay-at-home orders and fear of the virus. Many were told that they could not return to work and received no compensation. Unvaccinated household workers were especially affected.

The decline in paid employment during the pandemic went hand in hand with an increase in unpaid employment and childcare (Seck et al., 2021). The International Labour Organization defines unpaid labour as "non-remunerated work carried out to sustain the well-being and main-tenance of other individuals in a household or the community, and it includes both direct and indirect care (i.e. routine housework)" (ILO, 2018, p. 3). Women have always carried the burden of unpaid labour. The ILO estimated that unpaid work accounted for "16.4 billion hours per day, with women contributing more than three-fourths of the total", which is "equivalent to 2.0 billion people working on a full-time basis without pay" (2018, p. 43). The time spent on unpaid domestic work and caregiving increased substantially for Caribbean women during COVID-19. During the pandemic, Caribbean women were already spending between 22 and 42 hours per week on unpaid domestic work and caregiving (ECLAC, 2021). A regional IDB online socioeconomic survey which showed that twice as many women compared to men reported increases in domestic chores and home-schooling children (ECLAC, 2021).

Labour market inequality is also substantial in the Caribbean, and COVID-19 led to further inequalities. In Jamaica, there is a 14 percentage point gap in labour market participation and a 5 percentage point gap in the unemployment rate. In July 2021, the overall labour participation rate was 13.6 percentage points higher for men than women (70.3% of men aged 15 or over are in the labour market compared to 56.7% of women). The unemployment rate is also vastly different, with 11.1 per cent of women out-of-work, compared to 6.3 per cent of men (STATIN, 2020).

Gender-Based Violence

As shown in Chapter 2, gender-based violence is one of the most sig-nificant threats to gender equality and women's rights in the Caribbean. This has been exacerbated by the pandemic and associated lockdown

Health Inequalities and COVID-19 133

measures and stay-at-home orders that were implemented to control the spread of the virus (Aziz & Moussa, 2021; Ravindran & Shah, 2020). Intimate partner violence, both sexual and physical, affected some 243 million women in the first year of the pandemic (Maji, Bansod & Singh, 2022). The UN estimates that there was a 30 per cent increase in GBV globally. In twelve countries tracked by the United Nations, the number of cases of violence against women and girls reported to various institutions increased by 83 per cent from 2019 to 2020, and cases reported to the police grew by 64 per cent. Reports like these were common in many other small-island developing states. Unfortunately, this is expected because of a notable finding within the violence-against-women literature that family members perpetrate most acts of violence against women. During lockdowns, some women, many of whom could be described as vulnerable, had to shelter in place with abusers. During the pandemic, the home became a very dangerous place for victims of domestic violence. Women were required to spend an inordinate amount of time, sometimes 24 hours, with partners. The stress is exacerbated for those who live in small houses and densely populated areas without open spaces (Campbell & Connell, 2021). These findings accord with what obtained during the Ebola crisis in West Africa, where in Guinea, for example, there was a reported 4.5 per cent increase in GBV and twice as many rapes (Chattu & Yaya, 2020).

The picture is no different for the Caribbean, where there was an increased risk of gender-based violence during the pandemic. In the first two quarters of 2020, which included the COVID-19 lockdown period, Barbados saw an increase of about 38 per cent in reported domestic violence incidents. In Jamaica, the number of reported cases of domestic violence increased by 100 per cent between 2007 and 2022 (from 4,000 to 8,000 cases). The Jamaica Information Service (2021) reported more than 700 new cases to the Victim Support Unit in March and April 2020 alone compared to previous months. In Guyana, where one in two women experience GBV, Help and Shelter, an NGO for victims of domestic violence, reported a 300 per cent increase in calls to the institution (Help and Shelter & Government of Canada, 2021). There was also a 140 per cent increase in cases of abuse of women and girls reported to the Trinidad and Tobago Police Service in 2020, compared with the same period the previous year (PAHO, 2021). These increases have had real consequences for women. Women who suffered from GBV during the pandemic were at greater risks of reproductive health disadvantages and, as suggested by studies in the past, higher rates of gynaecological problems, HIV and sexually transmitted infections, miscarriages, abortions, low birth weight and unwanted pregnancy (Campbell et. al., 2013; WIGB, 1999).

134 *Health Inequalities and COVID-19*

Research Findings: Impact of COVID-19 on Women

Childcare Responsibilities/Unpaid Employment

Most women in our study reported an increase in childcare responsibilities during COVID-19. This stems from a patriarchal culture that regards women as homemakers, wives and household managers. This is common in the Caribbean, where women are expected to perform traditional gender roles such as cooking, cleaning, caring for sick parents and providing childcare responsibilities. They are also expected to have full-time jobs. With school closures and women sheltering in place during COVID-19 because of stay-at-home orders, women found themselves, in some cases working without much assistance from their partners or husbands. Those who could afford help still suffered this burden of increased unpaid labour because their nannies and housekeepers were affected by government restrictions. For single women with children, the problem was even worse:

> As a single parent with no support, it has been horrible I have to carry my child everywhere with me and I have to take on all the childcare responsibilities. A man does not have this challenge, to say the least.
> (Respondent 1: 38 years old, employed, private sector, Jamaica)

Even though some men participated in caregiving roles during the pandemic, women still carried the burden of responsibility. Married women also found themselves disproportionately burdened by childcare responsibilities during the pandemic. Respondent 2, a Jamaican woman who is married, bemoaned the fact that men were not affected in the same way and did not treat online schooling and childcare responsibilities as important:

> The kids were at home for longer periods. I work from home so was not always productive with them home. I had full responsibility to help with online schooling. Daddy treated it like it was not that important.
> (Respondent 2: 42 years old, self-employed, private sector, Jamaica)

Respondent 3 from Trinidad and Tobago and Respondent 4 from Jamaica, shared similar sentiments:

> Men don't take much responsibility around the home so most of that will fall on the women especially with children being at home.
> (Respondent 3: 26 years old, self-employed, informal sector, Trinidad and Tobago)

> Ensuring food security and health security tends to be the female role in the family. Women are also the primary caregivers so those with

Health Inequalities and COVID-19 135

smaller children would have to undertake class monitoring, teaching and general child care while still carrying out their own jobs from home.
(Respondent 4: 53-year-old, employed, public sector, Jamaica)

These women were affected in multiple ways as they tried to balance work, online schooling, and day-to-day childcare requirements. Women found themselves taking on numerous roles all at once:

My children are home so I had taking on extra roles as worker, mother, teacher, care-giver and nurse.
(Respondent 5: 41-year-old, employed, public sector, Guyana)

These roles, especially home-schooling, which was new for many women posed difficulties and came with additional financial costs.

Face to face learning has been replaced by remote learning and as such, new arrangements had to be made to ensure that someone would be home with the child while I went to work. Additional arrangements had to be made to purchase gadgets.
(Respondent 6: 27 years old, self-employed, Jamaica)

Unlike women who could work remotely and stand in for their nannies who were also affected by COVID-19, essential workers had no such option. Some found themselves in double jeopardy and were forced to choose between work and childcare responsibilities. Women in the private sector also faced similar challenges.

The inability to engage with childcare facilities really affected me.
(Respondent 7: 39 years old, employed, private sector, Barbados)

Increased childcare responsibilities were a huge problem for me.
(Respondent 8: 43 years old, employed, informal sector Trinidad and Tobago)

In the early stages of COVID, childcare arrangements were affected when the child had to stay home. After that the increase in childcare arrangements and increase in prices for goods and services. All this with no increase in income.
(Respondent 9: 39 years old, employed, public sector, Jamaica)

The increased household burden, whether related to home-schooling, taking care of sick children or other routine tasks, placed on women in the Caribbean threatened their careers and economic status. It led to health and financial challenges and deepened inequalities. Increased unpaid labour and other pandemic measures left women with little time for leisure

136 *Health Inequalities and COVID-19*

and other activities they value. Women found it hard to achieve a work–life balance and were under constant pressure to take on additional care. Women found it difficult to cope under these circumstances, especially young, poor women and those employed in the informal sector or as essential workers.

The findings reflect ingrained sociocultural practices and ideas about a woman's place in society, her role in the household and the prevailing social relations of gender, all of which shaped the social experiences of women during the pandemic. These conditions created a "pandemic patriarchy" in the Caribbean and intensified the rights gap (Brysk, 2020). The pandemic showed that despite efforts towards gaining equal citizenship, Caribbean women are still tethered to sexual reproduction and caregiving roles. The household continues to be where "gender roles are both produced and performed through various means like the sexual division of labour" (Chauhan, 2021, p. 397). Moreover, even in households where both parents had a full-time job, women were still expected to play the role of mothers, teachers, nurses and nannies.

COVID provided an opportunity for a "reset" towards valuing and recognising women's unpaid work in the Caribbean. Despite this and "women's visible presence on the frontlines of the COVID-19 pandemic responses, the trends in COVID-19 have not led to greater recognition of women's roles in social reproduction, reproduction and care labour that sustain societies and economies" (Johnston et al., 2021). Women in the small-island developing states in the Caribbean continue to struggle against the unequal division of labour in the household. The same holds for other small-island developing states such as those in the Asian Pacific (Gunawardana & Elias, 2013).

Economic Impacts on Caribbean Women

COVID-19 significantly affected the economic well-being of women in the Caribbean. This manifested in various ways, from loss of employment to increased prices and invariably a higher cost of living. The government's response was hardly enough to cushion these impacts. Most research participants, irrespective of the Caribbean country they were from, shared some similar experiences. For some participants, the loss of employment affected them most. Respondent 10, a 36-year-old woman from Jamaica, caught the virus and subsequently resigned from her job:

> Contracting COVID-19 significantly impacted my health for months prompting the ultimate decision to resign from employ to prioritize physical and mental health. Financial strain ensued, and I had to personally cater to the children because of adjustments to childcare arrangements under State declarations. This financial strain and childcare adjustments also affected my personal relationships.
>
> (Respondent 10: 36 years old, employed, private sector, Jamaica)

The initial lockdown occurred after I had just left my job, another job was lined up but just before I started the lockdown began and the organization could not afford to take on another staff during this period. I took about 1 year to find employment.

(Respondent 11: 23 years old, employed, public sector, Guyana)

For the last two years, I have had to depend on loans and family. Unable to afford childcare outside of the house.

(Respondent 12: 26 years old, self-employed, private sector, Trinidad and Tobago)

Respondent 13 who became unemployed as a result of the pandemic complained about not being able to find another full-time job and expressed the view that she felt that men and women were impacted in different ways:

I was unemployed from January 2021, since then I was able to find a part time job ONLY. However, this is not the case for men. For example, my brother who is younger has worked during the lockdowns and stay-at-home orders. He was laid off Dec 31 and have gotten another job in less than two months. Without COVID-19 men are hired more easily and this remains the case with COVID- 19.

(Respondent 13: 27 years old, employed part-time, Barbados)

Respondent 1 from Jamaica also expressed similar views:

In this economy, men seem to have a greater chance at getting extra income and even raise in pay.

(Respondent 1)

Women have perennially complained about being excluded from opportunities and being unable to benefit from networking opportunities as much as men because of the "old boys' club." Women in the Caribbean seemed to have been differentially impacted by employment and income losses depending on what sector they worked in. Most employees in the public sector retained their jobs, while those who were either self-employed or employed in the private sector seemed to have been more adversely affected by the loss of income or employment. However, even women who retained their jobs soon found that their salaries were insufficient to cover basic needs such as food, electricity bills and childcare in light of increased prices and a general inability to meet basic needs. Respondent 14, a 22-year-old woman from Guyana, explained that she found it impossible to run her household because of the economic impacts of the pandemic. Similar challenges were expressed by Respondent 15:

138 *Health Inequalities and COVID-19*

Since this pandemic started, the prices on basic household items, groceries and other items have gone up. However, there has been no increase on my salary, so this has made it much harder for me to budget effectively with the same salary income. Paying of bills and maintaining a house has grown more difficult.

(Respondent 14: 22 years old, employed, private sector, Guyana)

Financially, the rising cost of living has significantly reduced my disposable income.

(Respondent 15: 31 years old, employed, public sector, Guyana)

Some self-employed women complained about being affected so negatively by the financial strain of COVID-19 that they sometimes considered closing their businesses. This was the case for Respondent 16, a 39-year-old self-employed Trinidadian woman:

COVID-19 affected me financially and mentally. Less money came in for a long time. It got real hard to pay basic bills. I lost money, nearly had to close down my business. That affected me mentally. Business compensation. Not enough to make a real difference.

(Respondent 16: 39 years old, self-employed, informal sector, Trinidad
and Tobago)

With children at home, women from lower socioeconomic backgrounds and single-parent households suffered even more since they had to spend more on food in the absence of school feeding programmes that accompanied the closure of schools and had to contend with increased food prices.

It has been terrible! As a single parent it has been hard to recover and to try to maintain career ambitions … At times it has been very disheartening. Limited finances have increased anxiety (mental health), Childcare is another spin off from finances and employment (lack thereof) goes back to finances.

(Respondent 1)

I have to spend more because the children were at home and they were eating out everything.

(Respondent 5)

My ability to meet basic needs such as food/groceries has been impacted significantly. Food prices have increased and so has utilities given remote learning and working.

(Respondent 6)

Health Inequalities and COVID-19 139

Even women from higher socioeconomic backgrounds found it challenging to afford costs related to childcare and tuition fees, food, rent and the cost of sanitisers and masks. Respondent 4, a 53-year-old Jamaican woman, expressed the view that

> Increased costs associated with sanitizers, masks, healthy diets plus what turned out to be food stocking due to curfews placed a tremendous financial burden. I missed normal obligations to take on the additional expenses. Was very stressful and costly. Child overseas had to give up job and school to return home on expensive repatriation flight. This led to increased household costs, increased reliance on me for school fees since child was no longer self-sufficient, increased burden to cover cost of lease for unoccupied apartment as leases can't be broken.
>
> (Respondent 4)

Not only were women affected by increased financial strain and the burden of unpaid work, but they also found themselves having to work more hours at their jobs. This significantly affected essential or front-line workers, who worked long hours without compensation for extra hours or extended hours without consideration for their other responsibilities and the need for leisure.

> There was suddenly no separation between work and home. My boss expected me to work throughout day, without any acknowledgement that the work day typical starts at 8 a.m. and ends at 5 p.m. The demands on my time were unfair and I was constantly being asked to join long zoom meetings then deliver the same work output having spent so much time in these meetings.
>
> (Respondent 25, 36 years old, employed, public sector, Trinidad and Tobago)

> I am an essential worker, who works in policy and at the beginning of the pandemic when everything was so uncertain, I worked from morning until sometimes 11 p.m. in the night. But I was never compensated for these extra hours, although I had to work these extra hours and my family suffered as a result as did my mental health.
>
> (Respondent 26, 35 years old, employed, public sector, Jamaica)

Women suffered severely from the economic impacts wrought by the pandemic. Women were affected by unemployment, precarious employment and new work practices that increased demands to adjust to new working arrangements and work longer hours. Women were also affected by increased prices, brought about by inflation and supply chain issues in the global marketplace. Some women even struggled to afford their rent

140 *Health Inequalities and COVID-19*

and basic food items. The pandemic revealed the vulnerability of women's socioeconomic status in the Caribbean, confirming that women are more likely to be affected by the social and structural determinants of health (Khalatbari-Soltani et al., 2020). Given high food prices and the impact of inflation, women of lower socioeconomic status in the Caribbean experienced more significant food shortages owing to COVID-19 restrictions.

Consequently, 56 per cent of female-headed households were affected. In order to cope, these households were forced to consume smaller meals or fewer meals per day (CAPRI, 2021). The International Labour Organization, in light of the impacts of COVID-19 on labour participation, asserted that Latin America and the Caribbean must include special measures to promote the return to work of women who were affected by unemployment, significant exits from the workforce and demands for unpaid care. Governments in the Anglo-Caribbean responded, in considerable measure, through one-off cash payments, but this was hardly enough to cushion the effects and was not tailored to the particular needs of women. In Jamaica, the government offered cash payments to households earning below a certain income threshold and businesses. In Guyana, households received a one-off cash grant of $25,000 and food hampers. Most respondents felt that the government's response was inadequate:

> The Government was in a position to do way more, but nevertheless did less. While financial assistance was awarded, this was inadequate. A one-time pay off could not sufficiently off-set the financial impacts COVID-19 has caused. The government took a very loose approach with regards to lockdown measures. Not only did they fail to implement a successful lockdown measure, but the curfews that were implemented had no significant effect. As said policy makers were the main ones breaching them. This encouraged civilians to do likewise which resulted in extreme spikes in the cases. Even when the country experienced rapid surge in cases, curfews were being reduced, and removed.
>
> (Respondent 27: 26 years old, employed, public sector, Guyana)

These impacts will likely continue for women as Caribbean countries try to tackle inflation and deal with the economic fallout from COVID-19. As an early response to the pandemic, most Caribbean countries made requests to the IMF for emergency financial assistance under the Rapid Credit Facility to help address the balance of payments and other challenges posed by COVID-19. Even before the total onslaught of COVID-19, governments made a desperate attempt to help businesses and households adapt to the economic downturn (Campbell & Connell, 2021).

Health Inequalities and COVID-19 141

The economic impacts of the pandemic on women confirm that structural reforms are needed to encourage women's participation in non-traditional areas and away from part-time contracts and the informal sector. A reduction in the pay gap is also needed to protect women and provide equal employment opportunities. Without these changes, men will continue to hold higher-paying jobs and be more likely than women to participate in the labour force.

Mental and Physical Health

Our findings show that the pandemic had the biggest impact on women's physical and mental health. Many women suffer from mental health issues and challenges related to depression, anxiety, isolation and lack of social contact. The pandemic significantly curtailed women's ability to socialise with friends and family members. Additionally, some women reported being fearful of contracting the virus. The fear of death, unemployment for some women and increased stress associated with increased childcare and unpaid labour were all issues that affected women's mental and physical health. At the same time, women found themselves without time for self-care and mental health.

Respondents 17 from Jamaica and 18 from Guyana complained about depression brought on by factors, including limited interaction with loved ones and stories of death in the media.

> I was depressed and crying constantly because of lack of social inter-actions and continuous news of death. Being away from people and not able to hug friends caused a mild continuous state of depression.
> (Respondent 17: 28 years old, employed, Jamaica)

> The first weeks being home was so relaxing but then coming months it began to take a toll on me mentally. I was depressed and rarely left the house to even go outside for some fresh air. I was disassociated from my family.
> (Respondent 18: 27 years old, employed, public sector, Guyana)

Depression was not the only mental health challenge for women resulting from the pandemic. Women also complained about anxiety attacks and being scared about a disease for which very little information was available at the beginning of the pandemic. Participants not only worried about themselves but also about their family getting sick:

> It has affected me mentally, in terms of getting constant anxiety attacks from fear of my family and contracting the virus and not knowing the outcome of how our bodies may react. It was just a scary experience that made me paranoid about everything.
> (Respondent 19: 26 years old, employed, public sector, Guyana)

142 *Health Inequalities and COVID-19*

This fear was shared by other women:

> Mentally, I worry for myself and family constantly as I fear one or all of us becoming ill or even succumbing to this virus. Financially, increased cost of living makes it harder to meet basic needs or to even maintain a savings account for rainy days.
>
> (Respondent 20: 29 years old, employed, public sector, Guyana)

Women's mental health was also affected by worrying about unemployment and the inability to pay their bills. Women also complained about other illnesses brought on by the experience of the pandemic:

> My mental health has been exacerbated from the stress of being unemployed and struggling to meet my financial obligations. As a result, this took a toll on my personal relationships and physical health: i.e., my blood pressure was slightly elevated in Nov 2021.
>
> (Respondent 21: 27 years old, self-employed, Barbados)

For many women, it was a combination of factors that caused negative impacts on their mental health. The idea of a new normal and the uncertainty of their place in this new order also caused women to worry:

> Following one routine every day, being stuck in the house most of the time and the inability to live the way things were before are all having negative impacts on my mental health. Knowing that there is a possibility that this is always going to be the new normal has made me feel like just existing is all I will be doing for the rest of my natural life. I had so many dreams of what I want and will be but most of it seems impossible now. Finances, the prices of items are constantly raising and the salary increases aren't. More expenses every month, it's like there isn't a break in life.
>
> (Respondent 14)

While loneliness and limited social contact proved challenging for women both mentally and emotionally, others longed for personal space and time away from children and childcare responsibilities.

> Although I am an introvert, there was a need for connection with loved ones face to face Everyone in the same environment so not enough time for personal time and to take care of my mental health. I had to stay with kids as no childcare available.
>
> (Respondent 9)

Health Inequalities and COVID-19 143

While I like solitude, too much of it leaves room for depression. Where childcare is concerned new arrangements (as mentioned in 4b) had to be made for remote learning.
(Respondent 22: 27 years old, employed, Jamaica).

One self-employed woman from Barbados described her experience as "mentally draining," "psychologically hard to deal with" and "mentally exhausting." Other women surveyed for the study shared similar experiences:

The experience has been mentally draining. The increasing responsibility to work from home while providing child rearing duties was double the workload and total family income was reduced due to spouse's inability to work.
(Respondent 23: 39 years old, employed, private sector, Barbados)

Extended periods of restricted movement was psychologically hard to deal with. Too much time together with spouse was not healthy. Too much time away from friends equally so.
(Respondent 8)

It was challenging having everyone at home at the same time 24/7 during lockdowns. It made me physically and mentally exhausted.
(Respondent 24: 38 years old, self-employed, informal sector, Jamaica)

Some women also bemoaned that they had to spend excessive time with their husbands or spouses. In contrast, at least two women believed that the pandemic and lockdown measures brought them closer to their spouses. Some also worried that their male spouses were into risk-taking behaviour and were less likely to get tested for COVID-19. This increased their fear of infection and the possibility of getting severely ill from COVID-19. The pandemic significantly challenged women's mental health. Women were constantly worried about the unknown and all the uncertainties surrounding COVID-19, especially at the start of the pandemic. Women also worried about their health, families' well-being, and economic circumstances.

The social isolation that came with lockdown measures and curfews meant that women could not seek out normal ways of reducing stress and anxiety. In the absence of state-led efforts and programmes to help them cope, many women were forced to deal with these mental health challenges independently. This is typical in the Caribbean, where limited human and financial resources have acted as barriers to implementing effective mental health programmes and access to specialist mental health providers (Walker et al., 2022). There are limited mental health facilities in countries such as Guyana, Trinidad and Tobago and Jamaica. This has created a gap between the number of individuals with diagnosable

144 *Health Inequalities and COVID-19*

psychiatric disorders and those receiving treatment (Kohn et al., 2004; Hickling, 2005). Approximately 60 per cent of people diagnosed with mental illness have no access to treatment (Robinson et al., 2022). In Guyana, for example, there are only two inpatient rehabilitation facilities in the country and only one for women. The stigma attached to the disease also makes it difficult for women to report and seek help. Our findings confirm what has been found in other studies, that lockdown measures and increased childcare burdens led to mental health challenges for women and to lack of adequate domestic and emotional support.

Conclusion

COVID-19 and the response measures implemented by states to reduce the spread of the virus such as stay-at-home orders, curfews and the closure of schools affected Caribbean women in adverse ways. The pandemic significantly impacted women's physical and mental health, financial circumstances, income and childcare responsibilities, with differential impacts on poor, uneducated women who work in the informal sector. High levels of gender-based violence, social inequality, poor healthcare systems, labour market challenges, women's low economic status relative to men's and patriarchy shaped these impacts and affected women's ability to cope. But even before the pandemic, health inequality proved challenging for the Caribbean because of the social determinants of health, limited resources, poor healthcare infrastructure and lack of universal access to healthcare. Women in remote areas were also confronted by problems related to poor ambulance services, limited capacity to deal with health emergencies and difficulties with getting referrals to type-A hospitals, usually located in urban spaces that can better manage health emergencies. Women from a low socioeconomic background are likely to suffer more from these inadequacies since most of them do not have health insurance, cannot afford private care and must interact with a public health system that is neither adequately resourced nor sufficiently focused on a patient-centred, gender-sensitive healthcare.

References

Aziz, Z. A., & Moussa, J. (2021). COVID-19 and violence against women: Unprecedented impacts and suggestions for mitigation. In M. Kjaerum, M. F. Davis & A. Lyons (Eds.), *COVID-19 and Human Rights* (pp. 100–115). London: Routledge.

Bennett, N. R., Francis, D. K., Ferguson, T. S., Hennis, A. J., Wilks, R. J., Harris, E. N., & Sullivan, L. W. (2015). Disparities in diabetes mellitus among Caribbean populations: A scoping review. *International Journal for Equity in Health* 14(1), 1–17.

Bluedorn, J. C., Caselli, F., Hansen, N. J., Shibata, I., & Mendes Tavares, M. (2021). *Gender and Employment in the COVID-19 Recession: Evidence on*

Health Inequalities and COVID-19 145

*"She-cessions."*IMF Working Paper. Retrieved on June 13, 2023, from https://www.imf.org/en/Publications/WP/Issues/2021/03/31/Gender-and-Employment-in-the-COVID-19-Recession-Evidence-on-She-cessions-50316.

Boniol, M., McIsaac, M., Xu, L., Wuliji, T., Diallo, K., & Campbell, J. (2019). *Gender Equity in the Health Workforce: Analysis of 104 Countries*, WHO/HIS/HWF/Gender/WP1/2019.1. Geneva: World Health Organization.

Braveman, P., Arkin, E., Orleans, T., Proctor, D., & Plough, A. (2017). *What is Health Equity? And What Difference Does a Definition Make?*Princeton, NJ: Robert Wood Johnson Foundation.

Brysk, A. (2022). Pandemic patriarchy: The impact of a global health crisis on women's rights. *Journal of Human Rights* 21(3), 283–303.

Burki, T. (2020). The indirect impact of COVID-19 on women. *Lancet Infectious Diseases* 20(8), 904–905.

Campbell, J. C., Lucea, M. B., Stockman, J. K., & Draughon, J. E. (2013). Forced sex and HIV risk in violent relationships. *American Journal of Reproductive Immunology* 69, 41–44.

Campbell, Y., & Connell, J. (Eds.) (2021). *COVID in the Islands: A Comparative Perspective on the Caribbean and the Pacific*. Singapore: Springer.

CAPRI (2021). *Insult to Injury: The Impact of COVID-19 on Vulnerable Persons and Businesses*. Kingston, Jamaica: Caribbean Policy Research Institute.

Chattu, V. K., & Yaya, S. (2020). Emerging infectious diseases and outbreaks: Implications for women's reproductive health and rights in resource-poor settings. *Reproductive Health* 17(1), 1–5.

Chauhan, P. (2021). Gendering COVID-19: Impact of the Pandemic on Women's Burden of Unpaid Work in India. *Gender Issues* 38(4): 395–419. Retrieved on November 8, 2022, from https://doi.org/10.1007/s12147-020-09269-w.

Colafella, K. M. M., & Denton, K. M. (2018). Sex-specific differences in hypertension and associated cardiovascular disease. *Nature Reviews Nephrology* 14(3), 185–201.

Cook, G., John, A., Pratt, G., Popat, R., Ramasamy, K., Kaiser, M., Jenner, M., *et al.* (2020). Real-world assessment of the clinical impact of symptomatic infection with severe acute respiratory syndrome coronavirus (COVID-19 disease) in patients with multiple myeloma receiving systemic anti-cancer therapy. *British Journal of Hematology* 190(2), e83–e86.

Crimmins, E. M., Kim, J. K., & Solé-Auró, A. (2011). Gender differences in health: Results from SHARE, ELSA and HRS. *European Journal of Public Health* 21(1), 81–91.

Cunningham-Myrie, C., Younger-Coleman, N., Tulloch-Reid, M., McFarlane, S., Francis, D., Ferguson, T., & Wilks, R. (2013). Diabetes mellitus in Jamaica: Sex differences in burden, risk factors, awareness, treatment and control in a developing country. *Tropical Medicine & International Health* 18(11), 1365–1378.

Desai, S., Deshmukh, N., & Pramanik, S. (2021). Precarity in a time of uncertainty: Gendered employment patterns during the Covid-19 lockdown in India. *Feminist Economics* 27(1–2), 152–172.

Dlamini, N. J. (2021). Gender-based violence, twin pandemic to COVID-19. *Critical Sociology* 47(4–5), 583–590.

Eaton, N. R., Keyes, K. M., Krueger, R. F., Balsis, S., Skodol, A. E., Markon, K. E., & Hasin, D. S. (2012). An invariant dimensional liability model of gender differences in mental disorder prevalence: Evidence from a national sample. *Journal of Abnormal Psychology* 121(1), 282–288.

146 Health Inequalities and COVID-19

ECLAC (2021). *The Burden of Unpaid Care Work on Caribbean Women in the Time of COVID-19*. Retrieved on November 8, 2022, from https://www.cepal. org/en/events/burden-unpaid-care-work-caribbean-women-time-covid-19.

Flor, L. S., Friedman, J., Spencer, C. N., Cagney, J., Arrieta, A., Herbert, M. E., Stein, C., *et al.* (2022). Quantifying the effects of the COVID-19 pandemic on gender equality on health, social, and economic indicators: A comprehensive review of data from March, 2020, to September, 2021. *The Lancet*, 399(10344), 2381–2397. Retrieved on November 8, 2022, from https://doi.org/10.1016/S0140-6736(22)00008-00003.

Gaviria, S. L., & Rondon, M. B. (2010). Some considerations on women's mental health in Latin America and the Caribbean. *International Review of Psychiatry* 22(4), 363–369.

Gulliford, M. C., & Mahabir, D. (1998). Social inequalities in morbidity from diabetes mellitus in public primary care clinics in Trinidad and Tobago. *Social Science & Medicine* 46(1), 137–144.

Gulliford, M. C., Mahabir, D., & Rocke, B. (2004). Socioeconomic inequality in blood pressure and its determinants: Cross-sectional data from Trinidad and Tobago. *Journal of Human Hypertension* 18(1), 61–70.

Gunawardana, S., & Elias, J. (2013). *Global Political Economy of the Household in Asia*. Basingstoke: Palgrave Macmillan.

Hall, B. J., & Tucker, J. D. (2020). Surviving in place: The coronavirus domestic violence syndemic. *Asian Journal of Psychiatry* 53, 102–179.

Hawkes, S., Pantazis, A., Purdie, A., Gautam, A., Kiwuwa-Muyingo, S., Buse, K., Tanaka, S., Borkotoky, K., Sharma, S., & Verma, R. (2022). Sex-disaggregated data matters: Tracking the impact of COVID-19 on the health of women and men. *Economia Politica* 39(1), 55–73.

Help and Shelter & Government of Canada (2021). *Ending Gender-Based Violence Requires Collective Effort*. Retrieved on November 8, 2022, from https://www.international.gc.ca/world-monde/stories-histoires/2021/guyana_collective_effort-guyana_effort_collectif.aspx?lang=eng.

Hennis, A., Wu, S., Nemesure, B., Li, X. & Leske, C. M. (2002). Diabetes in a Caribbean population: Epidemiological profile and implications. *International Journal of Epidemiology* 31, 234–239. Retrieved on November 8, 2022, from https://doi.org/10.1093/ije/31.1.234.

Hickling, F. W. (2005). The epidemiology of schizophrenia and other common mental health disorders in the English-speaking Caribbean. *Revista Panamericana de Salud Pública* 18(4–5), 256–262.

Howitt, C., Hambleton, I. R., Rose, A. M., Hennis, A., Samuels, T. A., George, K. S., & Unwin, N. (2015). Social distribution of diabetes, hypertension and related risk factors in Barbados: A cross-sectional study. *BMJ Open* 5(12), e008869.

ILO (2018). *Care Work and Care Jobs for the Future of Decent Work*. Geneva: International Labour Office.

ILO (2020a). *The COVID-19 Response: Getting Gender Equality Right for a Better Future for Women at Work*. Geneva: International Labour Organization.

ILO (2020b). *Tourism in the English and Dutch Speaking Caribbean: An Overview and the Impact of COVID on Growth and Employment*. Retrieved on November 8, 2022, from https://www.ilo.org/wcmsp5/groups/public/—americas/—ro-lima/—sro-port_of_spain/documents/publication/wcms_753077.pdf.

Jamaica Information Service (2021). *Statement on Gender Based Violence (GBV) and 2021 Spotlight Workplan*. Retrieved on November 8, 2022, from https://jis.gov.jm/statement-on-gender-based-violence-gbv-and-2021-spotlight-work-plan/.

Johnston, M., Davies, S. E., True, J., & Riveros-Morales, Y. (2021). "Patriarchal reset" in the Asia Pacific during COVID-19: The impacts on women's security and rights. *Pacific Review* 36(3), 1–28.

Kabeer, N., Razavi, S., & Rodgers, Y. (2021) Feminist economic perspectives on the COVID-19 pandemic. *Feminist Economics* 27(1–2), 1–29. doi:10.1080/13545701.2021.1876906.

Khalatbari-Soltani, S., Cumming, R. C., Delpierre, C., & Kelly-Irving, M. (2020). Importance of collecting data on socioeconomic determinants from the early stage of the COVID-19 outbreak onwards. *Journal of Epidemiol Community Health* 74(8), 620–623.

King, J., & Devonish, D. (2022). Mental health and COVID-19 perceptions in a predominant black population in the Eastern Caribbean: An exploratory study of residents of Barbados. *Journal of Mental Health Training, Education and Practice* 17(2), 92–109. Retrieved on November 8, 2022, from https://doi.org/10.1108/JMHTEP-07-2021-0085.

Kohn, R., Saxena, S., Levav, I., & Saraceno, B. (2004). The treatment gap in mental health care. *Bulletin of the World Health Organization* 82(11), 858–866.

Kontis, V., Bennett, J. E., Rashid, T., Parks, R. M., Pearson-Stuttard, J., Guillot, M., Asaria, *et al.* (2020). Magnitude, demographics and dynamics of the effect of the first wave of the COVID-19 pandemic on all-cause mortality in 21 industrialized countries. *Nature Medicine* 26(12), 1919–1928.

Lang, J. M., & Stover, C. S. (2008). Symptom patterns among youth exposed to intimate partner violence. *Journal of Family Violence* 23(7), 619–629.

Lee, S., Schmidt-Klau, D., & Verick, S. (2020). The labour market impacts of the COVID-19: A global perspective. *Indian Journal of Labour Economics* 63(1), 11–15.

McCartney, G., Popham, F., McMaster, R., & Cumbers, A. (2019). Defining health and health inequalities. *Public Health* 172, 22–30.

Maharaj, R.G., Alexander, C., Bridglal, C.H., Edwards, A., Mohammed, H., Rampaul, T., Sanchez, S., Tanwing, G., & Thomas, K. (2010). Abuse and mental disorders among women at walk-in clinics in Trinidad: A cross-sectional study. *BMC Family Practice* 11(26) Retrieved on November 8, 2022, from https://doi.org/10.1186/1471-2296-11-26.

Maji, S., Bansod, S., & Singh, T. (2022). Domestic violence during COVID-19 pandemic: The case for Indian women. *Journal of Community & Applied Social Psychology* 32(3), 374–381.

Ministry of Health and Wellness, Jamaica (2018). *Jamaica Health and Lifestyle Survey* III. Retrieved on November 8, 2022, from https://www.moh.gov.jm/wp-content/uploads/2018/09/Jamaica-Health-and-Lifestyle-Survey-III-2016-2017.pdf.

Ministry of Health and Wellness, Jamaica (2021). *Covid-19 Clinical Management Summary for Friday, January 14, 2022*. Retrieved on November 8, 2022, from https://www.moh.gov.jm/page/75/?option=com_docman&task=cat_view&gid=70&limit=5&order=date&dir=DESC&Itemid=74.

Mittal, S., & Singh, T. (2020). Gender-based violence during COVID-19 pandemic: A mini-review. *Frontiers in Global Women's Health* 1(4). Retrieved on November 8, 2022, from https://doi.org/10.3389/fgwh.2020.00004.

148 Health Inequalities and COVID-19

Miyamoto, I. (2020). *COVID-19 Healthcare Workers: 70 Per Cent are Women.* Retrieved on November 8, 2022, from http://www.jstor.org/stable/resrep24863.

Nadeem, E., Lange, J.M., Edge, D., Fongwa, M., Belin, T., & Miranda, J. (2007). Does stigma keep poor young immigrant and US-born Black and Latina women from seeking mental health care? *Psychiatric Services* 58(12), 1547–1554.

Nayak, B. S., Sahu, P. K., Ramsaroop, K., Maharaj, S., Mootoo, W., Khan, S., & Extravour, R. M. (2021). Prevalence and factors associated with depression, anxiety and stress among healthcare workers of Trinidad and Tobago during COVID-19 pandemic: A cross-sectional study. *BMJ Open* 11(4), e044397. Retrieved on November 8, 2022, from https://doi.org/10.1136/bmjopen-2020-044397.

PAHO (2021). *Trinidad and Tobago Build Capacity to Respond to Gender-Based Violence under the Spotlight Initiative.* Retrieved on November 8, 2022, from https://www.paho.org/en/news/20-8-2021-paho-trinidad-and-tobago-builds-capacity-respond-gender-based-violence-under.

Pappa, S., Ntella, V., Giannakas, T., Giannakoulis, V. G., Papoutsi, E., & Katsaounou, P. (2020). Prevalence of depression, anxiety, and insomnia among healthcare workers during the COVID-19 pandemic: A systematic review and meta-analysis. *Brain, Behavior, and Immunity* 88, 901–907.

Patrick, S. W., Henkhaus, L. E., Zickafoose, J. S., Lovell, K., Halvorson, A., Loch, S., Letterie, M., & Davis, M. M. (2020). Well-being of parents and children during the COVID-19 pandemic: A national survey. *Pediatrics* 146(4). Retrieved on June 13, 2023, from https://publications.aap.org/pediatrics/article/146/4/e2020016824/79686/Well-being-of-Parents-and-Children-During-the?autologincheck=redirected.

Piquero, A. R., Jennings, W. G., Jemison, E., Kaukinen, C., & Knaul, F. M. (2021). Domestic violence during the COVID-19 pandemic: Evidence from a systematic review and meta-analysis. *Journal of Criminal Justice* 74, 101–806.

Ravindran, S., & Shah, M. (2020). *Unintended Consequences of Lockdowns: COVID-19 and the Shadow Pandemic.* Cambridge, MA: National Bureau of Economic Research.

Robinson, E., Sutin, A. R., Daly, M., Jones, A. (2022). A systematic review and meta-analysis of longitudinal cohort studies comparing mental health before versus during the COVID-19 pandemic in 2020. *Journal of Affective Disorders* 296, 567–576. doi:10.1016/j.jad.2021.09.098.

Seck, P. A., Encarnacion, J. O., Tinonin, C., & Duerto-Valero, S. (2021). Gendered impacts of COVID-19 in Asia and the Pacific: Early evidence on deepening socioeconomic inequalities in paid and unpaid work. *Feminist Economics* 27(1–2), 117–132.

Seedat, S., & Rondon, M. (2021). Women's wellbeing and the burden of unpaid work. *BMJ (Clinical Research Editon)* 374(1972). Retrieved on November 8, 2022, from https://doi.org/10.1136/bmj.n1972.

Sobers-Grannum, N., Murphy, M. M., Nielsen, A., Guell, C., Samuels, T. A., Bishop, L., & Unwin, N. (2015). Female gender is a social determinant of diabetes in the Caribbean: A systematic review and meta-analysis. *PloS One* 10(5), e0126799. https://doi.org/10.1371/journal.pone.0126799.

STATIN (2020). *The Jamaican Labour Market: Impact of COVID-19.* Retrieved on November 8, 2022, from https://statinja.gov.jm/covidPDF/Jamaican%20Labour%20Market%20Impact%20of%20COVID-19.pdf.

UN Women (2021). *Summary Status of Women and Men Report-The Impacts of COVID-19.* Retrieved on June 13, 2023, from https://caribbean.unwomen.org/

sites/default/files/Field%20Office%20Caribbean/Attachments/Publications/2021/
20210413%20Summary%20Report%20COVID-19%209%20interactive.pdf.

Waldron, E. M., Burnett-Zeigler, I., Wee, V., Ng, Y. W., Koenig, L. J., Pederson, A. B., Tomaszewski, E., & Miller, E. S. (2021). Mental health in women living with HIV: The unique and unmet needs. *Journal of the International Association of Providers of AIDS Care* 20. Retrieved on November 8, 2022, from https://doi. org/10.1177/2325958220985665.

Walker, I. F., Asher, L., Pari, A., Attride-Stirling, J., Oyinloye, A. O., Simmons, C., Potter, I., *et al.* (2022). Mental health systems in six Caribbean small island developing states: a comparative situational analysis. *International Journal of Mental Health Systems* 16(1), 1–16.

WHO (2008). *Closing the Gap in a Generation: Health Equity through Action on the Social Determinants of Health*. Geneva: WHO Commission on Social Determinants of Health.

WHO (2019). *Barbados: Meeting the Health Needs of Its Adolescents*. Retrieved on November 8, 2022, from https://www.who.int/news/item/14-08-2019-barbados-m eeting-the-health-needs-of-its-adolescents#:~:text=Overallper.

WHO (2021a). *Social Determinants of Health*. Retrieved on November 8, 2022, from https://www.who.int/health-topics/social-determinants-of-health#tab=tab_1.

WHO (2021b). *Second Round of the National Pulse Survey on Continuity of Essential Health Services during the COVID-19 Pandemic*. Retrieved on November 8, 2022, from https://www.who.int/publications/i/item/WHO-2019-n CoV-EHS-continuity-survey-2021.1.

WHO (2022). *COVID-19 Pandemic Triggers 25 Per Cent Increase in Prevalence of Anxiety and Depression Worldwide*. Retrieved on November 8, 2022, from https:// www.who.int/news/item/02-03-2022-covid-19-pandemic-triggers-25-increase-in-pre valence-of-anxiety-and-depression-worldwide.

WHO-AIMS (2008). *WHO-AIMS Report on Mental Health System in Guyana*, Geor- getown, Guyana: WHO and Guyana Ministry of Health. Retrieved on November 8, 2022, from https://cdn.who.int/media/docs/default-source/mental -health/who-aims-country-reports/guyana_who_aims_report.pdf?sfvrsn=945ffe d0_3&download=true.

WIGB (1999). Ending violence against women. *Issues in World Health* 11, 1–44.

Xavier, J. (2021). *Voices of St. Lucian Women*. Retrieved on November 8, 2022, from https://caribbean.unwomen.org/en/digital-library/publications/2022/02/voices-of-sai nt-lucian-women-a-study-of-the-impact-of-covid-19-on-frontline-workers-small-ent repreneurs-pre-school-teachers-and-hospitality-workers-0.

6   Conclusion

In this book, we have examined critical gender equality challenges in the Anglo-Caribbean, including gender-based violence, abortion rights, underrepresentation of women in politics and the impact of COVID-19 on women. Most of these are not new challenges and originate in patriarchal and colonial systems of power, traditional gender roles and economic disadvantages that have persisted for decades. Although progress towards affording women equal citizenship has been made, women are still struggling to achieve gender parity and sexual autonomy. The chapter on political underrepresentation shows how Caribbean women have struggled to enter the political arena, increase their numbers or remain in politics due to structural and systemic barriers. Increasing the number of women in politics is critical, but how this should be done continues to attract debate. One way is through legislative quota, which Guyana has done. Another approach which is clear from the interviews we conducted with women in Jamaica, Trinidad and Tobago and Barbados is to take deliberate steps to remove barriers to entry and make the political arena less of an "old boy's club." It is equally important for men to share in childcare responsibilities and unpaid labour. Our interviews with female politicians have shown that household and childcare labour still disproportionately affect women. Women are generally considered the backbone of the family and are responsible for raising children and taking care of the home. Supply-side barriers dominated the challenges we identified, which include family obligations/commitment, lack of networks/support systems for women, lack of financial support/political financing, role congruency and gender stereotypes and violence against women in politics. Violence against women in politics was most dominant in Jamaica and not as central in Barbados. Having identified the barriers to women's political participation in the Anglo-Caribbean, we highlighted at least two key solutions: providing financial support/funding and strong support networks for female politicians. We also outlined critical attributes and traits that female political aspirants and women in politics are encouraged to possess to survive in politics.

Another gender challenge we examined in this book is gender-based violence, which is prevalent in the Caribbean and has become known as the shadow pandemic. We have tried to fill a gap in the literature by

DOI: 10.4324/9781003130987-6

Conclusion 151

examining GBV against LGBTQ women in the Caribbean and the inadequacy of laws, which currently do not provide sufficient protection. Because LGBTQ people have multiple identities, violence against them can be even more complex, raising questions about the need for greater attention to intersectionality. Attacks can go unreported because of fear of discrimination and lack of recognition of LGBTQ rights in many countries in the Anglophone Caribbean, where buggery laws criminalise same-sex/same-gender relationships. In some countries in the Anglophone Caribbean, such as Jamaica, Barbados and St Vincent and the Grenadines, domestic laws implicitly or explicitly exclude LGBTQ relationships either through a requirement of marriage or connection as biological parents, whereas others require that both victim and abuser be of opposite sexes.

Abortion rights are another vexing subject in many Caribbean countries. This has become even more topical and controversial in light of the overturning of Roe v. Wade by the Supreme Court in the US. The Jamaican case is an interesting one for several reasons. Jamaica maintains an 1864 colonial law that has never been amended or repealed. It robs women of their bodily autonomy and contributes to maternal mortality and morbidity by pushing poor women to seek unregulated abortions. Successive political administrations have used collaborative governance to debate and facilitate multi-sectoral discussions on abortion laws in Jamaica. Unfortunately, collaborative governance was perhaps doomed to failure from the outset. Most of the groups participating in Joint Select Committees of parliament hold sharply divergent views on the issue of abortion. There is a strong Christian lobby, and many Jamaicans hold conservative positions on abortion, despite an increasing number of Jamaicans identifying as secular. Gender-based organisations and women's groups have supported a pro-choice agenda.

We also examined the impact of COVID-19 on women in four countries in the Caribbean, an area that has not received sufficient attention. The gendered implications of the pandemic have proved incredibly challenging in the Caribbean because of high levels of gender-based violence, social inequality, poor healthcare systems, labour market challenges, women's low economic status relative to men's and a patriarchal culture that places the burden of childcare on women. COVID-19 intensified these challenges and created new ones. Many women lost their jobs, mental-health issues soared and women took on the increasing burden of childcare and unpaid labour were exposed to domestic violence as they were forced to shelter in place with their abusers. In addition, access to important services for women was curtailed during the pandemic. Most governments implemented cash payment programmes as part of their COVID-19 response efforts. While these payments provided some immediate relief for individuals and families affected by the pandemic, they were hardly sufficient to address the full scope of the economic impact.

152 *Conclusion*

Much has changed, but much remains the same, especially in countries where economic questions are interrelated with gender ones. Where economies perform poorly, it is more difficult for women to gain gender parity. Similarly, in countries with poor health systems and developmental challenges, gender inequality in health can prove more challenging to resolve. Feminist academics in the Caribbean continue to struggle with how to move the gender equality project forward. Caribbean women have made gains in education, the labour market and sports, especially. Women's political representation has also increased, but not enough to achieve equality. Moreover, the Caribbean is far from solving one of the most violent representations of patriarchy and women's unequal citizenship: gender-based violence. Gendered power relations and gender norms continue to constrain women's freedom and full citizenship. Even with the advances made, the state has failed to correct these failures, partly because the state is itself a part of the problem and also because powerful groups, the Christian lobby in particular, continue to exert a disproportionate influence on decisions about gender and women's autonomy. Through struggles and citizenship from below, Caribbean women have won important rights and have continued to challenge gender inequality, with varying success.

Index

Page numbers in **bold** refer to tables.

ableism 7, 15, 90
abortion and collaborative governance 74–6
"abortion on demand" 80
Abortion Policy Review Advisory Group 74–6, 78
ageism 6–7, 15, 90
Agrawal, A. 777
Ahn, M. 74
Aleksanyan, 129
alienation 41–2, 49
altruism 56
anal sex 98, 112, 117
androcentrism 111
Anglo-Caribbean: definition of rape 112–14; disadvantage 90–2; domestic violence laws 107–11; forms of violence and sexual oppression 116–17; fundamental human rights 1–4; gender-based violence laws 102–3; gender-based violence legislation **104–5**; gross indecency 114–16; historical overview of women in politics 31–6; homophobic laws **99**; increasing female participation in politics 51–8; invisibility of LGBTQ women 107–16; right to vote 21–2; sexual offences legislation 105–7, 111–16; summary of challenges to women 150–2; violence against female politicians 48–51; violence against LGBTQ people 98–101; women in national parliaments **34**; women's agency 11–13; women's citizenship 8–11; see also gendered impact of COVID-19 on women

Ansell, C. 73
anti-abortion lobbies 67–70
anti-sodomy provisions 98
antisocial disorders 129
anxiety 128–30, 141
arthritis 127
assets 54–8
asthma 127
autonomy 9, 67–9, 84–5, 150–2

Bailey, Amy 2
Baldwin, E. 74
Balogh, S. 74
Barbados Labour Party 52
barriers, biases, boys' club 21–66; see also underrepresentation of female politicians
Barriteau, Eudine 2–3, 11, 29
Barrow-Giles, C. 31
Bean, D. 96
Beijing Platform for Action 1995 2, 21, 72, 102
Biholar, R. 9–10, 111–12, 114
Bill Johnson poll 100
Black Feminism 5
bodily performance 12
Bradshaw, Santia 36
Breiding, M. J. 97
buggery 91, 98–100, 114, 116

cardiovascular diseases 127
Caribbean Community 1
Caribbean Development Research Services 100
Caribbean Institute for Women in Leadership 30

154 *Index*

Caribbean perspectives on barriers to women 29–30
CARICOM *see* Caribbean Community
CARICOM Charter of Civil Society 102, 105
carnival 12
Cates, W., Jr. 71
CEDAW *see* Convention on Elimination of Discrimination Against Women
CGR *see* collaborative governance regimes
challenges for female politicians 36–51; *see also* deterrents for female politicians
challenges for gender equality 67–89; *see also* illegality of abortion rights (Jamaica)
character assassination 48–50
Charles, Eugenia 3, 33, 49
Charter of Fundamental Rights and Freedoms 106
Charter of Rights 102, 110
Chen, L. 97
child custody 98
child pornography 102, 106
childcare responsibilities and COVID-19 134–6
Christian lobby 68–9, 76–85, 151–2; power of 80–4; *see also* failure of collaborative governance
Christian values 80
cis-normativity 111
cisgender 10, 91, 96–7, 106, 111, 116
CIWiL *see* Caribbean Institute for Women in Leadership
Clark, J. 48
Clarke, Rupert 13
classism 90–91
coercion 93, 97, 109
cohabitation 106, 108–9
collaboration 69
collaborative governance approaches 67–89; *see also* illegality of abortion rights (Jamaica)
collaborative governance regimes 77
collective resistance 12–13
Collins, Iris 32
Collins, P. H. 6
colonial systems of power 150–2
colonialism 2, 7, 15, 40, 78, 90, 96
colourism 91
Commonwealth Parliamentary Association 30

compliance 129
confidence 24–5, 47, 55–6
consensus-building mechanisms 69
consequences of illegality of abortion rights 70–3
Convention of Belém do Pará 93, 102
Convention on Elimination of Discrimination Against Women 21–3, 93, 102, 110–11
Convention on the Rights of the Child 102
Cooper, C. 12
Couzens, J. 91
COVID-19 and women 3–4, 125–49; *see also* gendered impact of COVID-19 on women
Creasy, Stella 53
Crenshaw, Kimberlé 5–7
Criminal Law Amendment Act 1885 98
critical mass theory 21, 36, 59
Critical Race Theory 4–5, 92
cruelty 97
cultural attitudes towards women's roles 22, 46
curfews 125
Cuthbert-Flynn, Juliet 76, 78
cyber-stalking 109

Darcy, R. 48
de jure equality 21
debating abortion rights 67–89; illegality of abortion rights (Jamaica)
Declaration on Elimination of Violence Against Women (UN) 3, 92–4
decolonisation 96
decriminalisation of homosexuality 115
defamation 48
defining "spouse" 108–9
definition of rape in Anglo-Caribbean 112–14
demand-side barriers to female political representation 27–9
"Demarginalising the Intersection of Race and Sex" 5
Democratic Labour Party 52
depression 127–30, 141
deterrents for female politicians 36–51; domestic roles/responsibilities 36–41; lack of networks/support 41–3; political financing/funding 44–5; role congruency/gender stereotypes 46–8; violence against women 48–51
diabetes 127–8
dignity 57–8

Index 155

Disabilities Act 2014 107
disadvantage 1, 90–2
discrimination 5–8, 27–8, 37, 47–8,
  94, 130
domestic roles/responsibilities 24,
  36–41
domestic violence 3–4, 93–4
Domestic Violence Act 2006 108
Domestic Violence Act 2022 109
domestic violence legislation 103–5,
  107–11; invisibility of LGBTQ
  women in 107–11
Domestic Violence (Protection Orders)
  Act 1992 92, 103, 108–9
Dominica Freedom Party 33
double bind for women 24–5, 36–41
dropping out 126
Dunn, L. A. 73

Easton, D. 73
Ebola crisis 133
economic diversification 1–2
economic impacts of COVID-19 131–2,
  136–41; on Caribbean women 136–41
education 24
election cycle 76–84; *see also* failure of
  collaborative governance
electoral reform 51
electoral violence 30
Emerson, K. 74
empathy 57
empowerment 27
enslavement 31, 68
erotic agency 12
exclusion 31, 107
exposing pre-existing health
  inequalities 125–6
externalisation of emotion 129

failure of collaborative governance
  76–84; Christian lobby 80–4;
  political cycle 84; public opinion
  79–80; state power 77–9
Farin, S. L. 72
Federal Energy Regulatory
  Commission (US) 74
female genital mutilation 93
female political representation 24–9;
  demand-side barriers to 27–9;
  supply-side barriers to 24–7
femicide 93, 95
feminism 2, 5, 43, 82
FGM *see* female genital mutilation
foetal impairment 72

forms of violence 116–17
Fourth World Conference on Women
  1995 2–3, 21, 72
funding 26, 44–5

Gardner, Paul 13
Garvey, Amy 2
Gash, A. 73
Gaskins, J. 116
gaslighting 93
GBV *see* gender-based violence
gender balance 52
gender challenges 1–20; gender equality
  as fundamental human right 1–13;
  overview 13–15
gender equality as fundamental human
  right 1–13; intersectionality 4–8;
  women's agency 11–13; women's
  citizenship 8–11
gender markers 111, 117
gender norms 80–4, 97–8
gender paradox 127
gender stereotypes 37, 46–8
gender-based violence 7–9, 92–4, 96,
  102–3, 112–14, 125–6, 132–3, 150–1;
  and COVID-19 132–3; laws in
  Anglo-Caribbean 102–3; *see also*
  violence against women and girls
gender-based violence legislation in
  Anglo-Caribbean **104–5**
gendered impact of COVID-19 on
  women 125–49; death rate from
  COVID-19 129–33; exposing
  pre-existing health inequalities
  125–6; health inequalities in
  Caribbean 127–9; lockdowns,
  curfews, closure of schools 144;
  research findings on impact 134–44;
  social determinants of health 127
General Orders of the Public Service
  1970 44
Gibson, Stella 13
Gilchrist, S. 26
glass ceiling 11, 33, 35
global barriers to women in politics
  23–9; demand-side barriers 27–9;
  supply-side barriers 24–7
global South 1, 12
global violence against LBGTQ
  women 96–8
government inaction 77
grievous sexual assault 106
Grimes, D. A. 71
gross indecency 98, 100, 114–16

156 *Index*

Hankivsky, O. 6
Hanna, Lisa 76
Haraldsson, A. 29
harassment 48–9, 106
hard labour 98–9
"hard" political issues 48
Hassan, Zuleikha 53
hate crimes 97–8
hate speech 98, 101
HDT *see* Human Dignity Trust
health equity 127
health inequalities and COVID-19
  125–49; *see also* gendered impact of
  COVID-19 on women
hegemonic masculinity 96
Henry-Wilson, Maxine 2, 29–30
heteronormativity 91, 101, 111
heterosexuality 10, 96–7
historical overview of barriers to
  women 31–6
HIV 126, 129, 133
Hoehn-Velasco, L. 72
Hogwood, B. W. 73
home-schooling 132
homicide 95
homophobia 7–8, 15, 90–1, 98, 100
homophobic laws in Anglo-Caribbean **99**
homosexuality 10, 91, 110, 115
"horse-race" coverage 28–9
Human Dignity Trust 92
Human Rights Watch 91, 101
hyper-masculinity 101
hypercholesterolaemia 128
hypertension 127–8

IADB *see* Inter-American
  Development Bank
ICPD *see* International Conference on
  Population and Development
illegality of abortion rights (Jamaica)
  67–89; abortion and collaborative
  governance 74–6; anti-/pro-abortion
  views 67–70; collaborative
  governance 73–4; consequences of
  70–3; failure of collaborative
  governance 76–84; retention of 1864
  law 84–5
ILO *see* International Labour
  Organization
IMF *see* International Monetary Fund
Immigration Act 115–16
impact of abortion 72
impact of COVID-19 *see* gendered
  impact of COVID-19 on women

imperialism 12, 98
incest 72, 74, 80, 83, 114
increasing female political participation
  51–8
indecent assault 99–100
indigenous peoples 4–6, 94
institutional barriers 44–5
institutionalisation of gender power 11
integrity 58
Inter-American Convention on the
  Prevention ... of Violence Against
  Women 3, 102
Inter-American Development Bank 95
Inter-Parliamentary Union 26, 33
internalisation of emotion 129
International Conference on
  Population and Development 72–3
International Labour Organization
  131–2, 140
International Monetary Fund 140
interpersonal violence 90
intersectional analysis of LGBTQ
  women 90–124; *see also* invisibility
  of LGBTQ women
intersectionality 4–8, 23, 54, 116–17
intimate partner violence 3–4, 90, 93–4,
  129–30, 133–4
*Intimate Partner Violence in Five
  CARICOM Countries* 94
intimidation 30, 49, 58, 101, 109
invisibility of LGBTQ women 90–124;
  domestic violence legislation in
  Caribbean 103–5; forms of violence
  and systems of oppression 116–17;
  gender-based violence 92–4;
  gender-based violence laws in
  Anglo-Caribbean 102–3; global
  violence against LGBTQ women
  96–8; invisibility in domestic
  violence laws 107–11; invisibility in
  sexual offences legislation 111–16;
  sexual offences legislation in
  Anglo-Caribbean 105–7; violence
  against LGBTQ people in Caribbean
  98–101; violence against women in
  the Caribbean 94–6; violence against
  women and girls 90–2
IPU *see* Inter-Parliamentary Union
IPV *see* intimate partner violence
irrationality 46

J-FLAG *see* Jamaica Forum for
  Lesbians, All-Sexuals and Gays
Jagan, Janet 33

Index   157

Jamaica Forum for Lesbians,
  All-Sexuals and Gays 91, 101
Jamaica Gleaner 67–9, 71, 94–5, 100
Jamaica Health and Lifestyle survey 128
Jamaica Labour Party 30, 32, 34–5, 41,
  49, 76, 84
Jamaican Information Service 133
Jamaican Labour Market 131
Jamieson, K. 25
Jim Crow laws 116
JLP *see* Jamaica Labour Party
Johns, A. 80
Johnson Smith, Kamina 68–9
Johnson Survey Research Ltd 80
Johnson-Myers, Tracy-Ann 50–1
Joseph, T. D. S. 31

Kalla, T. D. 24
Kallis, G. 77
Kiparsky, M. 77

labour market inequality 132
lack of networks/support 41–3, 59
legalising abortion 72–6
legislation in Anglo-Caribbean 90–124;
  see also invisibility of LGBTQ
  women
Lemos, M. C. 77
Leon, Rose 32
lesbianism 6, 13, 49, 91, 94, 96–8,
  107–8, 116–7
Leslie, C. R. 116
LGBT rights 80–4
LGBTQ women 90–124; *see also*
  invisibility of LGBTQ women
life imprisonment 14, 70, 100
limited social contact 142
lockdown 125, 132–3, 140, 144
Love March Movement 67
Lovenduski, J. 22–3

Mahmood, S. 12
Mahoney, B. 91
Male and Female He Created Them 10
marginalisation 8, 23, 41, 90, 94, 100
marital rape 80–4, 113
Mason, Sandra 36
Massiah, Jocelyn 40
maternal mortality 71, 74–5, 151
Mathurin Mair, Lucille 2
Matland, R. E. 24, 27–8, 48
matriarchy 40–1
measures taken during COVID-19
  pandemic 144

media coverage 28–9, 48
medical complications 71
Medical Termination of Pregnancy Act
  1983 72
mental health and COVID-19 141–4
mentorship programmes 41–4
Miller, A. M. 77–8
misoprostol 70
Model Legislation on Domestic
  Violence 103, 105
Mohammed, Patricia 2, 29
morbidity 71, 127
Mottley, Mia 3, 33, 35–6, 49, 110
murder 80–4; *see also* Christian lobby

Nabatchi, T. 74
"national culture" 9
National Family Planning Board 80
National Intimate Partner and Sexual
  Violence Survey 97
Nazareth Moravian Church 13
NCDs *see* non-communicable diseases
need for "thick skin" 55, 58–9
networking 54, 56
non-binary people 10, 107
non-communicable diseases 126–8
non-consensual penile–vaginal sex 112–14
Norgaard, R. 77
Norris, P. 22–3, 28
Nurses Council of Jamaica 75
NVivo 22

obesity 127–8
occupational orders 103
Offences Against the Person Act 1864
  14, 67–73, 75–7, 84–5, 98, 115, 151
"old boys' club" 41, 43, 137, 150
oppression 90, 101, 116–17
oral sex 106, 112, 117
Ouellet, V. 26
"Out of Many, One People" 91
outing 97–8

PAHO *see* Pan American Health
  Organization
Palmer-Adisa, Opal 68, 83
Pan American Health Organization 127
pandemic patriarchy 136
Parliament Arbitration Act 1989 52
party subvention 52
passion 56–7
patriarchy 2–4, 14, 27, 33, 68, 78, 98,
  150–2; and colonial systems of
  power 150–2

158 *Index*

Patterson, Wynante 74–5
People's National Party 30, 35, 41, 49–50, 76, 83–4
Persad-Bissessar, Kamla 3, 33, 36, 49
Pesko, M. 72
physical health and COVID-19 141–4
pigmentocracy 91
"place" in society 49
PNP *see* People's National Party
policy space in Caribbean 73–4
political cycle 84
political financing/funding 44–5
political violence 27, 30, 48–51
post-traumatic stress disorder 129–30
poverty 74–5, 101, 126–7, 131
power of Christian lobby 80–4
power dynamic 77
Prevention of Discrimination Act 1997 107
pro-abortion lobbies 67–70
pro-life groups 79
proportional representation 28, 51
prostitution 115–16
protection orders 103
psychiatric disorders 143–4
psychological violence 27
public opinion 79–80, 100
Public Service (Conduct and Ethics of Officers) Code 45
public–private life dichotomy 24, 36–8
PV *see* political violence

qualitative study of female underrepresentation 21–66; *see also* underrepresentation of female politician

race discrimination doctrine 5–6
racism 7, 12, 15, 68, 90
Rainbow Times 91
Ramkeesoon, Gema 2
rape 72, 80–4, 93, 95, 112–14, 900; definition of 112–14
Rapid Credit Facility 140, 151
recipe for survival in politics 55–8
Red Thread 13
Reddock, Rhoda 2, 29
regional constitutions 102–3
registration fees 45
religious orthodoxy 96
research findings on impact of COVID-19 134–44; childcare responsibilities/unpaid employment 134–6; economic impacts on women

136–41; mental/physical health 141–4
resistance 31
responsibilities of women 36–41, 134–6; and impact of COVID-19 134–6
retention of 1864 abortion law 84–5
Rhodes, R. A. W. 73
right to abortion 4
risk-taking behaviours 143
RJR-Gleaner Don Anderson poll 80
Robinson, Tracy 2, 9
Roe v. Wade 67, 71, 151
role congruency 46–8, 59
Roman Catholic Church 79
Roseman, M. J. 77–8
Rosenbluth, F. 24

same-sex consensual sex 114–16
same-sex relationships 90–1, 93, 107–10, 113–14, 116, 151
schools closures 125, 130, 134
Schulz, K. F. 71
Scott, T. A. 77
segregation 116
self-doubt 55
self-efficacy 25
self-governance 31
self-inducing abortion 70
serious indecency 100, 114–15
Serra, N. E. 97
sexism 29, 90, 96
sexual abuse 13, 93–4
sexual exploitation of a child 106
sexual grooming 106
Sexual Harassment (Protection and Prevention) Act 2021 106
Sexual Offences Act 1992 100, 113
Sexual Offences and Domestic Violence Act 1991 103
sexual offences legislation 105–7, 111–16; in Anglo-Caribbean 105–7; definition of rape 112–14; gross indecency 114–16; invisibility of LGBTQ women in 111–16
sexual orientation 91, 94, 96–8, 105–7, 110
Sexual Orientation Amendment Bill 2003 111
sexual/reproductive rights 69, 77, 80–1, 84–5
sexuality 49, 90
sexually transmitted diseases 133
Shepherd, Verene 2, 29, 96
Shiab, N. 26

Index 159

Shvedova, N. 24, 48
Simpson-Miller, Portia 3, 33, 35, 49
Sistren Theatre Collective 13
skin colour 90–1
slapping 93
slavery 2, 31, 40, 96
social determinants of health 127
social impacts of COVID-19 131–2
sodomy 98–100, 115–16
"soft" political issues 48
solutions for increasing female
    participation 51–8; assets 55–8
Spence, Rudy 79
spheres of power 76–84; *see also* failure
    of collaborative governance
Staff Orders for Public Service
    Officers 45
stalking 90, 97
state power 77–9
Statistical Institute of Jamaica 131
stay-at-home orders 125, 132–4
stereotyping 25, 29–30, 37, 52, 59,
    116–17
stigma 98
stoning 101
stroke 127
substance abuse 129
subversion 12
supply-and-demand model 22–3, 36–7
supply-side barriers to female political
    representation 24–7, 150
Swers, M. 26
systems of oppression 7, 116–17

Tambourine Army 13
tenancy orders 103
Termination of Pregnancy Act 75–6
thematic analysis 22
Thomas, C. W. 77
Thomas, David 67
Thomson, D. 26
transphobia 7, 15, 90, 97
types of health inequality 127–9

Ulibari, N. 74
UN *see* United Nations
UN Human Rights Council 110
UN Population Find 73
UN Women 8, 13–15, 26–7, 30, 131
UNAIDS survey 101
underrepresentation of female
    politicians 21–66; Anglo-Caribbean
    historical perspectives 31–6;
    Caribbean perspectives 29–30;

challenges/deterrents for female
    politicians 36–51; global barriers to
    women in politics 23–9; increasing
    women's participation 51–8; women
    in world's population 21–3; women's
    involvement in decision-making 59
UNICEF 2
United Nations 21–2
Universal Declaration of Human
    Rights 1, 102
universal suffrage 29, 31–2
University of the west Indies 72
unlawful sexual connection 106
"unnatural crimes" 98–100, 114
unpaid employment and COVID-19
    134–6

Vassell, Linette 2, 29–30
Vatican 10
VAWG *see* violence against women and
    girls
VAWIP *see* violence against women in
    politics
victimisation 49, 94
Victoria Jubilee Hospital 71, 74–5, 78
violation of gender role expectations 35
violation of human rights 90
violence against female politicians
    48–51
violence against LGBTQ people
    98–101
violence against women and girls 50,
    90–6, 103
violence against women in politics 26–7
"visiting relationship" 110
vulnerability 90, 133

Walters, M. L. 97
Wängnerud, L. 29
Watson Williams, C. 94
WE-Change *see* Women's Empowerment
    for Change
Weekes, Paula-Mae 36, 59
Welch, S. 48
well-being 105, 125–49
WHO *see* World Health Organization
Wilkinson, D. 91
Williams Institute 97
winner-take-all system 51
withdrawal 129
women and COVID-19 129–33;
    gender-based violence 132–3; social
    and economic impacts 131–2
women with disabilities 4–5, 7

160 *Index*

women and formal political participation **32**
women in national parliaments in Anglo-Caribbean **34**
women in politics *see* underrepresentation of female politicians
women in positions of political power in Caribbean **34**
women as symbols 59
women in world's population 21–3
women's agency 11–13
women's citizenship 8–11

Women's Empowerment for Change 12–13
women's involvement in decision-making 59
Women's Political Caucus 54–5
women's violence against women 90–124; *see also* invisibility of LGBTQ women
work–life balance 136
World Bank 93
World Health Organization 8–9, 71–2, 94, 127
World Population Review 95

Milton Keynes UK
Ingram Content Group UK Ltd.
UKHW020751231124
451456UK00007B/47